Elements of Parametric Design

Elements of Parametric Design

Robert Woodbury

with contributions by

Onur Yüce Gün, Brady Peters and Mehdi (Roham) Sheikholeslami

Routledge
Taylor & Francis Group

LONDON AND NEW YORK

First published 2010
by Routledge
2 Park Square, Milton Park, Abingdon, Oxon, OX14 4RN

Simultaneously published in the USA and Canada
by Routledge
270 Madison Avenue, New York, NY 10016

Routledge is an imprint of the Taylor & Francis Group, an informa business

©2010 Robert Woodbury

Typeset in URW Garamond and Bitstream Vera Sans by Robert Woodbury
Printed and bound in India by Replika Press Pvt. Ltd.

British Library Cataloguing in Publication Data
A catalogue record for this book is available from the British Library

Library of Congress Cataloging-in-Publication Data
A catalog record has been requested for this book

ISBN10: 0-415-77986-3 (hbk) ISBN10: 0-415-77987-1 (pbk)

ISBN13: 978-0-415-77986-9 (hbk) ISBN13: 978-0-415-77987-6 (pbk)

To Gwenda, Ian and Cailean

Contents

CONTENTS

Foreword

Parametrics is more about an attitude of mind than any particular software application. It has its roots in mechanical design, as such, for architects it is borrowed thought and technology. It is a way of thinking that some designers may find alien, but the first requirement is an attitude of mind that seeks to express and explore relationships.

Embedded in this method of exploration is the idea of capturing *design history* and returning it in an editable form – that can be varied and then re-played. The power of the concept is the belief that design history can be extrapolated to produce *design futures*. Sometimes it can – but this requires much practice to achieve a level of   uency which still allows intuition to play its part.

As a concept parametrics is far more likely to be understood by a musician than by an artist. This is because the musician is dedicated to rehearsing for performance – which is an essential characteristic of a virtuoso in parametrics. To the artist on the other hand the accumulation of technique is incidental to the production of an artefact, which is the result of direct interaction with a medium. For this activity there is no written score that can be fine tuned and re-played. However, at the highest level of   uency we may yet see a generation emerge who can "sketch with code".

Parametrics should perhaps be clearly labelled with a warning along the lines of "drink deep – or taste not". So the best advice might be to make your choice before reading further – or just allow your curiosity to guide you!

— Hugh Whitehead

The beginning of the third millennium brings growing recognition that the practice of building design will change more rapidly than in preceding decades. With increasing economic pressure, established practice gives way in favour of tight integration of design and delivery as well as innovation in sharing risks and rewards. In parallel, climate change reinvigorates deep concern about our excessive use of resources, rebalancing values of capital costs and long term design performance. Integrated design teams make simultaneous, interrelated design decisions across disciplines and project phases. Such decisions concern interconnected subsystems with interfaces that propagate change through the overall system and allow the design team to create many design alternatives. In addition, investment in validation of design assumptions through analysis or simulation cycles can further reduce risks.

With parametric modeling, early design models become conceptually stronger than conventional CAD models and less constrained than building information models. Parameters express the concepts contained in these new models and give interactive behaviour to building components and systems. This means a change in how tools need to support design activities. For example tools like Bentley Systems GenerativeComponents offer a uid transition between a CAD-like modeling-based design approach on one side and a scripting-based design approach on the other side. These new parametric systems support a shift from one-off CAD-modeling to thinking in and working with geometric concepts and behaviour. Instead of building a single solution, designers explore an entire parametrically described solution space.

The new parametric tools challenge CAD work practices – practitioners and students alike must learn how to use such tools well. We know that quality of learning depends on quality of teaching. The author of this book, Dr. Robert Woodbury, has been teaching GenerativeComponents workshops for several years, while intellectually penetrating the mere instrumental layer of tool use and elevating his teaching to a new layer of concepts. Dr. Woodbury and his students chose the motif of patterns to explain this conceptual layer, to unravel its components behaviours and to provide new functions useful for parametric design. Initial results appeared online at www.designpatterns.ca and now are revised for this book. Dr. Woodbury also reviews geometric foundations in a quick but thoroughly understandable way because they are instrumental to designing with parameters. Interspersed are practice case studies illustrating types of design this new generation of tools can help designers achieve.

I have enjoyed witnessing Dr. Woodbury s teaching of GenerativeComponents over the past years and refer to his design patterns frequently. I hope that this book will inspire instructors in their teaching of parametric design and invoke practitioners and students imaginations about new approaches to design.

— Volker Mueller

Acknowledgements

It takes a community to write a book. Though the conception, writing and any errors are mine, I am deeply indebted to many people for ideas, technical help and personal support.

First of all, Onur Gün, Brady Peters and Roham Sheikholeslami bring practice perspectives and fresh voices to their respective sections. Thank you guys!

Throughout my career, I have been blessed with great teachers and mentors. Ron Brand, Gulzar Haider, Jim Strutt, Livius Sherwood, Steve Tupper, Chuck Eastman, Irving Oppenheim, Steve Fenves, Art Westerberg, Mark Allstrom, John Dill and Tom Calvert each taught me enduring and important lessons. I am largely a self-taught writer (and it probably shows). Chris Carlson, Mikako Harada and Antony Radford each helped me sharpen whatever craft I have.

The basis for the book is the ongoing *Patterns for Parametric Design* project in my research group at Simon Fraser University. Without Yingjie (Victor) Chen, Maryam Maleki, Zhenyu (Cheryl) Qian and Roham Sheikholeslami, there would be no patterns and no book. Victor especially has tolerated and met my incessant demands for amendments to the pattern website s programs.

Through many conversations, writing sessions and too much email, Robert Aish and Axel Kilian helped me discern the main themes and structure of the book. I treasure both the intellectual context they provide and, especially, our many differences of opinion about parametric design. In reviewing the book Lars Hesselgren, Axel Kilian, Ramesh Krishnamurti, Volker Mueller, Makai Smith, Rudi Stouffs and Bige Tunçer pointed out its numerous errors and aws (which I hope I have corrected). Diane Gromala gave indispensable advice on design and typography. Maureen Stone sharpened several graphical tools. The book has hundreds of figures. Roham Sheikholeslami helped immensely in the horrible task of wresting a semblance of visual coherence from unruly symbolic beginnings. Makai Smith, Volker Mueller and the rest of the Bentley team put up with many questions and much nagging about their systems.

Ideas need tempering. SmartGeometry provides the crucible. There is nothing like a room of 200 practical people to tell you when your ideas and explanations don t work. Over the years Maria Flodin at Bentley brilliantly organized many events – I couldn t do your job Maria, and all of us in SmartGeometry are in debt to you.

In 2004, Caroline Mallinder, then at Taylor & Francis, first approached me with the idea for a book. Her gentle persistence kept the idea in my field of view. My editors, Francesca Ford, Georgina Johnson and Jodie Tierney have given me far too much latitude in time and graphical control. I hope I have not given them too many headaches in return.

I spent much of a sabbatical writing and thank the School of Interactive Arts and Technology at Simon Fraser University (SFU) for this precious time. The Interdisciplinary Research in the Mathematical and Computational Sciences Centre at SFU loaned me a quiet office in which I could avoid my usual tasks at SFU. My departmental colleagues put up with me being distracted for many months and I thank them for their patience. In the summer of 2009, Don and Donna Woodbury lent me their boathouse to edit the book. The sound of wind and waves motivates both work and afternoon naps. In the fall of 2009, I visited Osaka University as the recipient of the Tee Sasada Award. My gracious host Professor Kaga Atsuko gave me less work to do than she might have. I was able to accomplish much writing in a beautiful place.

I ve stretched my family s patience. I m a hermit when I write, ignoring far too much of the rich life around me. Being the wonderful positive people they are, my children still talk to me. I am sure that Gwenda looks forward to having her husband back from his literary affair. Minnie the dog wants more walks.

This work was partially supported through the Canadian Natural Science and Engineering Research Council Discovery Grants Program; Bentley Systems, Incorporated; the MITACS Accelerate program; the Networks of Centres of Excellence program through the Canadian Design Research Network and the Graphics, Animation and New Media Network; and the BCcampus Online Program Development Fund.

Oh, yes. $\LaTeX$, which invokes joy and despair in equal measure. I could not have written this book without it.

I am deeply grateful for all of this support.

Author's note

Neither fish nor fowl.

Any *Elements of...* book had better be about practice. And it must be useful and accurate. I write in two worlds. Computer-aided design depends utterly on mathematics and computing. Designers use it to expressive ends. Bringing the two together forces compromise and I ve leaned towards design throughout.

I use unusual mathematical notation throughout the book. My mathematician friends may cringe when they see it, but I made a deliberate choice. Designers generally don t do mathematics – they see it, use it and move on. The notation visually describes the objects it denotes: points $\dot{p}$ have dots, vectors $\vec{v}$ have arrows and frames $^A_B\mathsf{T}$ express both their name and where they sit. Between established convention and clarity for non-mathematicians, I choose the latter every time.

Many references that should appear do not. Again, this is by choice. To get into the bibliography, most books have passed the same test I would hope to pass with this one. Clarity over completeness. Explanation over erudition. Utility over intellectual virtuosity. I aim to explain. This means that I have often left out much detail that would be essential in an academic tome. In doing so, I have selected the material offering the best explanation. For example, the chapter on curves uses the simplest equations and remains with them throughout. It is far from complete; hopefully its omissions let its few key ideas shine through.

The book s longest chapter explains its elements as *Patterns for parametric design*. It contains little computer code – a book is the wrong medium. Programs should be online and executable. The website `www.elementsofparametricdesign.com` provides working code for each of the patterns (and more).

Many people in this world cannot distinguish among red, green and blue. Yet computer-aided design systems freely use these colours to signal direction and type. To address the most common color vision deficiencies (deuteranomaly and deuteranopia), I have avoided using red and green together. The principal exceptions – coordinate systems (aka frames) – appear with their *x*-axes drawn slightly thicker and with a gap between the end of line and arrow head.

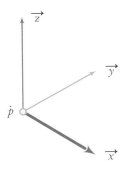

Chapter 1

Introduction

Design is change. Parametric modeling represents change. It is an old idea, indeed one of the very first ideas in computer-aided design. In his 1963 PhD thesis, Ivan Sutherland was right in putting parametric change at the centre of the Sketchpad system. His invention of a representation that could adapt to changing context both created and foresaw one of the chief features of the computer-aided design (CAD) systems to come. The devices of the day kept Sutherland from fully expressing what he might well have seen, that parametric representations could deeply change design work itself. I believe that, today, the key to both using and making these systems lies in another, older idea.

People do design. Planning and implementing change in the world around us is one of the key things that make us human. Language is what we say; design and making is what we do. Computers are simply a new medium for this ancient enterprise. True, they are the first truly active medium. As general symbol processors, computers can present almost limitless kinds of tools. With craft and care, we can program them to do much of what we call design. But not all. Designers continue to amaze us with new function and form. Sometimes new work embodies wisdom, a precious commodity in a finite world. To the human enterprise of design, parametric systems bring fresh and needed new capabilities in adapting to context and contingency and exploring the possibilities inherent in an idea.

What new knowledge and skill do designers need to master the parametric? How can we learn and use it? That is what this book is about. It aims to help designers realize the potential of the parameter in their work. It combines the basic ideas of parametric systems with equally basic ideas from both geometry and computer programming.

It turns out that these ideas are not easy, at least for those with typical design backgrounds. Mastering them requires us to be part designer, part computer scientist and part mathematician. It is hard enough to be an expert in one of these areas, yet alone all. Yet, some of the best and brightest (and mostly young) designers are doing just that – they are developing stunning skill in evoking the new and surprising. Mostly, the book is about the idea that *patterns* are a good tool for thinking about and using parametric modeling. Patterns are themselves another old idea. A *pattern* is a generic solution to a shared problem. Readers with architecture backgrounds will find this definition more modest and limited than is common in the field. It is perhaps more familiar to those with a software background. Using patterns to think and work may help designers master the new complexity imposed on them by parametric modeling.

Patterns work when grounded in practice. I m not an architectural practitioner. So I asked three young and thoughtful practitioner/researchers to demonstrate how they and their firms resolved novel and complex design situations using parametric modeling. Onur Yüce Gün, Brady Peters and Roham Skeikholeslami responded with well-considered and crafted chapters.

My hope is that the book s ideas and explanations foster both understanding and meaningful action in the human enterprise we call design.

The idea of the book originated in 2003, when Robert Aish suggested to me that both new and expert designers needed better explanations of parametric design. In 2005 and 2006, three of us, Robert, Axel Kilian and I met several times to draft ideas for a possible book. Our aim was both broad and high. Events transpired for each of us so that authorship took different directions. For me, the result narrowed our original aspirations into this book. Perhaps its focus and voice will be useful in what is surely a growing body of research, writing and computer code about parametric design.

Who should read this book?

If you are a practitioner using parametric design, you will find many manuals and tutorials, both in print and online. Mostly, these provide lists of commands or detailed, keystroke-by-keystroke instructions to achieve specific tasks. These may help you see what the tool can do, but are unlikely to teach much about how you can adapt it to new situations or how to extend your skills. They show you how to do small things, but leave the next steps to your imagination and skill. For you, the book provides foundational geometry for expressing your own models and models of computing particular to parametric systems. Mostly though, it provides patterns, which you can adopt and adapt to the problems at hand. The trick to using the book is to see patterns in your problem, that is, to learn to divide your work into parts that can be cleanly and clearly resolved and then combined into a whole. The case studies may help you see how others have woven parametric thinking and design into entire projects.

If you are a student learning parametric design, your aim is the practitioner s craft. Everything relevant to the practitioner applies to you too. Design can only be learned by doing. "Talkitecture" is a derogatory term, reserved for those who discuss but do not draw. Don t draw it onto yourself. You need more; particularly, you need to understand how parametric systems work; how their structure makes them perform and how people have used and are using them to do design. The middle chapters of the book may have special meaning for you.

If you are a teacher, you will find strategies here. I believe that we teachers do our best work when we attend to all aspects of design, from vocational skill, through technique and strategy, and all the way to helping our charges discover their muse. The book aims mostly at the middle ground, at linking underlying skills with the higher order understanding needed for good design. Patterns do yeoman s work in this enterprise, at least for the hundreds I have taught and the dozens of tutors who have worked with me in pattern-oriented courses.

If you are a CAD system developer, I believe that you will find some of what is missing in contemporary systems. Without exception, the market provides systems with wonderful capability, cleverly constructed and often with nifty human-computer interfaces. Largely because the needed knowledge is not yet available, current systems are of little help with strategizing, re ecting and developing individual and group practice. As software design patterns have done for software engineering, perhaps the patterns here can suggest new ways of solving the compositional problems that are at the heart of making systems scale in complexity, both of model size and human use.

Almost all who use parametric modeling are amateur programmers . I use the word "amateur" in its literal and complimentary sense, describing one who has interest and skill in an area, but who lacks formal education in it. Amateur and professional programmers differ in more than expertise. Amateurs tend to work on programs that relate to current work tasks, write short programs, use simple data structures and create sparse documentation. Amateurs prefer a copy-and-modify style in their programming work, in which they find, skim, test and modify code until it works for the task at hand. Amateurs satisfice – they leave abstraction, generality and reuse mostly for "real programmers". Professionals might decry such practices, but they cannot change them. Amateurs program because they have a task to complete for which programming is a good tool. The task is foremost, the tool need only be adequate to it. Amateurs write most programs used in our world. Yet almost all programming tools are designed for the professional and are overly complex for the tasks amateurs attempt. If, like almost all designers, you are an amateur programmer, you will find in the book s patterns ideas and techniques for achieving your programming tasks.

It is ironic that this book for amateurs is itself a work of amateur programming. Almost all of its figures were created using GenerativeComponents®, itself a parametric modeling system. Rather than rely on the tedious and limited image export capabilities available in the host system at the time, I wrote a system that output code from the parametric modeler to the TikZ/PGF graphics macro package in the LaTeX package in which I typeset the book. This system has three parts. The first is DR, a graphics package much simpler than TikZ/PGF, that provides just the functions I needed. DR translates function calls to TikZ/PGF calls. The second is code in the parametric modeler s scripting language that uses the DR package to describe figures for the book. The third is an Excel® spreadsheet interface to the parametric modeler, so that all of the figures can be described in a single Excel® worksheet. Outside of this sytem, I programmed many macros in LaTeX, largely to gain control over page layout. This sometimes messy code suffices for producing the book. Though I know how to make it general (and know how much work that would take), I focused on the book. The code will need work if it is ever used for another purpose. So be it.

Lastly in this introduction, I must explain the title. In 1919, William Strunk first published *The Elements of Style*,[1] a brilliant, and brilliantly short, book giving strategies for effective writing. Much in that book pertains to writers today. Its clear imperative voice is remarkably similar to much writing about design patterns. Strunk himself borrowed the title; in 1857, John Ruskin (1857) had published the wordy and minimally graphical *Elements of Drawing*. Seeing an obvious good idea, many other authors have undertaken *The Elements of...* books on topics ranging across colour (Itten, 1970), cooking (Ruhlman, 2007), ecology (Smith and Smith, 2008), graphic design (Williams, 2008)[2], interaction design (Garrett, 2002), mentoring (Johnson and Ridley, 2008), programming (Gamma et al., 1995), rhetoric (Maxwell and Dickman, 2007; Rottenberg and Winchell, 2008), typography (Williams, 1995, 2003; Bringhurst, 2004) and, of course, writing (Flaherty, 2009). Strunk and all subsequent authors had a strong precedent in *Euclid s Elements* written *circa* 300BC. A work and writing style could not be more deeply embedded in our culture. Absent an original idea, go with one that works. So I took Euclid s and Strunk s leads, with a twist. I make two points in omitting the "The". First, the field is young, and I would commit a ludicrous error in implying that I cover anything like a complete set of ideas. Second, my premise for design patterns is that they are important only if useful, and useful only if used. The way people use patterns is to try them out, re ect on them and change them. For me, the set will never be complete. The definite article "The" might well be replaced by the indefinite "Some". But no article is shorter still.

---

[1] My personal copy is the 1959 edition, (Strunk and White, 1959)

[2] I have included Robin Williams books *Non-Designer s Design Book*, *The PC is Not a Typewriter* and *The Mac is Not a Typewriter* in this list. Though not one uses *Elements* in its title, each is completely within the genre and each is a very good book, too!

Chapter 2

What is parametric modeling?

The archetypal design medium is pencil and paper. More precisely: pencil, eraser and paper. The pencil adds and the eraser subtracts. Add a few tools, like a T-square, triangle, compass and scale, and drawings can become accurate and precise models of a design idea. Designers are used to working in this mode; add marks and take them away, with conventions for relating marks together.

Conventional design systems are straightforward emulations of this centuries-old means of work. *Parametric modeling* (also known as *constraint modeling*) introduces a fundamental change: "marks", that is, *parts of a design*, relate and change together in a coordinated way. No longer must designers simply add and erase. They now *add, erase, relate* and *repair*. The act of *relating* requires explicit thinking about the kind of relation: is this point *on* the line, or *near* to it? *Repairing* occurs after an erasure, when the parts that depend on an erased part are related again to the parts that remain. Relating and repairing impose fundamental changes on systems and the work that is done with them.

Many parametric systems have been built both in research laboratories and by companies. An increasing number are present in the marketplace. Certainly the most mature parametric system is the spreadsheet, which operates over a usually rectangular table of cells rather than a design. In some design disciplines, like mechanical engineering, they are now the normal medium for work. In others, such as architecture, their substantial effects started only about the year 2000.

The first computer-aided design system was parametric. Ivan Sutherland s PhD thesis on Sketchpad (1963) provided both a propagation-based mechanism and a simultaneous solver based on relaxation. It was the first report of a feature that became central to many constraint languages – the *merge operator* that combines two similar structures into a single structure governed by the union of all the constraints on its arguments.

Hoffmann and Joan-Arinyo (2005) provide an overview of different kinds of parametric systems. Each is defined by its approach to constraint solving, and each has its own characteristics and implications for design work. *Graph-based* approaches represent objects as nodes in a graph and constraints as links. The solver attempts to condition a graph so that it divides into easily solvable sub-problems, solves these problems and composes their answers into to complete solution. *Logic-based* approaches describe problems as axioms, over which search for a solution occurs by applying logical inference rules. *Algebraic* approaches translate a set of constraints into a non-linear system of equations, which is then solved by one or a variety of techniques. Constraints must be expressed before they can be solved. Large designs can embody thousands of constraints, which must be clearly expressed, checked and debugged as design proceeds. In addition to their contributions to solving constraints, several research projects have focused on devising clear languages for expressing constraints. Borning s ThingLab (1981) had both graphical and programming constructs for constraints. At the same time, Steele and Sussman (1980) reported a LISP-based language for constraints. *Constraint languages* such as ASCEND (Piela et al., 1993) use a declarative object-oriented language design to build very large constraint models for engineering design. *Constraint management systems*, for example, Delta Blue (Sannella et al., 1993) provides primitives and constraints that are not bundled together and with which the user can overconstrain the system, but must give some value (or utility) for the resolution of different constraints. In this system, a constraint manager does not need access to the structure of the primitives or the constraints. Rather its algorithm aims to find a particular directed acyclic graph that resolves the most highly valued constraints.

Propagation-based systems (Aish and Woodbury, 2005) derive from one aspect of Hoffmann and Joan-Arinyo s graph-based approach. They presume that the user organizes a graph so that it can be directly solved. They are the most simple type of parametric system. In fact, they are so simple that the literature hardly mentions them, focusing rather on more complex systems that address problems beyond those directly solvable with propagation. Discussed in more detail later in this chapter, propagation arranges objects in a directed graph such that known information is upstream of unknown information. The system propagates from knowns to compute the unknowns.

Of all types of parametric modeling, propagation has the relative advantages of reliability, speed and clarity. It is used in spreadsheets, data ow programming and computer-aided design due to the efficiency of its algorithms and simplicity of the decision-making required of the user. Propagation systems also support a simple form of end user extensibility through programming. This simplicity exacts a price. Some systems are not directly expressible, for instance, tensegrity structures. Also, the designer must explicitly decide what is known and order information from known to unknown. Propagation s simplicity makes it is a good place from which to start building an acount of parametric modeling. The rest of this chapter explains the basic structure and operation of a propagation-based parametric modeling system.

It is useful to be precise with language. The following section defines terms needed for accurate dicsussion of parametric modeling systems. These terms are generic. Any particular propagation-based system has a similar description, though some details will vary.

Graphs are *nodes* connected by *links*. In a *directed graph*, the links are arrows; they explicitly link *arrow tail* or *predecessor* to *arrow head* or *successor* nodes. *Paths* or *chains* are sequences of nodes, each except the last linked to the next node in the path. A graph is *cyclic* if it has paths in which nodes recur.

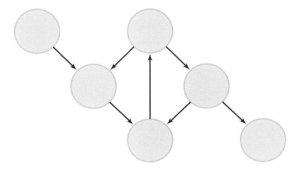

2.1: A graph has a collection of nodes joined by links. In a directed graph, links join tail (predecessor) to head (successor) nodes. This graph is both directed and cyclic.

In parametric modeling, nodes have *names*. Further, the nodes are *schemata*, that is, they are objects containing *properties*. Each property has an associated *value*, accessed by *dot notation*, that is, by appending to a schema name a period followed by the property name. For example, p.X accesses the X property of point p and has the value stored in that property.

```
Point p
{
   CoordSystem:  cs;
   X:            3.0;
   Y:            4.0;
   Z:            1.0;
}
```

2.2: A schema for a point named p, with properties for its coordinate system and *x*, *y* and *z* coordinates. The value of the CoordSystem property is the name of a coordinate system node elsewhere in the model that contains the point. Using dot notation, p.X identifies the X property of p and equals 3.0.

The algorithms needed are most simply described by considering only nodes with a single property. Dot notation accesses the single property of such a node, for example, n.Value gives the data held in the Value property of node n. By convention, for single-property nodes, the name of the node itself returns the data in its single property.

A *constraint expression* is a well-formed formula comprising objects, function calls and operators. The objects comprise numbers and property values given with dot notation. When evaluated, constraint expressions result in values.

Constraint expression	Result
3.0	3.0
Sin(30.0)	0.5
false	false
true	true
3.0+Sqrt(5.0)	approximately 5.236067977
p.X + 3.0	the X property of p + 3.0
p.X > 1.0 ? true : false	either true or false depending on the X property of p.
p	the node named "p"
p.CoordSystem.Y	the Y property of the CoordSystem property of p
distance(p,q)+1.618	the distance between p and q plus 1.618

2.3: Examples of constraint expressions.

Property values can be constraint expressions, which in turn can use, that is, *contain* properties from other nodes. Such properties are said to be *contained* by both the property and expression in which they occur. They define the links in the graph. The system ensures that properties and their expressions are evaluated whenever their contained properties change value. Informally, we say that data *ows into* a node when its constraint expressions are evaluated. Nodes (properties) used in a constraint expression are predecessors of the node (property) holding the expression. Links in the graph record that a successor node has a constraint expression that uses a property value from a predecessor node. In single-property nodes, links directly encode property predecessors and successors.

A property can *have* (or be *assigned*) an explicit value or an expression using no property values; such properties are called *graph-independent*. Alternatively it can have a constraint expression using one or more property values from other nodes; such are called *graph-dependent* properties.

A *source node* has no graph-dependent properties and thus no predecessor nodes. A *sink node* is used in no constraint expressions; it has no successor nodes. An *internal node* is neither source nor sink. A node can be both source and sink. A subgraph has its own source and sink nodes.

The system maintains graph consistency by evaluating the expressions in each property. We say that it *evaluates a node* by evaluating all node s properties and thus all its contained expressions. It must choose an order of evaluation so that a property is evaluated *after* all of its predecessor properties have been evaluated. The graph thus cannot have any cycles, else a node would have to be evaluated in order for it to be evaluated, leading to a contradiction of the algorithm s need for prior evaluation of predecessor nodes.

A *parametric design* (or just *design*) is an *directed graph* of the nodes and links above. A *well-formed* design has no cycles – it is a *directed acyclic graph*.

A *chain* is an ordered set C of nodes, with each node $c_i, 0 < i < |C|$ in the chain being an immediate successor of c_{i-1}.

The system uses three algorithms: one *orders* the graph, one *propagates values* through the graph and one *displays* the results.

The first algorithm requires a well-formed parametric model and produces a total ordering of the graph nodes. It finds a sequence of nodes such that a node occurs in the order only after all of its predecessor nodes. Such a sequence is called a *topological order*, many of which may exist for a given graph. It does not matter which of the possible total orders is chosen. For a given graph, this algorithm need only be run once.

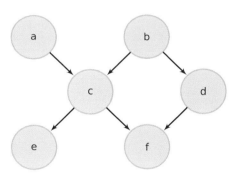

2.5: The tuple ⟨ b,d,a,c,f,e ⟩ is a topological sort – a sequence such that all predecessor nodes of any node occur before the node in the sequence. A graph can have many such, for example, ⟨ a,b,c,d,e,f ⟩, ⟨ a,b,c,d,f,e ⟩ and ⟨ b,a,c,e,d,f ⟩ are among the possible sorts for this graph. Any one suffices as a result of the sorting algorithm, though there may be advantages in the user interface for choosing one over another.

2.4: Nodes c_0 ... c_8 form a chain.

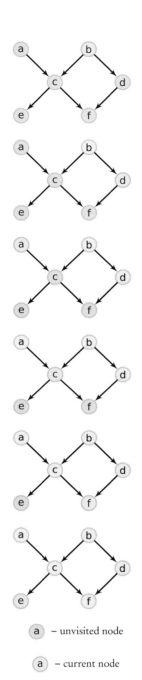

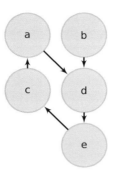

2.6: In a graph with cycles a node can be predecessor of itself. Such a graph cannot be sorted topologically. A naïve algorithm that tried to evaluate it would loop infinitely.

The second algorithm is propagation. In its most simple form, it evaluates each node in a sequence by evaluating its contained constraint expressions. More sophisticated and faster versions of this algorithm only evaluate those nodes that are successors of the nodes that have changed.

A graph models a usually infinite collection of *parametric design instances* (or just *instances* when clear in context), each of which is defined by assigning values to the graph-independent properties of the graph. To compute an instance order its graph and propagate values throughout it. Both algorithms are simple and efficient, enabling interaction with large models. For instance, the ordering algorithm is topological sort, with worst case time complexity of $O(n + e)$ where n is the number of nodes and e is the number of links in the graph. The propagation algorithm has time complexity $O(n + e)$, presuming that the internal node algorithms are $O(1)$. (The O function is called big-Oh and describes the running time or memory requirement of an algorithm as the size n of inputs grow. Informally, a time complexity of $O(n)$ means that, as n grows, a plot of the running time of the algorithm remains below some non-vertical straight line on the graph. If an algorithm is $O(1)$ the running time is independent of the size of the input n.)

The third algorithm displays the graph symbolically (that is, as nodes and links) and as a model in 3D. A useful, though not universal, convention for symbolic views is to arrange the nodes such that the links ow in a consistent direction (up, down, right or left). Such arrangements reveal the inherent ow of data through a propagation graph. The system invokes the propagation and display algorithms continuously. When the model is sufficiently small that each cycle of these algorithms takes less than approximately 1/30 of a second, designers feel like they are directly interacting with the parametric model.

For systems of one-property nodes the ordering algorithm can be viewed equally as ordering properties and nodes. Multi-property nodes are more complex. Figure 2.8 shows that such a node can be viewed as containing (or *condensing*) a collection of single property nodes and as replacing those nodes in a graph.

a – unvisited node

a – current node

a – visited node

2.7: Using the topological sort ⟨ b, d, a, c, f, e ⟩, the propagation algorithm visits each node in sequence. It evaluates the graph-dependent properties in each node.

16

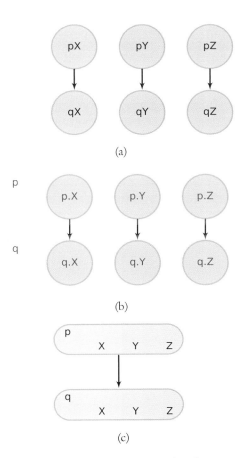

(a)

(b)

(c)

2.8: Multi-property nodes can be viewed as collections of single-property nodes. (a) A parametric model comprising six nodes, representing the coordinates of two points, with one point being a simple translation of the other. (b) Nodes p and q collect the respective single-property nodes. (c) The prior single-property nodes become properties in p and q. One link joining p and q replaces the three prior single-node links.

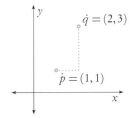

2.9: Point $\dot{q}$ is a simple translation of point $\dot{p}$, in this case $\dot{q}_x = \dot{p}_x + 1$ and $\dot{q}_y = \dot{p}_y + 2$. When $\dot{p}$ moves, so does $\dot{q}$.

A problem arises in that an acyclic graph of single-property nodes can become cyclic when it is condensed into multi-property nodes. For example, consider two points $\dot{p}$ and $\dot{q}$, with the y coordinate of $\dot{q}$ being assigned the x coordinate of $\dot{p}$ and the y coordinate of $\dot{p}$ being assigned the x coordinate of $\dot{q}$. Points $\dot{p}$ and $\dot{q}$ will always define a line segment at 135° to the origin, with its endpoints equidistant from their nearest axis. This graph is acyclic when it comprises single-property nodes, but becomes cyclic when points $\dot{p}$ and $\dot{q}$ are condensed into nodes. Further, if multi-property nodes are used from the outset, then some models that "should" be expressible are not due to the acyclic constraint of the topological ordering algorithm (Algorithm #1). Some practical solutions to this problem are to define the sorting and propagation algorithms to work over properties; or to accept the inexpressibility of some apparently sensible models. There are advantages and disadvantages to both approaches.

Propagating over properties yields a larger and more "complete" range of expressible models and often faster model updating. It can create problems in user interfaces, which most often rely on the acyclic constraint to make model visualizations readable. Propagating over multi-property nodes can simplify the user interface, but also can result in slower updates and confusion when a modeling step that "should" work fails for no apparently sensible reason.

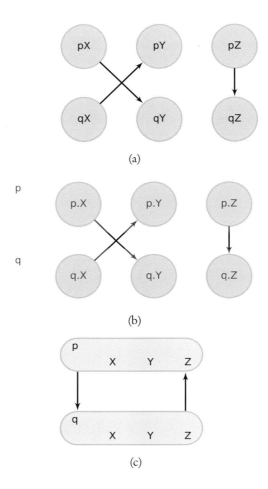

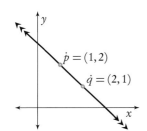

2.11: The y property of point $\dot{p}$ depends on the x property of point $\dot{q}$ and vice versa. When $\dot{p}_x = \dot{q}_x$, $\dot{p}$ and $\dot{q}$ coincide, otherwise they define a line at 135° to the x-axis.

2.10: Condensing single-property nodes into multi-property nodes can produce cyclical graphs. (a) A parametric model comprising six nodes, representing the coordinates of two points, with the y coordinates of each point being the x coordinate of the other. (b) Points p and q collect the respective single-property nodes. (c) The prior single-property nodes become properties in p and q. The three links joining the single-property nodes are replaced by two links joining p and q to form a cycle.

Multi-property nodes present major advantages in what computer scientists call *encapsulation* and *data abstraction*. With them, data describing a distinct conceptual object can be stored in one logical place; multiple operations can be defined over this data; logical relations among the data can be automatically maintained; and data access can be made uniform. Figure 2.2 on page 13 shows a simple multi-property node comprising a coordinate system and the three coordinates needed to define a point. It demonstrates two key ideas: first, that properties can contain (refer to) other multi-property nodes (the cs held in the CoordSystem property); and second, that nodes can be *typed*.

Dot notation extends to properties holding multi-property nodes. For example, the *path* notation p.CoordSystem.X accesses the x coordinate of the coordinate system held in p.CoordSystem.

Typed nodes are *instances* of *types*. A type is a template specifying a property set and a set of *update algorithms* for computing properties defined within the type.

We take a type and its set of properties to represent a concept or object in the world. It is useful to distinguish between the nodes and their properties and the corresponding objects and properties to which they refer. By convention, we render nodes and properties in a sans-serif font and their corresponding objects in *italicized* (mathematical) notation. For example, a node named p of type Point might have properties X, Y and Z. The corresponding point $\dot{p}$ has coordinates $\dot{p}_x$, $\dot{p}_y$ and $\dot{p}_z$ respectively. The node p *represents* the concept or object $\dot{p}$.

An update algorithm uses some node properties to compute others. In the scope of a node, those properties whose values are computed by an update algorithm are *node-dependent* (or just *dependent* when clear in context). Node-dependent properties are successors to the input properties to the update algorithm. The node-dependent properties are determined by the update algorithm and cannot have a user-defined value or expression attached to them. All other properties are *node-independent* (or just *independent*). An instance of a type selects one of the available update algorithms as an *active update algorithm*.

```
Point p
 update byCartesianCoordinates
{
   CoordSystem: cs;
   X:           q.X + 2.0;
   Y:           3.0 * 2.0;
   Z:           1.0;
   Azimuth:     dep Atan2(X,Y)      = 51.13;
   Radius:      dep Sqrt(X*X + Y*Y) = 5.0;
   Height:      dep Z               = 1.0;
}
```

2.12: A node of type Point with a ByCartesianCoordinates update algorithm may have a user-defined constraint expression in each of its X, Y or Z properties. In contrast, the constraint expressions in its Azimuth, Radius or Height properties are given by its update algorithm. In this figure the CoordSystem and X property are graph-dependent and the Y and Z properties are graph-independent.

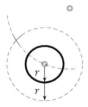

Even objects as simple as points have multiple update algorithms. For instance, a point node might include its containing coordinate system CoordSystem, its X, Y and Z coordinates and, in cylindrical coordinates, its Azimuth, Radius and Height. A ByCartesianCoordinates update algorithm would require that the CoordSystem, X, Y and Z properties be defined and use these to compute the point node s Azimuth, Radius and Height properties. Conversely, using a ByCylindricalCoordinates update algorithm would use the CoordSystem, Azimuth, Radius and Height properties to compute values for its X, Y and Z properties.

```
Point p
 update byCartesianCoordinates
 {
   CoordSystem:  cs;
   X:            3.0;
   Y:            4.0;
   Z:            1.0;
   Azimuth:      dep Atan2(X,Y)      = 51.13;
   Radius:       dep Sqrt(X*X + Y*Y) = 5.0;
   Height:       dep Z               = 1.0;
 }
```

```
Point q
 update byCylindricalCoordinates
 {
   CoordSystem:  cs;
   X:            dep Radius*cos(Azimuth) = 3.0;
   Y:            dep Radius*sin(Azimuth) = 4.0;
   Z:            dep Height              = 1.0;
   Azimuth:      51.13;
   Radius:       5.0;
   Height:       1.0;
 }
```

2.13: Different update algorithms imply different sets of node-dependent and node-independent properties. The two points p and q are at the same location. Using the ByCartesianCoordinates update algorithm, the properties CoordSystem, X, Y and Z are independent. The node-dependent properties are marked with the keyword dep. Using the ByCylindricalCoordinates update algorithm, CoordSystem, Azimuth, Radius and Height are independent.

A node may use several nodes in its contained expressions, that is, it can be a successor of several nodes. It can also use several properties from each used node; a link thus indicates that one or more properties from a predecessor node are used in the expressions within a node.

2.14: Steps in constructing a line through a point $\dot{p}$ and tangent to a circle $\hat{c}$ with centre $\dot{c}$ and radius r. Find the intersection $\dot{s}$ of two circles, with centres at $\dot{p}$ (radius $|\overrightarrow{pc}|$) and $\dot{c}$ (radius $2r$). Intersect the circle $\hat{c}$ and $\overline{sc}$ to find the tangent point.

```
Point p
  update byCartesianCoordinates
  {
    CoordSystem: cs;
    X:           (p0.X+p1.X)/2.0;
    Y:           (p0.Y+p1.Y)/2.0;
    Z:           (p0.Z+p1.Z)/2.0;
  }
```

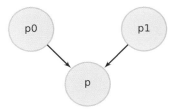

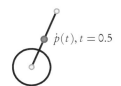

2.15: A node may depend on several nodes and several properties within itself. For instance, the constraint expressions in point p use the properties in points p0 and p1, which, by this fact, are predecessors of p. Evaluating these expressions places the point $\dot{p}$ equidistant from and collinear with points $\dot{p}_0$ and $\dot{p}_1$, that is, the midpoint of a line segment between $\dot{p}_0$ and $\dot{p}_1$.

Constraint expressions can be written in a way that expresses the flow of data. In the example above, $\dot{p}$ depends on $\dot{p}_0$ and $\dot{p}_1$, by taking the average, that is, the expression, $\dot{p} = \frac{\dot{p}_0 + \dot{p}_1}{2}$. Reversing the order of the expression and using an arrow to indicate data flow gives the following expression.

$$\frac{\dot{p}_0 + \dot{p}_1}{2} \rightarrow \dot{p}$$

This vector equation expands to an equation for of its coordinates. These are shown below as parametric modeling constraint expressions.

```
(p0.X + p1.X)/2 → p.X

(p0.Y + p1.Y)/2 → p.Y

(p0.Z + p1.Z)/2 → p.Z
```

Data flow visualization of constraint expressions provides a more accurate view of property values; one that reverses their usual reading. In programming, the common view of a property value is that it *holds* or *contains* the object it names. In parametric modeling, a more insightful view is that a property value *uses* the nodes named within it. Such nodes are predecessors of the property in the model. Dot notation therefore gives access to only those parts of a model that precede (are upstream from) the property. An expression in dot notation records a chain of nodes, starting at the bottom of the chain. The notation provides no direct way of discovering the nodes (properties) that use a particular node (property). If provided, such *back links* must be computed by the modeler itself.

2.16: An alternative construction sequence for a line through a point $\dot{p}$ and tangent to a circle $\hat{c}$ with centre $\dot{c}$. Draw a circle centred on the midpoint of $\dot{p}$ and $\dot{c}$. Intersect this circle and the circle $\hat{c}$ to find the tangent point.

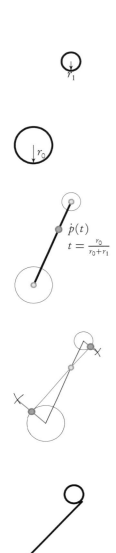

Propagation is by far the most simple form of parametric modeling. Over other bases for modeling, it has the major advantage of generality. Update algorithms can compute anything (or at least, anything computable), whereas other schemes restrict their domain, for example, to real-valued expressions. With it, many constructs that designers would like to use become difficult to express. For example, computing the two lines tangent to two circles requires a multi-step geometric construction unless a specific update algorithm for such lines exists. Some constructions require cyclical networks and these can only be solved with global graph techniques. The number of potentially useful update algorithms boggles the mind and would devastate any user interface that tried to provide them all. Even if a huge set of algorithms could somehow be made available and accessible in a system, geometry is too big a topic and design too adventurous an enterprise to be fully covered. The reality is that designers will work at the boundaries of any system and need a combination of techniques to do so. Two key techniques are *geometric construction* and *programming*.

Geometric construction involves making sequences of simple operations to solve problems. It is the child of the compass and straight-edge constructions of Euclidean geometry, but adds the entire set of parametric update methods to the primitive operations of this ancient system. Almost all constructions can be done in different ways. For example, Figures 2.14 and 2.16 show distinct ways to construct a tangent from a point to a circle. While brevity is important (see Figure 2.16), sometimes longer solutions are easier to find and may give new and perhaps valuable insight (see Figure 2.14). Once a good geometric construction has been discovered, it can be used in other, more complex constructions, for example, in finding the tangent line between two circles (see Figure 2.17).

Programming is writing algorithms that either build models or work as update algorithms in their own right. Both construction and programming are foreign to most designers. The last half of the 20th Century saw a dramatic decline in teaching the closest geometric topic, descriptive geometry; and a modest and erratic introduction of programming. Parametric modeling and contemporary design conspire to demand both of these skills. Before addressing either of the technical skills of programming or geometry, the next chapter outlines how designers are using parametric modeling as they work.

2.17: To construct a line tangent to two circles find the parametric point $\dot{p}(t)$ between the circle centres that divides the centre-to-centre distance proportional to the circle radii. Using $\dot{p}(t)$ replaces several steps of Euclidean construction. Use Figure 2.14 or 2.16 to construct the tangents from $\dot{p}(t)$ to each circle.

Chapter 3

How designers use parameters

The generic description of parametric modeling in the previous chapter defines important technical terms and structures, but does not speak to the effects of such a system on design work. This chapter sketches how parametric design work changes what designers do and what they must think about while they are doing it. The treatment is mainly descriptive. It derives from the properties of parametric systems themselves; from my own knowledge of computation and design; but mostly from working, over several years, with designers using and learning parametric systems.

3.1   Conventional and parametric design tools

In conventional design tools it is "easy" to create an initial model – you just add parts, relating them to each other by such things as *snaps* as you go. Making changes to a model can be difficult. Even changing one dimension can require adjusting many other parts and all of this rework is manual. The more complex the model, the more work can be entailed. From a design perspective, decisions that should be changed can take too much work to change. Tools like these can limit exploration and effectively restrict design.

On the other hand, erasing conventional work is easy. You select and delete. Since parts are *independent,* that is, they have no lasting relationship to other parts, there is no more work to do to fix the representation. You might well have to fix the design, by adding parts to take the place of the thing erased or adjusting existing parts to fit the changed design.

Since the 1980 s, conventional tools have used the ubiquitous generic concepts of *copy, cut* and *paste.* These combine erasure and addition of parts to support rapid change by copying and repositioning like elements. Copy, cut and paste work in conventional design precisely because of part independence.

Parametric modeling aims to address these limitations. Rather than the designer creating the design solution (by direct manipulation) as in conventional design tools, the idea is that the designer establishes the *relationships* by which parts connect, builds up a design using these relationships and edits the relationships by observing and selecting from the results produced. The system takes care of keeping the design consistent with the relationships and thus increases designer ability to explore ideas by reducing the tedium of rework.

Of course, there is a cost. Parametric design depends on defining relationships and the willingness (and ability) of the designer to consider the relationship-definition phase as an integral part of the broader design process. It initially requires the designer to take one step back from the direct activity of design and focus on the logic that binds the design together. This process of relationship creation requires a formal notation and introduces additional concepts that have not previously been considered as part of "design thinking".

The cost may have a benefit. Parametric design and its requisite modes of thought may well extend the intellectual scope of design by explicitly representing ideas that are usually treated intuitively. Being able to explain concepts explicitly is a part of at least some real understanding.

Defining relationships is a complex act of thinking. It involves strategies and skills, some new to designers and some familiar. The following sections outline some of these strategies and connect them with what designers already have in their repertoire. The first section, entitled *New Skills,* outlines the small-scale, technical knowledge and craft in evident use by effective parametric modeling practitioners. The second section, entitled *New Strategies,* steps slightly closer to design to sketch the new tasks that designers can and do undertake with the new tools. Both sections are descriptive, not normative. By this I mean they are based on observing and working with designers using parametric modelers, not on surmising what designers might, in some sense, need to know.

3.2   New skills

Drawing is a skill. Combining multiple orthographic and perspective sketches to reveal the implications of a design idea is strategy. Here are six skills held by those who know and use parametric tools. Some have analogues to historical design skills. Others are new to design. Parametric mastery requires them all.

3.2.1   Conceiving data flow

Caveat: The examples in Sections 3.2.1 to 3.2.4 are very simple, almost trivial. This is deliberate. Through simplicity, I hope to explain crucial principles that are easily obscured. **Reader, please bear with me.**

The detailed explanation of propagation-based systems in Chapter 2 reflects a real need to understand propagation in use. Data flows through a parametric model, from independent to dependent nodes. The way in which data flows deeply affects the designs possible and how a designer interacts with them. This can be illustrated with a very simple example: a three-room rectangular plan drawn with lines representing walls. In the figures that follow, the propagation graph represents only the dimensions of the rooms; the lines would, in turn, depend on the nodes in this graph. In Figure 3.1, room dimensions are related by open dimension chains. Figure 3.2 shows the same set of rooms, with the additional relationship that $room_1$ is always square. Here the graph has an new link (between w_1 and h_1) and one fewer source node (h_1). In Figure 3.3, $room_1$ remains square and is a constant proportion of the overall width. This makes w_1 an internal node and introduces the proportional constant a as a new source node.

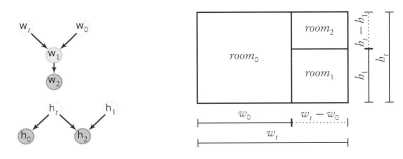

3.1: The plan has $room_{0...2}$. Each $room_i$ has a width w_i and a height h_i. The total width is w_t; the total height is h_t. Dimensions w_t and w_0 are independent. Dimensions w_1 and w_2 are dependent: $w_t - w_0 \rightarrow w_1$ and $w_1 \rightarrow w_2$. Dimensions h_t and h_1 are independent, whereas h_0 and h_2 are dependent: $h_t \rightarrow h_0$ and $h_t - h_1 \rightarrow h_2$. An increase in h_t results in $room_1$ remaining the same height: $room_0$ and $room_2$ expand to take up all of the new space. For graphical clarity, the floor plans omit the simple relations of equality between dimensions where such are implied by the drawing, for instance, $w_2 = w_1$.

(a) – source node   (a) – internal node   (a) – sink node

Conceiving, arranging and editing dependencies is the key parametric task.

To make things more complex, dependency chains – several nodes in sequential dependency – tend to grow. Figure 3.4 expands the examples above it to include the points and lines representing the floor plan. It shows that long dependency chains are the norm, and that visualizing the graph can become difficult.

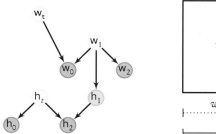 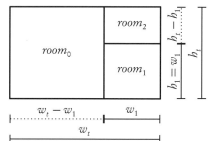

3.2: The main interactive difference between this design and that of Figure 3.1 is that $room_1$ is always square and its size is explicitly controlled. The propagation graph is distinctly different.

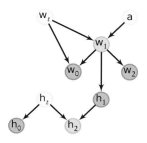 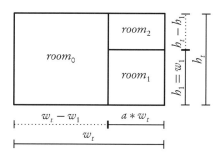

3.3: In addition to the constraints in the design in Figure 3.2, the ratio between w_t and w_1 remains constant: $a * w_t \rightarrow w_1$.

Designers use dependencies in combination to exhibit some desired aggregate form or behaviour. Dependencies may correspond to geometric relationships (for example, between a surface and its defining curves), but are not restricted to this and may in fact represent higher order (or more abstract) design decisions. Parametric approaches to design aim to provide designers with tools to capture design decisions in an explicit, auditable, editable and re-executable form.

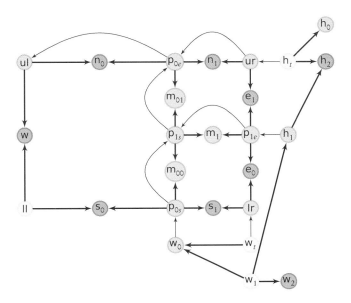

3.4: Adding the points and lines defining the oor plan increases both the length of the dependency chains, the overall graph complexity, the difficulty of inventing short, clear, descriptive names, and, especially, the challenge of achieving a readable graph layout. This diagram is based on that of Figure 3.2. It changes the layout of the nodes in the prior graph and breaks the convention of uniform direction of data ow in favour of a layout that mimics the location of points and lines in the oor plan. Some arcs are curved to avoid intervening nodes. Arcs whose sole purpose is to carry coordinate information are thin. External walls are labeled with n, e, s and w (for *north, east, south* and *west*); and internal walls are prefixed with the character m (largely because this character was not used elsewhere). Finally the node ll (for *lower left*) is presumed to be at (0,0); if it were locatable anywhere, arcs would have to go from it to other nodes in the graph.

3.2.2   Dividing to conquer

For very good reasons, designers organize their work as *near-hierarchies,* that is, recursive systems of parts with limited interactions between parts. This is a near-universal claim, and it is easy to test. Think of a designed object that is so organized, for example, an automobile organized into body, drive train and electrical systems. Now think of a designed object that is a non-near-hierarchy in some way, either by having only one part or by having extremely complex interactions among its parts. Compare the relative difficulty of imagining each. **See?**

One of the many reasons for near-hierarchies is that the limited interactions among system parts enables a divide-and-conquer design strategy – divide the design into parts, design the parts and combine the parts into an entire design, all the while managing the interactions among the parts. The strategy works best when the interactions are simple.

Parametric modeling enables, indeed almost requires, a divide-and-conquer strategy. In building a parametric design, it is easy to keep adding nodes to the graph. A moment comes though, when the graph is too complex to fully grasp. At a much earlier moment, it becomes difficult to explain the graph to another, or to resume work on it after an inevitable interruption (in this situation, there really is "another" – it is you, after you've taken a break and come back with a different memory state). Using a divide-and-conquer strategy is to organize a parametric design into parts so that there are limited and understandable links from part to part. Directional of data flow assures a hierarchical model, with parts higher in the flow typically being assemblies – organizing concepts. Parts at the bottom of the flow usually correspond to physical parts of the design.

Returning to the three-room floor plan, even this seemingly simple design could be given a hierarchical structure. Figures 3.5 and 3.6 show that a decision to model the three rooms in two *wings*, assigning each room to one of the wings, has profound effects on the plans obtainable, particularly when the number of rooms in each wing increases.

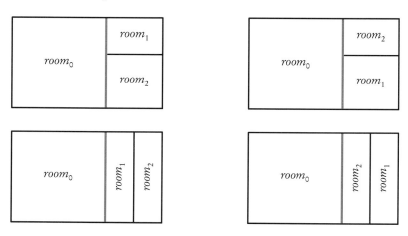

3.5: All possible arrangements of an organization into two wings with $room_0$ in the west wing and $room_1$ and $room_2$ in the east wing.

Skilled designers spend much time on developing and refining the near-hierarchical structure of their models. They arrive at parametric design as able practitioners of divide-and-conquer – architects usually organize designs (especially at the construction documentation phase) into technical subsystems. In conceptual design, common design schema separately play on space and tectonics. But skills transfer poorly across domains. The divide-and-conquer of parametric modeling requires knowledge from both the design domain and about how to structure parametric designs so that data flows from part to part in a clear and explainable manner.

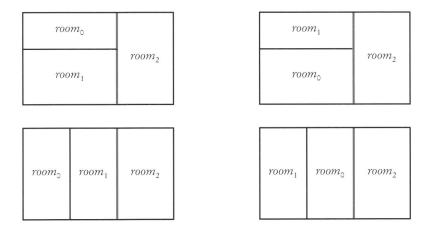

3.6: All arrangements of an organization into two wings with $room_0$ and $room_1$ in the west wing and $room_2$ in the east wing.

3.2.3   Naming

Parts have names. This is designerly practice, not physical law. But there is a good reason for this – names facilitate communication. "The column at grid location E2:S4" is a more reliable way of identifying a particular column than "that square mark a third or the way across and halfway up the sheet".

Parametric modelers spend much time in devising and refining the names of their parts. Simply renaming the rooms and dimensions of the three-room oor plan shows why they do this. Figure 3.7 is identical to Figure 3.2 in all respects, except that the nodes and rooms have been given arbitrary names.

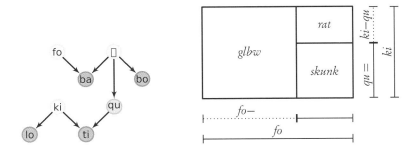

3.7: Confusion reigns with arbitrary names. Even though this figure and Figure 3.2 are identical except for names, it takes much more effort to understand this one.

3.2.4 Thinking with abstraction

The word "abstraction" is laden, that is, its meaning depends on context.

Designers and computer scientists use the term differently.

An abstraction describes a general concept rather than a specific example. In common usage, abstraction is associate with vagueness; it may be hard to infer much from an abstract idea. In design, abstract ideas are often protean, that is, they are used as a base from which to generate many alternatives. In this role, both connotations of the word apply: a general concept can be realized in many ways, and a vague concept can be given many interpretations, each of which may have multiple realizations.

In computer science, abstraction has the first meaning: an abstraction describes of a class of instances, leaving out inessential detail. Computer scientists (and their craftful cousins, programmers) are constantly seeking formalisms and code that apply in many situations. In fact, the utility of a computational idea is deeply linked to its generality – the more often it applies, the more useful it becomes). Designers too know and practice such abstraction. Dimensional modules, structural centrelines and standard details all are media for abstract design ideas.

To abstract a parametric model is to make it applicable in new situations, to make it depend only on essential inputs and to remove reference to and use of overly specific terms. It is particularly important because much modeling work is similar, and time is always in short supply. If part (remember divide-and-conquer?) of one model can be used in another, it displays some abstraction by the very fact of reuse. Well-crafted abstractions are a key part of efficient modeling. For example, in   oor plans comprising rectangular rooms, two good abstractions are to consider the rooms and the walls respectively as as nodes. Using rooms as nodes (Figure 3.8) creates two independent subgraphs in the design, one for west-to-east relations and one for north-to-south relations.

When walls are nodes, as in Figure 3.9, the graph becomes a very simple tree structure of successive subdivisions, either vertical or horizontal, dividing an overall rectangular plan. Each of the four abstractions in this section, based on dimensions (Figures 3.1, 3.2 and 3.3); points and line segments (Figure 3.4); rectangles (Figure 3.8); and walls (Figures 3.9 and 3.10) represents layouts of two-dimensional rectangles; each offers advantages and disadvantages; and, sadly, each requires work to understand, develop and use. Computer scientists use the term *representation* to describe abstractions with mathematical proofs relating properties of the abstraction to properties of a class of objects.

An important form of abstraction for parametric modeling is *condensing* and *expanding* graph nodes. In any graph, a collection of nodes can be condensed into a single node; and graphs with condensed nodes are called *compound graphs*.

A condensed node can be expanded to restore the graph to its original state. Condensing and expanding implement hierarchy and aid divide-and-conquer strategies. Parametric modelers implement this strategy to create new kinds of multi-property nodes, to support copying and reuse of parts of a graph and thus to build user-defined libraries of parametric models. See Section 3.3.7 on p. 45.

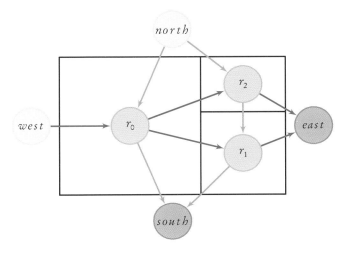

3.8: The *loosely-packed arrangement of rectangles (LOOS) representation* (Flemming, 1986, 1989). Treating each rectangle as a graph node creates two separate subgraphs in the design (west-to-east and north-to-south). There are four distinguished nodes (called *north, east, south* and *west*) that bound the actual rectangles in the design. Each internal node carries two minimum dimensions: one for the west–east direction and one for the north–south direction. The node computes a location of the wall consistent with these constraints. One such algorithm computes every vertical (horizontal) wall location as being as far west (north) as it can possibly be. In addition to its simple graph, the LOOS representation has the benefit of being able to represent every possible layout of rectangles, and provides relatively simple operations for inserting and deleting rectangles.

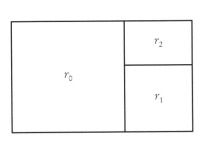
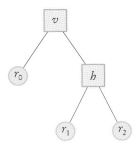

3.9: In the *subregion representation* (Kundu, 1988; Harada, 1997), the representation is a simple tree, with each square node representing both a rectangular region and either a vertical (v) or horizontal (h) wall dividing the region and each round node representing a specific rectangle. This representation is extremely simple and has an easily understood dimensioning scheme; each v and h node contains an independent parameter.

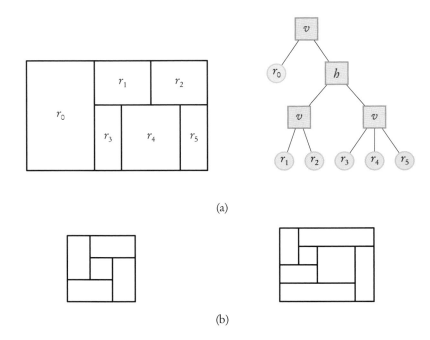

(a)

(b)

3.10: The subregion representation can (a) simply represent complex arrangements of rectangles, and provides a natural hierarchy of regions. Every v and h node of the tree contains a single parameter that specifies the proportion at which the larger rectangle is subdivided. However, walls must completely divide a region; (b) shows that some arrangements cannot be represented at all.

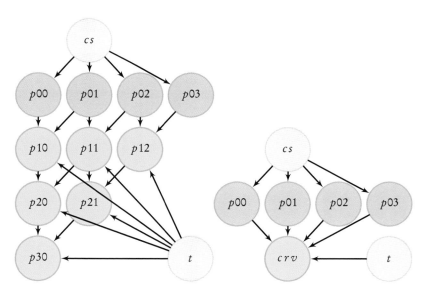

3.11: The graph on the left condenses to the compound graph on the right. The selected collection of nodes (in red) on the left becomes the single selected node on the right.

3.2.5   Thinking mathematically

Whether conventional or parametric, a CAD model is a set of mathematical propositions. A line object is a statement that the segment between its end points is a part of the model. Mathematical calculations are routinely made by the system: putting new points on the active plane, placing a line tangent to a circle through a point and specifying a point as the centroid of a polygon each model basic mathematical inferences. Designers do more than make collections of propositions: they make *proofs* of their designs. By using constructions such as grids, snaps, circle intersections and tangents, they construct mathematical proofs that the designs thus specified are consequent to their base assumptions. Of course, designers seldom look at their work in this way, and mathematicians might cringe to consider such special-purpose constructions as meaningful proofs. But the analogy stands; in some sense, designers "do" mathematics. Practically though, designers *use* mathematics more than they *do* mathematics. To use mathematics is to begin with established mathematical fact and to rely on it to make a construction or, even more loosely, as a metaphor for a design move. To do mathematics is to derive theorems (new mathematical facts) by inference from prior known statements. The difference is in both intent and practice. A designer sets out to create a design, a description of a special artefact suited to purpose. A mathematician seeks to discover new and general facts from old or new paths of inference to already known facts. Design work is more like McCullough s (1998) digital craft and less like Lakatos s (1991) cycle of proof and refutation. We can quibble about how similar (or not) these two acts are, but there is an essential difference in license taken and understanding sought. Using mathematics to do design requires far less understanding than doing mathematics for its own sake. Note the word "requires". Some designers choose to delve into the mathematics of their work. Sometimes such apparent distraction becomes core to developing a body of work. Other times it follows the time-honoured tradition of curiosity as its own reward.

Design has always had practitioners who take more than slight steps towards mathematical maturity. Gothic buildings can be understood and were evidently designed as complex sequences of geometric construction proceeding from a few key dimensions. Traditional Persian Rasmi domes result from projecting a drawing onto a predetermined dome geometry. In Persian, the verb for drawing and the word "rasmi" have the same linguistic root. DaVinci s Vitruvian Man drawing is the centrepiece of a collection of notes on Vitruvius s *The Ten Books on Architecture* (Pollio, 2006).

Palladio (1742; 1965) expounded on and (sometimes) used proportional systems in his building plans and elevations. Antoni Gaudí limited his form-finding mostly to developable surfaces, to great sculptural effect. Le Corbusier espoused *The Modular*, a manifesto on the play of the golden ratio $\phi = (1 + \sqrt{5})/2$, also the solution to the equation $1/\phi = \phi/(1 + \phi)$, and in turn the division of a line segment such that the small and large parts are in the same ratio as the large part to the whole. Canadian architect James W. Strutt (see Figure 3.2.6) based

Salisbury Cathedral.
Source: Bernard Gagnon.

A sequence of Rasmi domes in *Nasir-Al-Molk Mosque,* Shiraz, Iran. Projection from a base drawing is the main generator for Rasmi domes.

Source: Babak Nikkhah Bahrami.

Da Vinci s *Vitruvian Man.*
Source: Luc Viatour.

his life s work on the play of sphere and polyhedral packings and their duals. Geometric construction and visual clarity are signatures for Foster + Partners. These are statements of historical fact, not judgments on the work obtained. Valuing design for using geometry is circular reasoning at best.

Parametric systems can make such mathematics active. By coding theorems and constructions into propagation graphs and node update methods, designers can experience mathematical ideas at play. The once dry ideas of surface normals, cross products, tangencies, projections and plane equations become an essential part of the modeler s repertoire. Active and visual mathematics can become means and strategy to the ends of design.

Modern mathematics is too vast for the lifetime of a single mind. Indeed, it seems too vast for an entire industry. New geometric operators appear slowly in CAD, leaving much design possibility unexplored. For example, in 2009, the mesh subdivision and refinement techniques common in animation systems were only beginning to appear in CAD. The field of computational geometry provides such basic constructs as convex hulls, Voronoi diagrams and Delauney triangulations that would enable new avenues of exploration were they in the CAD toolkit. Parametric modeling enables new mathematical play. Designers know about something these other fields – their demands may well push system developers to richer tools. Section 3.3.5 outlines some of the new strategies in contempory parametric design. Chapter 6 explains some of the fundamental mathematics needed to master parametric modeling.

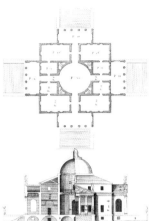

Palladio s *Villa Rotunda*.
Source: Palladio (1965).

3.2.6   Thinking algorithmically

A parametric design is a graph. Its graph-dependent nodes contain either or both update methods and constraint expressions. Both are *algorithms* and can be changed by users, at least in principle. Long practice in using, programming and teaching parametric systems shows that, sooner or later, designers will need (or at least want) to write algorithms to make their intended designs.

It is useful to consider what an algorithm is. There are many definitions. Berlinski (1999) (whose book you should read!) writes on page *xix*

Geometrically Antoni Gaudí s, *Temple Expiatori de la Sagrada Família* is an exploration of the possibilities of developable surfaces.

Source: Paolo de Reggio.

> An algorithm is
>
> > a finite procedure,
> >
> > written in a fixed symbolic vocabulary,
> >
> > governed by precise instructions,
> >
> > moving in discrete steps, 1,2,3,...,
> >
> > whose execution requires no insight, cleverness, intuition, intelligence or perspicuity,
> >
> > and that, sooner or later, comes to an end.

Berlinski s definition is less formal than those you will find in dictionaries and computer science texts, but contains all of the accepted essential elements of an algorithm. Design highlights two of its aspects. The first is "procedure": an algorithm is a process that must be specified step-by-step. Designers largely describe objects rather than processes. The second is "precise": one misplaced character means that an algorithm likely will not work. In contrast, designerly representations are replete with imprecision – they rely on human readers to interpret marks appropriately. It is hardly surprising then that many designers encounter difficulty in integrating algorithmic thinking into their work, in spite of over 30 years of valiant attempts to teach programming in design schools. It is even less surprising that computer-aided design relegates programming to the background. Almost all current systems have a so-called *scripting language*. These are programming languages; developers call them scripting languages to make them appear less foreboding. In almost all of these, to use the language your must remove yourself from the actual task and your accustomed visual, interactive representation. You must work in a domain of textual instructions. This is not surprising either – algorithmic thinking differs from almost all other forms of thought. But the sheer distance between representations familiar to designers and those needed for algorithms exacerbates the gap.

In both conventional and parametric systems, the scripting language can be used to make designs. The language provides functions that can add, modify or erase objects in a model. In addition, parametric systems bring the algorithm closer to design models. They do this by localizing algorithms in nodes of a graph, either as constraint expressions or as update methods. However, designers still must grasp and use algorithmic thought if they are to get the most out of such systems. Chapter 4 summarizes the programmer s craft and shows how and why programming is built into parametric modeling.

3.3   New strategies

Conceiving data ow; dividing to conquer; naming; and thinking abstractly, mathematically and algorithmically form the base for designers to build their parametric craft. In this section, I describe strategies that my research group has observed over several years of running courses and workshops in parametric modeling. Our observation techniques have ranged from informal interaction and journaling to structured *participant observer* studies (Qian et al., 2007).

3.3.1   Sketching

The sketch occupies a near sacred place in the design pantheon. A library of books attests to its importance to design, extolls its protean virtues and urges students to learn this all-important skill. Toothy paper and the 2B pencil are among the saints of architectural hagiography. Irony aside, all design teachers know that the student who sketches well tends to do well in the studio; and

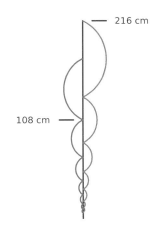

The core of the Modulor. The *red series* originates with dimension of 108 cm (putatively at navel height); the *blue series* with 216 cm (the top of an outstretched arm). Each is geometric in the golden ratio $\frac{1+\sqrt{5}}{2}$. Corbusier rounded imperfectly—the Modulor dimensions are not in the golden ratio to the nearest integer.

James W. Strutt s *Rochester House* is based on a close packing of rhombic dodecahedra.
Source: James W. Strutt Family.

The *Albion Riverside* apartments by Foster + Partners combines multiple trigonometric functions to compose an overall form.
Source: Chris Kench.

that pencil sketching remains a vital and important tool for design. But what is a sketch? In *Sketching User Experiences*, Bill Buxton (2007) crafts a thorough argument for the qualities and uses of sketches in interaction design. In the chapter *The Anatomy of Sketching* (pp. 111–120), he posits 11 qualities of design sketches. For Buxton sketches are (or have) *quick; timely; inexpensive; disposable; plentiful; clear vocabulary; distinct gesture; minimal detail; suggest and explore rather than con rm; appropriate degree of re nement;* and *ambiguity.* Of these, only clear vocabulary, distinct gesture and appropriate degree of refinement make any reference to the media conveying a sketch. All of the other eight (and much of these three) refer rather to the role of sketches in the design process. Buxton does not have the only or final word on sketching in design, but his voice is both recent and clear. To paraphrase his words: Designers have always sketched. It is how they do their work.

We have known since McLuhan that media and content deeply intertwine; the carrier and carried cannot be pulled apart. Well-mastered, the skill of pencil sketching meets all of Buxton s criteria. But when *taken in their own terms,* so do other media and tools. Unencumbered with the 2B religion, students use the media at hand, and today such media are mostly digital. These fresh newcomers consistently do work that meets all of Buxton s criteria – see Figure 3.12. And their eyes are different. What old-timers like Buxton and I might see as overly determined and graphically definite, the new generation sees as ambiguous and free. If you don t like it, change it! The digital generation might well add the word *dynamic* to Buxton s list.

Parametric models are, by their nature, dynamic. Once made, they can be rapidly changed to answer the archetypal design question: "What if...?" Sometimes a single model replaces pages of manual sketches. On the other hand, parametric models are definite, complex structures that take time to create. Too often, they are not quick. A challenge for system developers is to enable rapid modeling, so that their systems can better serve sketching in design.

3.3.2 Throw code away

Designers do design, not media. Unless they get seduced by the siren of the parametric tool, they model just what they need to the level of confidence and completeness they need. From project to project, day to day or even hour to hour, they tend to rebuild rather than reuse. In stark contract, much of the toolkit of computer programming (and parametric modeling is programming) aims at making clear code, reducing redundancy and fostering reuse. In the world of professional programming, these aims make eminent sense. In the maelstrom of design work, they give way to such simple devices as copying, pasting and slightly modifying entire blocks of code. Professional programmers would be horrified by such acts. Designers are delighted if the resulting model works, right now.

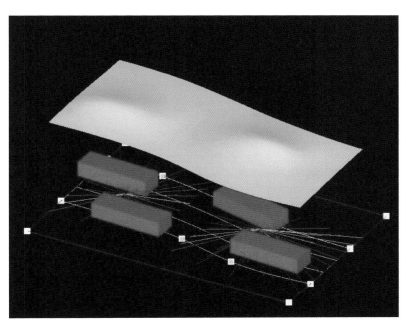

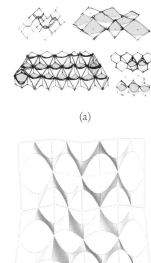

(a)

(b)

(c)

3.12: The initial sketches ((a) & (b) in the margin) led to this parametric sketch, whose purpose was to build and understand how a surface could react to objects underneath it. The screen elements spanning the surface (c) were built, literally, on top of the sketch. The relatively low resolution of the sketch image re ects its ephemeral role in the design process – whatever gets saved in the moment determines the historical record.
Source: Mark Davis and Stephen Pitman.

At the 2007 ACADIA conference, Brady Peters presented a paper on the design and construction of a roof over the courtyard of the Smithsonian Institution Patent Office Building (Peters, 2007) by Foster + Partners. During his talk, he showed some of the computer code that generated the design alternatives. It was highly repetitive. Entire blocks of almost identical code appeared again, and again. To an audience question (OK, it was from me) about why he, as a skilled programmer, would not have made his code more clear, he responded simply "I didn t need to do that." Peters wasn t being lazy or uncraftful; he was being a designer. Throw-away code is a fact of parametric design.

3.3.3   Copy and modify

Designers may throw their own models away, but will invest considerable time in finding existing models and using them in their own context. This is hardly surprising. References such as *Architectural Graphics Standards* (Ramsay and Sleeper, 2007a) and their recent digital versions (Ramsay and Sleeper, 2007b) provide exemplary details that, for much design, are the foundation for detailed work. In an engineering design domain, Gantt and Nardi (1992) report script finding and reuse as an important mode of work. Given the additional work that must go into a parametric model, we should expect to see an intellectual trade in models and techniques. As both a learning and enabling tool, existing code reduces the job of making a model. It is typically easier to edit and change code that works than it is to create code from scratch, even if what it produces differs from current intentions. The key is the word "works", that is, code that produces a result. Starting with a working model and moving in steps, always ensuring that the model works, is often more efficient than building a model from scratch.

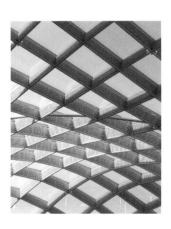

3.13: The roof over the courtyard of the *Smithsonian Institution Patent Office Building*. Source: Nigel Young / Foster + Partners.

3.14: Details of the Smithsonian courtyard roof.
Source: Nigel Young /
Foster + Partners.

Copy-and-modify is the flip side of throw-away code. Designers show natural reluctance to invest sufficient work in making code that will be clear to others, but they are happy to use such code when it is available. This makes "good" code a treasured community resource. The copy-and-modify strategy requires a community of practice that generates the code. The World Wide Web fosters such communities. Enabled by the fact that pages are written in human-readable HTML (and other languages), web designers often mine existing pages for code snippets that show to achieve a particular effect. In design, the practice communities are less well developed, but such groups as SmartGeometry have built necessary precursor networks. Vendor publications of books with worked examples partially fill the need for such models and code.

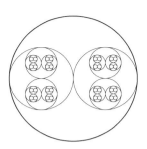 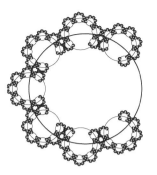

3.15: The figure on the left was copied and modified by a designer learning recursion to create the figure on the right.
Source: Dieter Toews.

3.3.4   Search for form

Parametric modeling opens new windows to design. Nowhere is this more evident than with curves and surfaces. These are naturally parametric objects; mathematically they are defined as parametric functions over sets of control points. Conventional systems provide these mathematically motivated controls. In contrast, parametric systems enable a new set of controls to overlay the basis controls. This creates endless opportunities to explore for forms that are not practically reachable otherwise. To the technically-minded, such exploration can appear as play that is both aimless and ungrounded. A broader and longer perspective reveals serious purpose in the play. The history of design can be read as a constantly changing process of exploring for new form-making ideas, using whatever tools and intellectual concepts are at hand. New languages and styles of design require such exploratory play, especially at their early stages. Figure 3.17 shows recent exploratory work by Aranda\Lasch.

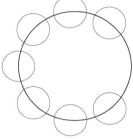

3.3.5   Use mathematics and computation to understand design

Understanding mathematics (especially geometry) and computation can bring some design concepts into sharp focus. Working with such formal descriptions restricts the range of forms that can be expressed, but links them in a common logic that may be worth the cost paid. For example, taking sections of a toroidal surface yields a surprisingly rich language of form, with the benefit of planar faceting and a limited set of edge lengths for facets.

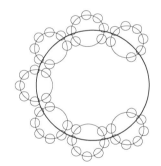

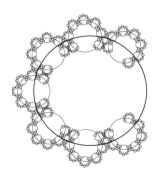

3.16: The same design shown at increasing recursive depth.

3.17: The quasi-series is about the pursuit of orders that are rigorously modular but wild – almost out of order. Quasicrystals, a new phase of matter discovered in 1984, represent this kind of material structure that hovers on the edge of falling apart. Unlike a regular crystal, whose molecular pattern is periodic (or repetitive in all directions), the distinctive quality of a quasicrystal is that its structural pattern never repeats the same way twice. It is endless and uneven, but it can be described by the arrangement of a small set of modular parts. This furniture piece explores an aperiodic assembly in wood. Source: Aranda\Lasch, fabrication by James Moore.

Sometimes you need to understand the underlying mathematics to effectively create a model. Hierarchy is a time-honoured architectural design strategy, yet has limited support in most CAD systems. The intellectual key to hierarchy is recursion, which occurs when a program invokes itself. (See Section 8.16 below and Figure 3.15.) With recursion, parts can be made to directly resemble the wholes they compose.

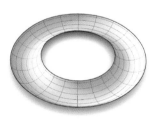

3.18: Sections cut from a torus.

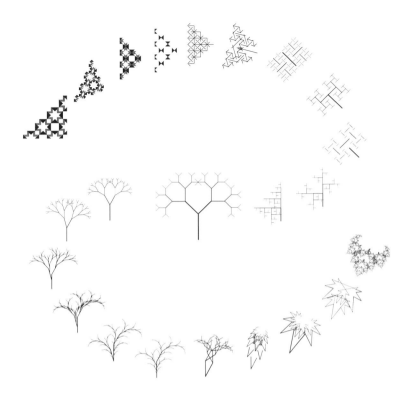

3.19: A single recursive structure with minor variations produces a wide range of designs. The central diagram demonstrates the basic tree structure of two motifs replicating at each recursive level. Along the upper branch, the location of the motifs changes with each successive figure. For the last four figures, the motif changes from a line to a triangle and only the final level of motifs appears. In the lower branch, only location changes; the line motif remains the same. In the final figure on this branch, the number of levels in the recursion increases and only the final level of motifs appears.
Source: Woodbury (1993).

A geodesic curve is the shortest path on a surface that joining two points $\dot{p}$ and $\dot{q}$ also on the surface. For spheres, the geodesic curve between $\dot{p}$ and $\dot{q}$ is the shortest arc linking the two points taken from the *great circle* defined by the two points and the sphere centre. Discrete points along a sphere geodesic curve can be found by projecting points on the 3D line between $\dot{p}$ and $\dot{q}$ to the sphere s surface. Geodesic meshes can be generated by subdividing polyhedral faces and then projecting the new vertices onto the sphere. Figure 3.18 shows that successive subdivisions produce more sphere-like forms. On the other hand, subdivision can be cleanly understood as a recursive operation. Even such a qualitative understanding of geodesic concepts enables complex form making.

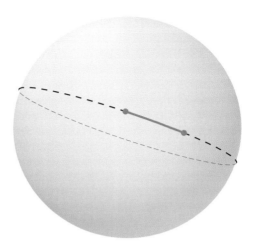

3.20: A geodesic curve on sphere is a fragment of a great circle.

Many contemporary parametric designers are exploring mathematically-based design strategies. I cannot help but notice a pattern. They browse the web and their social networks for math, picking ideas and playing them into design work. The reasoning chains (from pigeon-hole principle to permutations to binomial theorem to permutation cycles...) that structure classical mathematics learning and understanding are seldom part of the game. Designers mostly enter above the foundations, understand something of mathematical mechanism and move on to use it in design. Of course, there is co-evolution here. The web enables casual access (try doing it in a physical library of mathematics texts) and itself is conditioned by such use. It should come as no surprise that the constructive, recursive definition of the Bézier curve is much more common on the web than the Bernstein basis definition, in spite of revealing less mathematically. Visual construction trumps mathematical inference for design. As with algorithms, designers exhibit a copy-and-modify style in using mathematics. Even more quickly, they encounter limits. Just as a program may not even compile in the face of a minor coding error, a mathematical formula or theorem may break down completely with a seemingly minor change. There are no Pythagorean triplets for cubes, that is, there are no integer solutions to $a^3 + b^3 = c^3$. (This is an instance of Fermat s Last Theorem, proved only in 1995, that is, there is no integer solution to $a^n + b^n = c^n$ with $n > 2$.)

The mathematical knowledge available in libraries, especially those of research universities, staggers the mind. Much of this material can be accessed only by physically visiting, and relatively little can be understood without concentrated and sustained study of mathematical foundations. The World Wide Web and interactive software for working with mathematics have thrown open doors through which come a large crowd unfamiliar to the mathematically astute.

3.21: Starting with an icosahedron (20 equilateral triangular faces), successive subdivisions of each triangle make geodesic meshes that better approximate a sphere.

Online resources such as Wolfram s MathWorld (Weisstein, 2009) and many university courses provide immediate access to (sometimes carefully constructed) explanations that can help bridge to mathematical understanding. Packages such as Mathematica®️ and Maple™ are to mathematics what parametric modeling is to design – by making math active, they enable exploration and discovery.

3.3.6 Defer decisions

In design, accuracy measures how the design relates to the thing being designed. Precision measures how design parts relate to each other. Conventional systems require geometric precision and provide tools such as snaps to help achieve it. Without precise size and location, models look messy. They do not have the ambiguity and appropriate refinement of a sketch; they are just messy. I argue that, more than anything else, this need to commit to specific locations at the outset of modeling is what is least sketch-like about computer-aided design. A clear exception is the implicit modeling toolset widely used in animation and gaming. Implicit surfaces lie "somewhere near" their generating objects and provide rules to merge "nearby" surfaces together. Implicit modeling removes both the need for precision and the possibility of accuracy.

Parametric modeling introduces a new strategy: *deferral*. A parametric design commits to a network of relations and defers commitment to specific locations and details. The system maintains the prior decisions made. Deferral pervades parametric practice. Those new to parametric modeling often ask how to locate their initial points and lines. Those teaching delight in the answer: "It doesn t matter; you can change that later."

One of the earliest (and effective!) demonstrations of parametric modeling in architecture was the International Terminal Waterloo by Nicholas Grimshaw & Partners (see Figures 3.23 to 3.22). Lars Hesselgren crafted the original model in the I_EMS system. More than 15 years later Robert Aish used a similar model to demonstrate the CustomObjects system (which later became Generative-Components™). A salient site condition is that the train track curves through the station. A parametric model need not be initially constrained by this curve; fitting it to location can be deferred. Changing the order in which modeling and design decisions can be made is both a major feature of and deliberate strategy for parametric design. Indeed, a principal financial argument for parametric modeling is its touted ability to support rapid change late in the design process.

The Eden Project also by Nicholas Grimshaw & Partners, (see Figure 3.26), combined parametric modeling and geodesic geometry to address an unusual problem. The site was a quarry that remained active until very late in the design process. Consequently ground levels could not be predicted in advance. The geodesic geometry made it easy to extend and rearrange partial spheres, while parametric modeling shortened revision cycles.

3.22: The *International Terminal Waterloo* by Nicholas Grimshaw & Partners.
Source: James Pole.

3.23: The *International Terminal Waterloo* by Nicholas Grimshaw & Partners. The
station was designed around an existing path for the track system.
Source: Jo Reid and John Peck.

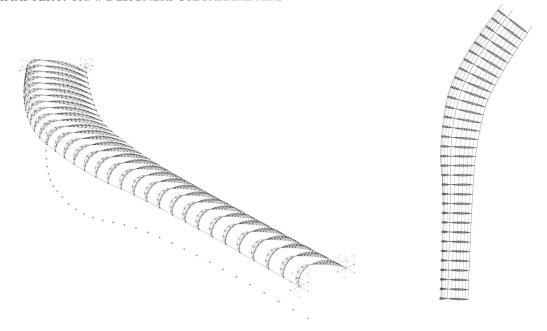

3.24: Using parametric modeling, the exact location of the structure can be changed at the very end of the modeling process.

3.25: Plan view of a parametric model of Waterloo Station.

3.26: The *Eden Project*, Cornwall, United Kingdom.
Source: ©2006 Jürgen Matern (http://www.juergen-matern.de).

3.3.7 Make modules

Propagation graphs can, and do, get big. Large size increases system update times and, more importantly, makes models hard to understand. Copying parts of a large graph and reconnecting them elsewhere in a model is prohibitively difficult. Reducing graph complexity and enabling reuse are the main reasons that systems universally provide module-making tools. The names and details of these vary from system to system, but their essence is the same. They provide a means to encapsulate a sub-graph as a single node with its own set of node-independent (input) parameters. Copying and reuse then reduces to making a copy of a single node and reconnecting its inputs as needed.

It takes much effort to make a module work well and communities of practice develop surprisingly sophisticated module-making techniques. Almost always, the process iterates; through successive attempts modelers converge on stability. Later in this book, the PLACE HOLDER pattern on page 218 shows one such community-developed technique for placing modules onto complex geometric constructions.

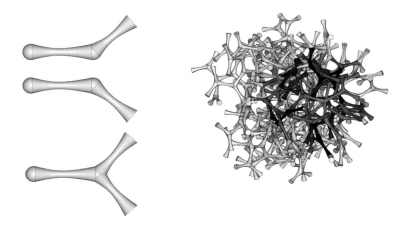

3.27: In a complex design with repeating elements, modules are a near-essential part of the modeling process. The design on the right is a programmatically arranged complex of the three modules on the left.
Source: Martin Tamke.

3.3.8   Help others

In *Gardeners and Gurus: Patterns of Cooperation among CAD Users,* Gantt and Nardi (1992) use the concept of the *gardener* to describe internal developers (and extenders) of CAD systems who are supported by their organization. Perhaps the peak example of gardening in architectural design in 2010 is the Specialist Modeling Group at Foster + Partners. This group employs many strategies to enable complex geometric and computational design work throughout the firm. From 2003 to the time of writing (2010) such gardening at a community scale was clearly evident in the SmartGeometry organization, in which more than 20 tutors volunteer a week of their time, year-after-year, to mentor students and practitioners new to parametric modeling. Of course, other rewards are at play: such events are superb places to meet peers, scout for employees and check out the latest work. From their offices and studios, some parametric practitioners (naming one or a few would be unfair – there are just too many good ones) freely share code and insight into modeling tasks. To them ow the rewards not just of fame, but more importantly, of new problems and approaches to solutions. Formalized or not, helping others is a clear strategy to at least some aspects of mastery.

3.3.9   Develop your toolbox

The parametric medium is complex, perhaps more so than any other media in the history of design. Using it well necessarily combines conceiving data ow; new divide-and-conquer strategies; naming; abstraction; 3D visualization and mathematics; and thinking algorithmically. These are the basics, and mastery requires more. We can expect that new technique and strategy will ow from the practices and schools that invest time and effort in the tools. Between the basics and the designs that are the focus and aim of professional work, lies a largely unexplored territory of what might be called *parametric craft*. I choose the word "craft" on purpose, to align with Malcolm McCullough s (1998) case for a developing digital craft. Some of his examples were of parametric models. Understandably, given the date and breadth of the book, McCullough merely hinted at the richness of parametric technique.

We can expect explorers in the new territory of parametric craft. Unlike the medieval sailors in whose portolanos we can see cartography slowly develop, the current explorers can learn from other fields that have undertaken similar voyages of discovery. There are numerous books on spreadsheets; some, like Monahan (2000), focus on strategies for spreadsheet design. Borrowing partly from film, computer animation has grown an extensive repertoire of technique. Software engineering has forged and polished a powerful tool. *Software Design Patterns* describe fragments of systems both functionally (by what they do) and structurally (by how they are composed of simpler structures). Their origins lie in architecture, particularly in Alexander s many works on pattern languages. In software, though, design patterns have a new and philosophically different logic and application. They have come to occupy a pragmatic place between the technical description of computer languages and the overall organization of a complex computer program. In software, design patterns record demonstrably useful ideas for system design. I have both adopted and adapted software design patterns as a basis for expressing the new parametric craft.

We can expect, as with the medieval nation-states, that some of the parametric portolanos will be kept strictly private. But practices and universities alike will come to use and value only those that are public. I devote much of this book to a small, initial set of design patterns. My aim is to begin what I hope will be a long and fruitful process of developing an explicit, shareable and learnable craft of parametric design. Before patterns must come programming and geometry – the practical manifestations of algorithms and mathematics for much of design. Explaining particular patterns relies on a few key ideas from each of these very large fields.

Chapter 4

Programming

Algorithms are realized as *programs*, which in turn are written in precise and prescribed *programming languages*. Almost universally, designers learn to think algorithmically by learning a programming language to accomplish design work. Anyone who has become a good programmer will tell you that, at some time, they focused intensely on programming and spent a great deal of time learning to do it well. The term "programming language" itself gives a hint as to why this is so. Just as the most effective way to learn a new natural language is to immerse yourself in the daily life of native speakers of that language, the best way to learn programming is to work intensely with a programming language to the near exclusion of other forms of thought. But even when a designer has expended all of this effort and has become an accomplished programmer, there will be aspects of algorithmic thinking still unlearned. This happens because there are general language-independent concepts to master. Computer scientists learn these through a combination more abstract algorithmic descriptions and programming in multiple languages. In fact, most computer scientists would assert that the science of computing is quite separate from programming skill. In particular, they will claim that not all programmers are computer scientists and (more reluctantly) that not all computer scientists are programmers. Like drawing in design, programming is the craft skill by which much of computer science is done.

Programming is not a monolith. It is a multi-faceted skill mostly taught in sequence. At every stage in the sequence you rely on concepts learned earlier. Importantly, at every stage you can accomplish *some* work with what you know. Almost all books and courses on programming languages progress through such a sequence of concepts each realized as short programs. Sequences are startlingly similar across books, courses and languages. Every programming language is, in fact, a concrete realization of the general concept of the algorithm, and inherits much of its structure from that source. It is a strange and frustrating experience to read such books as an expert in computing. By the term "expert", I mean one who both understands abstract algorithmic concepts and demonstrates effective programming skill. The expert wants a concept explained in general terms. A book almost always explains only by specific examples in its focus language. Of course, hundreds of authors are unlikely to be wrong. They use this concrete style of writing because it works to teach programming as it is usually taught in schools – as an isolated skill. It does presume that people learn computing ideas at first almost exclusively by learning a language. Skills-based learning makes it doubly hard to simultaneously master difficult abstract ideas. The tragedy in this all-too-common structure is that, without dedicated and formal study, it is hard to rise above the particulars of a language to see the general, powerful concepts at play.

This book is not an introduction to computer programming. Hundreds of books exist, and dozens of languages have new books published every year. It aims rather to help the amateur (and often self taught) designer/programmer become better at combining parametric modeling and programming to do more effective design work. This chapter presents a brief sketch of the sequence of concepts typically encountered in a programming language and outlines what each step in the sequence enables the designer/programmer to accomplish. For the novice, it might provide an principled overview, so often missing in basic programming books. For the expert, its brevity might help in reviewing and connecting key ideas.

4.1   Values

A *value* is a piece of data. Values are the basic objects over which computations occur. In computing in general, a value can be any *symbol*. Practically though, values usually come in kinds (or types, see Section 4.7 below). Most computer languages support a suite of such kinds, for example:

5	an integer
3.14159	a real number
⟦f⟧	a character
⟦aalto⟧	a string
false	a *Boolean,* either true or false

4.2   Variables

A *variable* is a container that holds a *value.* It has a *name.* We use variables to hold onto data so that we can use the data later. The nodes in a parametric model are, in fact, variables. They hold values, often multiple values (as shown in Section 4.8 below). In the following list, the variable name comes first, then the value it contains, then the value s kind of object. Variables names can (and often should) be long. A good (and common) programming convention, called *camel casing,* or *camelCasing,* makes memorable names by adding several words together with no spaces and by capitalizing the first character of each word. The word "camel" refers to the "humps" in the variable names so created.

$$
\begin{aligned}
\texttt{a=5} \quad &\text{an integer} \\
\texttt{SIRatio=1.414} \quad &\text{a real number} \\
\texttt{buildingPart = ⟦elevator⟧} \quad &\text{a string} \\
\texttt{qua = true} \quad &\text{a Boolean}
\end{aligned}
$$

Variables enable *description*. With variables alone, a collection of data can be organized so that it makes sense to an external reader. Variables allow us to express a design as a collection of values.

By themselves, variables impose no ordering. A collection of variables, with no duplicates, can be considered in any order without changing the values held in the variables.

4.3   Expressions

An *expression* combines values, variables, *operators* and *function calls* that return values. Expressions are classified by the kind of value they return. For example, a Boolean expression returns a bit (either *true* or *false*). Expressions are units from which larger structures are built. Some examples of expressions include the following:

$$
\begin{aligned}
\texttt{a} \quad &\text{a variable is a simple expression} \\
\texttt{2 + (5 * 8)} \quad &\text{this arithmetic expression returns the value 42} \\
\texttt{(1 + sqrt(5))/2} \quad &\text{expressions can contain function calls} \\
\texttt{b + 1} \quad &\text{the variable b must be defined already}
\end{aligned}
$$

Expressions support *data dependency*. By using an expression, a piece of data can be computed from (made dependent upon) other pieces of data.

The values returned by expressions can be held by variables. This simple fact imposes a partial ordering on a set of variables. If an expression uses a variable, then that variable needs to be given a value *before* the expression occurs.

4.4   Statements

A *statement* is a unit of code that a language can execute. A program comprises a sequence of statements that are to be executed in the *given order*.

Statements can be *simple* (made of one statement) or *compound* (being a *block* made of a sequence of statements). Like a variable, a compound statement can be thought of as a container. In this case the container holds code.

A particularly important statement is the *assignment statement*, which *assigns* a value or the result of evaluating an expression to a variable. For example, the variable a may be assigned the value of the golden ratio.

```
a = (1.0 + sqrt(5))/2.0;
```

Two successive assignment statements with the same variable being assigned have the result of the second statement overriding the first. The statements

```
a = (1.0 + sqrt(5))/2.0;
a = 3.14159;
```

result in the variable a holding an approximation of the value of π, not ϕ the golden ratio.

Statements in a sequence, executed statement-by-statement, in the order given, capture key aspects of algorithms: ... *governed by precise instructions, moving in discrete steps* ... (remember Berlinski (1999)?). Together, variables, expressions and statement sequences enable a simple but useful form of algorithm.

Each parametric model node can be thought of as a program, that is, a sequence of statements. Each use of a value or of a constraint expression in a node property is equivalent to an assignment statement. Taken together, all of the individual node programs compose a larger program in which nodes must occur before they are used in another node s constraint expressions.

4.5   Control statements

The   ow of control of a program is the sequence of statements that are executed when the program is run. Programming languages provide a class of statements whose purpose is to change the   ow of control. The most simple of these is the if statement, which executes a block of code if some condition is true. Another example is the switch statement that provides a list of possible actions given the value of a variable.

```
if (a > 5.0)
  {
    // A sequence of statements goes here.
  }
```

4.1: When executed, an if-statement transfers the   ow of control into its code block *if* the Boolean expression comprising its condition is true.

More complex is the *for-loop*, which calls an *initializer* for a *control variable* and repeats a block of code until its *loop condition* fails. At the end of each stage the for-loop executes a *counting statement* (the control variable usually occurs in this statement – exceptions abound, but these are hackery). Typical programming languages provide several such statements, for example, foreach and while.

```
for (i=0; i<10; i=i+1)
//for (initializer; loop condition; counting statement)
  {
     // A sequence of statements goes here.
     // Usually, but not necessarily, these statements
     // use the variable i, so that each iteration
     // through the loop has a different effect.
  }
```

4.2: When executed, the for-loop initializes the control variable i and transfers control into the body of the loop. When it exits the body, it executes the counting expression, in this case it adds 1 to i. Then it tests the loop condition, in this case that i is less than 10. If true, it enters the loop body again.

Control statements enable programs to perform actions that depend on the *state of the program*, that is, the current variable assignments. Statements such as the for-loop facilitate expressing repeated similar actions as a single block of code, and thus can make programs much shorter, easier to maintain and sometimes more readable.

A simple list of statements can achieve a surprising amount. Just as in the real world where actions may depend on context, in programs, the computation may rely on data values. In the absence of control statements, programmers would have to write separate code for each situation and themselves determine which piece of code to use.

4.6   Functions

A function is a named block of statements, wrapped up in a box. See Figure 4.3. It has inputs (these are called *arguments*) that go into the box and returns values that leave the box. The code in the function acts on the inputs to compute the return values.

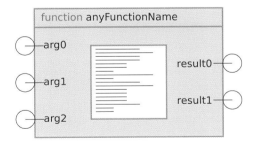

4.3: A function can be imagined as a box. The function is known by its name, in this case anyFunctionName. The arguments go into the left side of the box. The statements in the box use the arguments. The results exit the right side of the box as a result of executing the function. Unless there are side effects, the contents of the box are hidden from the containing program.

"Pure" functions have no effect other than to compute return values, that is, all of their action lies inside the box containing the function. Most programming languages though provide devices by which functions can have *side effects*. A side effect happens when a function either refers to or changes data outside its box. The most glaring example of a side effect happens when a function changes a *global variable*, that is, a variable that exists within the program as a whole and can be changed at any time by any function. As programs grow in size, side effects make them harder to understand and debug. Professional programmers will go to great lengths to avoid (or at least constrain) the use of global variables specifically and side effects generally.

Functions enable code reuse. Once defined, a function can be called throughout a program. The function itself is only stored once, reducing the length of code and, crucially, providing a single place for editing. To the rest of the program, a function is known only through its name and list of arguments. Programmers can, and do, change the code inside the function (to correct or improve it) and the rest of the program is not affected at all. This isolation of code by using an interface (the function arguments) is a simple form of what computer scientists call *encapsulation.*

Function calls enter programs as part of expressions. Every language includes a suite of predefined functions; programmers can define functions extending this set. Functions can call functions, enabling *composition* as a design tool for programming. Devising and refining layers of functions, each performing more specific work, is a key part of writing effective programs.

Functions are the first and simplest tool of *software engineering,* the discipline of building complex, reliable, maintainable and understandable programs.

In parametric modeling, a node can be thought of as a function call, in which an update method maps the inputs of the node to its outputs. Nodes can be drawn, and in some systems are so drawn, as function boxes with the arguments on one side and the returns on the other. Functions are the first and most simple device for building the modules of Section 3.3.7.

4.7 Types

Values have kinds. There are *numbers, characters, strings, bits* and others. *Types* organize these kinds by providing templates for their data and operators and functions that work with these templates. For example, the type integer gives a way to store integer numbers. It also provides such operators as +, −, *, /*, <, <=, >, >= and ==; as well as functions such as max(a,b) (the maximum of two integers) and print(a) (returns true or false and has the side effect of printing the integer named by a onto the screen). User-defined types can extend the range of templates available.

Typically, variables must be *explicitly declared* to be of a specific type (although some languages have a generic type that holds any value). Expressions usually require their operands and function calls their arguments to be of specific types.

```
double a,b,c;
Vector p,q,r;
// initializing a, b, p and q
// initialization code goes here. examples below
a = 3.141592654;
b = 2.718281828;
c = 1.618033989;
p.X = 1.0;
p.Y = 2.3;
p.Z = 1.5;
...
```

(a)

```
// statements with expressions using the + operator
// integer example
int b = 4;
int c = 5;
c = a + b;           // c is equal to 9

// string example
string a = ⬚⬚four⬚⬚;
string b = ⬚⬚five⬚⬚;
c = a + b;           // c is equal to ⬚⬚fourfive⬚⬚
```

(b)

```
function CrossProduct(Vector xVec, Vector yVec)
  {
    Vector zVec; // declaration of return value type
    // code to produce zVec, the result
    return zVec;
  }
```

(c)

```
// a call to the function CrossProduct
r = CrossProduct(p, q);
```

(d)

4.4: (a) Variables are declared to be of specific types. Programmers typically initialize them to a specific known value.
(b) The expression a + b implicitly requires its arguments to be of type integer, double or string. Operators that perform different operations depending on their input types are said to be *overloaded*.
(c) The function **CrossProduct** requires two objects of type Vector as input and returns an object of type Vector as output.
(d) Functions expose these type constraints when defined through their formal argument lists, but not in their actual argument lists when they are called.

Types enable a language compiler to perform some consistency checks prior to running a program, making some kinds of errors easier to find. Using explicit types helps as programs grow in size, but can hinder quick, exploratory coding.

4.8   Objects, classes and methods

Objects generalize values. Whereas a value typically has little or no internal structure (an integer is just a number), an object combines multiple values (or other objects) into a coherent collection. Objects have *properties* (sometimes called *slots*), that is, named parts. *Dot notation* accesses these properties. If P is a point, the object P.X refers to the property holding its X-coordinate. Like a function, an object is a container; it contains values and other objects, not code.

```
object anyPoint

    CoordinateSystem = anyCS
    XLocal = 3.0
    YLocal = 2.0
    ZLocal = 6.0
    Visible = true
```

4.5: An object can be imagined as a box. The object has a name, in this case anyPoint. The object s *properties* each have a name and a value. The values need not be primitive; they can be other objects, in this case, the CoordinateSystem property holds the value anyCS, itself an object.

Classes generalize types. A class is a template giving properties for objects of its class. An object can be an instance of a class – instances have all the properties specified in the class. The name of the class is its type. Each class property is of a particular type; only objects that are instances of that specified type can be held by the property. Classes are typically defined in *inheritance hierarchies* in which a class lower in the hierarchy has all of the properties of its parent(s) and may add additional properties. Almost all languages support *single inheritance*, in which a class may have only only one parent class. Mathematical and logical constraints make *multiple inheritance* difficult to include in languages and to use in programming practice.

```
object Point

    CoordinateSystem: CoordinateSystem
    XLocal: RealNumber
    YLocal: RealNumber
    ZLocal: RealNumber
    Visible: Boolean
```

4.6: A class too can be imagined as a box. The class has a name, in this case Point. The class s *properties* each have a name and a type. The types need not be primitive; they can be other classes, in this case, the CoordinateSystem property holds a value of the CoordinateSystem class.

Methods are essentially functions specific to a class. Many methods of the same name may exist in a class hierarchy, each defines a function. The call *signature*, that is the types of the arguments in the method call, determine which of these functions is actually called. Such methods are said to be *polymorphic* (meaning of multiple bodies). Polymorphism enables programmers to express similar operations with the same name, thus potentially simplifying code. The same dot notation used for properties applies to methods. If P is a point, the method call P.subtract(Q) returns the vector that is the result of subtracting Q from P. Dot notation for methods makes object properties and methods almost the same from a programming perspective. It aids encapsulation – a programmer using it need hardly be aware of the internal structure of an object, only of the set of methods defined over the object.

Objects, classes and methods present a double-edged sword to amateurs. Largely, they help programmers make big programs more robust and understandable. Used well, they can make programs truly beautiful (at least to the eyes of us nerdy programmers) – they are elegant and powerful programming tools. Most modern languages implement some aspects of objects, classes and methods. Like power tools, they require setup and this takes time and effort. In the contingent, rushed style of programming usual in parametric design, minimal classes, simple objects and "messy" functions often produce acceptable results.

4.9   Data structures, especially lists and arrays

Data structures allow programmers to organize data themselves. A data structure comprises types (or classes) and functions (or methods) that perform coherent operations on objects of these types (classes). The *linked list* (see Figure 4.7) gives a basic example in which its single type has two properties, one for the first element (the *head*) of the list it represents and the other for the rest (the *tail*) of the list. To access a member of a list, one must start with the head of the list. If the head is not the member sought, visit the tail, until the desired member is found.

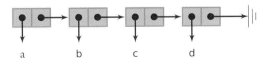

4.7: The linked list data structure comprises a single class (or type) often called List, ListElement or Cons containing two properties. The first property (called Head, First or Car) points to a value held at the place of the cell in the list. The second property (called Tail, Rest or Cdr), points to the rest of the list from that cell. The symbol ‖⌐ refers to the null list, and is often called nil. Instances of the List type are organized to represent structures including lists, trees, directed acyclic graphs and general networks.

Like a linked list, an *array* implements a sequence of objects. Unlike linked lists, access is by *index,* that is, position in the collection. Typically, array positions start at 0, so the expression a[0] gives the first element of the array and a[2] yields the third element.

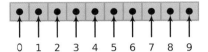

4.8: The array data structure comprises an ordered collection of cells and an associated *index set.* The cells hold data. By common convention the index set comprises the natural numbers, that is $0, 1, 2, 3, \ldots$. A member of the index set accesses the associated cell, for instance, 4 accesses the fifth member of the array. In most programming languages index sets start at zero, which creates linguistic, but not mathematical, difficulty in working with arrays. This quirk is a fact of history and programmers just have to get used to it.

Data structures are a key abstraction technique in programming. Once built, they can be used over and over again without worrying about how they do their job. Lists are just about the simplest data structure. They are easy to use, have a huge range of operations and functions and can hold values of any type. On the other hand, for some operations they are not very efficient and their very generality can make them hard to debug and maintain. Lists and arrays are well suited to quick, contingent programming in parametric modeling and are the first structure that modelers should learn to use and make.

4.10   Conventions for this book

Snippets of code appear throughout this book. The "language" to use for these was a difficult decision. The choices were three: an existing language, faithfully reproducing its syntax; the *pseudo code* used by computer scientists to express algorithms for publication; or a simplified language hopefully readable for many. I rejected the first two choices. The first requires the reader to know a specific language and might give the impression that the book is somehow about that language. The second, while precise and elegant, is not for amateurs, who often have not bridged to the abstractions required. The third lent itself to the license I needed, both to express ideas as simply as possible and to add some notation specific to parametric modeling. Here are some conventions:

`// comment`	Two forward slashes turn the rest of the line into a comment.
`p.X`	Dot notation accesses object properties.
`CamelCasing`	Camel casing is a convention, not a programming language feature. Used to combine words into names while maintaining readability.
`variableName`	Variable names begin with a lower-case letter and are otherwise CamelCased.
`TypeOrClassName`	Type or class names are pure CamelCase.
`Point p = new Point();`	A method with the same name as a class defines a *constructor* for that class. When called, it produces an instance of the class.
`p.ByCoordinates(1,4,3)`	Using `By` or `At` in dot notation signals that the method is a node update method.
`a = {1,3,6,3,8}`	The principle of *replication* is that a variable can hold a list or a single value. When a function is called on a list it applies to each element of the list in turn.

Replication (Aish and Woodbury, 2005) needs some explanation. A node s independent variables may be either *singletons* or *collections*. A collection has the interpretation that each object in the collection specifies a node in and of itself. When multiple variables representing independent nodes are collection-valued, collections propagate to variables representing dependent nodes in two distinct ways as shown in Figure 4.9. The first produces a collection of objects, of size equal to the shortest of the input collections, by using the ith value of each of the input collections as independent inputs. The second form generates the Cartesian product of the input collections. The Cartesian product $X \times Y$ of collections X and Y is the collection of all possible ordered pairs, taking the first member the pair from X and the second member from Y. For example, $\langle 1,2 \rangle \times \langle a,b,c \rangle = \{\langle 1,a \rangle, \langle 1,b \rangle, \langle 1,c \rangle, \langle 2,a \rangle, \langle 2,b \rangle, \langle 2,c \rangle\}$. Both cases result in a single node in the graph, with its elements being accessed through an array-indexing convention. The identification of singletons and collections supports a form of programming-by-example whereby the work done to create a single instance can be propagated to multiple instances simply by providing additional input arguments.

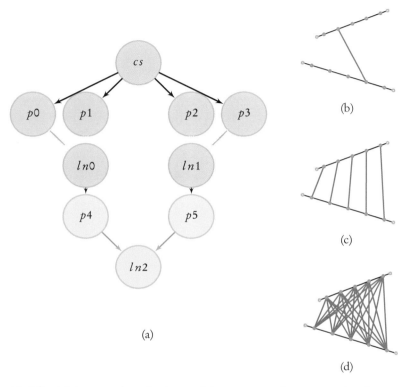

(a)

(b)

(c)

(d)

4.9: A line joining two point collections, each in turn expressed as a parametric point on a line. (a) A symbolic model representing the parametric points and connecting line. The same symbolic model represents (b), (c) and (d). The diagram (b) shows a line between the two parametric points with single index values (1 & 3) for the parameters of its defining points. (c) Each of the defining points of the result line uses all of the values in its input collections. The number of lines is equal to the length of the shortest collection. (d) A line collection under the Cartesian product interpretation of a collection joins each point in the first to each point in the second collection.

4.11   It's more than writing code

Programmers use the above language constructs (and others) to write programs. The act of programming itself has several facets.

To *design* code is to understand the problem, decompose the problem into parts, devise data structures and algorithms for the parts and compose the parts into an entire program design.

Coding translates a design into a program. It takes the abstract ideas of a design and turns them into precise instructions in some programming language. Code seldom works as written. Sometimes, coding and design go together, especially at early, exploratory stages of an idea.

Errors, which programmers call *bugs*, make themselves evident anytime from initial compilation to only after several years of use of a particular piece of code. Finding and fixing such bugs can be a fascinating intellectual activity in its own right. Without any slight to programmers, it is common that more time goes to *debugging* than any other part of the programming task. In fact, programmers will express real surprise when a piece of code works the first time as written!

A program may work, but may be unclear or may need to be used in a more general way. *Refactoring* is the process of *re-designing* code to improve its clarity and its interfaces to other code. Refactoring makes code more adaptable so that it can work in a range of situations.

Most good, large programs are built in *modules.* A module is a collection of data structures that implement a coherent and consistent behaviour. For example, in geometric computing, a common low-level module implements a concrete form of *vector spaces,* that is, collections of vectors that obey certain mathematical rules. Vector spaces rely on real number arithmetic in the language below and provide consistent vector operations to programming layers above. Vector space operations do not include any concept of location, as vectors are simply directions and magnitudes. Location is typically introduced in an *af ne space* layer above vector spaces. To design and program in modules is to conceive of the "world" being programmed as having multiple descriptions, each one in turn expressed as a description in some more atomic module. Designing and implementing systems made of modules is the focus of the discipline of software engineering.

A very important and surprisingly difficult programming skill is to abstract to the lowest level. If an operation or piece of data can be expressed without a domain-specific term, it should be. For example, inserting punched windows and doors into walls can be accomplished by devising a data structure specific to walls, into which holes are cut by special-purpose functions. More abstractly, walls can be represented as solids, in which case the hole-cutting operation can be conceived as the subtraction of a sweep of an outline representing a window or door from a solid representing a wall. In the latter case, details of the wall (its construction, thickness and shape,...) are invisible to the solid representing it. In turn, the hole-punching operation relies only upon the geometry of the solid.

Functions and data structures can be general or specific, complete or partial. To be general is to accommodate many cases. To be complete is to handle all cases in some logical class. For example, data structures and functions over vectors will be general as vectors are the basis for almost all computational geometry. A complete set of functions for vectors might take a very long time to write.

Most languages come with associated data structures and functions. These are almost always incomplete in some context and for some tasks. Programmers must write their own functions when needed. People who spend a lot of time programming will often build up personal collections of classes and functions, which they use and refine again and again in new projects.

Programming is algorithmic thinking in action. Two programs may express an identical algorithm, yet differ in fundamental ways. Above the basics lies a craft of programming, which takes time to master. The craft comprises concepts, constructs and skills. Parametric modelers are mostly amateur programmers. Their work patterns show a tendency to short code in which the craft manifests to a greater or lesser degree.

4.12 Combining parametric and algorithmic thinking

Programming enters parametric modeling in four distinct ways: parametric model construction, update method programming, module development and meta-programming.

Almost all conventional CAD systems have a programming language, either internal or accessible from the system. Designers program in these languages to build and edit models. Once built, models can be changed either by hand or by the action of other programs. Certainly, parametric thinking can and does engage programming of this sort. Programmers use some of the variables that are passed to functions as parameters that link to new parametric structures created in the program. An early CAD book, *The Art of Computer Graphics Programming: A Structured Introduction for Architects and Designers* (Mitchell et al., 1987) was essentially the reverse of this book. Through many examples, it showed how to build a parametric layer onto the top of a structured program. Parametric modeling inherits this programming mode but builds parametric models, that is propagation graphs, rather than fixed models.

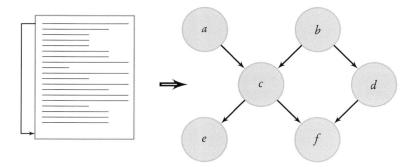

4.10: When executed, the block of code on the left creates or modifies the parametric model on the right. The arrow along the side of the code block represents the ow of control through the code when it is executed.

62

The second role of programming is in writing node update methods. This is like writing expressions in the cells of a spreadsheet. The expressions are called at each update of the spreadsheet to produce a value. Unlike the formulae in spreadsheets, update methods are written once and used many times by calling, not copying, the method. In this role, programs may be spread around a model, so that it becomes hard (though, with small programs, this is seldom needed) to visualize the code as a coherent collection. In this mode of work, each program stands on its own, at most calling other functions defined elsewhere.

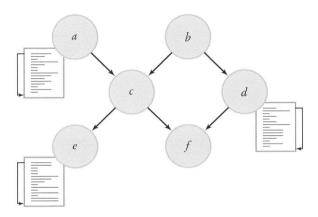

4.11: The nodes a, d and e have user-defined update methods. As propagation visits each model node, for example, in order $\langle b, d, a, c, f, e \rangle$, it executes the node update methods for each node in turn.

Creating a module requires design, coding, debugging, refining and maintaining a data structure and a suite of functions over that structure. Such new modules are needed if a system does not support a particular design task. For example, a layout module for rectangular rooms (see Figures 3.8 and 3.10) requires data structures representing rooms and walls, and functions for inserting, removing and dimensioning both. It can take a great deal of time to build such structures. Consequently, complete modules are a relative rarity in designer-built code. Once a serious commitment to parametric craft is made (or sneaks up through sustained work), it is inevitable that a designer/programmer will build her own modules. As with the master carpenter s jigs, clamps, racks and guides, these modules become an integral part of the parametric craft.

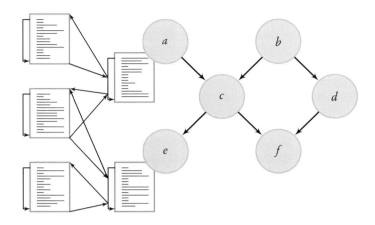

4.12: The code blocks on the left represent functions. They are called by the update methods on nodes *a* and *e*.

Meta-programming – programming the program – completes the set. It affects the whole, not the parts. Here the program affects or traverses the propagation graph itself. For instance, a design space explorer program takes a model and a small set of source nodes and systematically tries combinations of node values, updating the model for each combination and reporting the results, either on the screen, to files on the computer or to another process. Systems enabling meta-programming provide a set of functions that control *graph updates*. When called, these functions invoke the graph propagation algorithm starting either at the sources or at specified nodes. Graph updating provides a key entry point for techniques that can make a propagation-based parametric modeler perform cyclical calculations, perform systematic searches and produce animations.

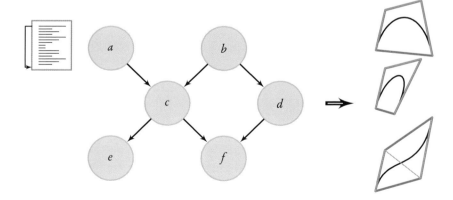

4.13: The code block on the left acts as a meta-program. It resets some of the graph-independent properties of the model, calls UpdateGraph() and records the result external to the system.

Building and using parametric models mixes propagation graphs and programs. Deciding when and how to employ each mode of work is itself part of the craft. Sometimes, clarity comes from the careful construction of new parts from old by building successive nodes in the graph. For instance, the two-circle tangent construction in Figure 2.17 builds and demonstrates a clear geometric method. On the other hand, a formula may be at hand that reduces this construction to a simple set of assignment statements, which is then wrapped in a function. Proficient parametric modelers routinely slip from modeling to programming and back.

4.13   End-user programming

Designers are not alone in facing increasing complexity in their tasks and tools. Many disciplines face a fundamental need and opportunity to do more with their computing tools. All encounter the fact that the graphical user interface, which makes computers so easy to use, also makes them hard to use powerfully.

The graphical user interface (GUI) has profoundly changed our engagement with computers. It does so by providing a shared visual metaphor that enables manual interactive tasks. It largely ignores computation s most vital aspect – the algorithm. Far too often, people must perform repetitive tasks through the GUI that could be completed more quickly and correctly with an algorithm. End-user programming tools promise to support people in expressing and using algorithms within computing tools such as spreadsheets, word processing tools, image systems and computer-aided design systems. However, useful end-user programming systems have been hard to achieve.

End-user programming systems aim to amplify work. They support domain specialists in doing work "better" (this means being more effective, efficient or replacing old tasks with new tasks). End users program to resolve unusual or repeated tasks. Their knowledge and skill lie within their domain and they have acquired programming ability as an adjunct. Further, they view their work as being primarily in their domain, rather than as the development of programs to support others (though many end-user programs are used by others). The point here is that the task comes first and programming is a means to its end.

Typically, end-user programmers work with specialized software. Writers use Emacs, Microsoft Word® or the Adobe Creative Suite®. Designers may use ArchiCAD®, AutoCAD®, CATIA®, form•Z®, GenerativeComponents®, Maya®, Revit®, Rhinoceros®, its add-on Grasshopper™or SolidWorks®. Game designers may use Cinema4D® or Virtools®. They program if the task at hand requires much repetitive work, involves redundant data or must cohere in some way; and when the tools available make work difficult to accomplish. Motivation increases for unique, high-value tasks; when the work repeats; or programs will be reused.

End-user programmers "come out" of their own domain to clarify, abstract and generalize. End-user programming is thus a form of meta-work, in which the programmer must reflect on the tasks at hand, develop, test and refine tools to aid it and then use those tools to accomplish the actual tasks.

End-user programming comes with costs. Increasing capability adds complexity. First introduced by Dertouzos et al. (1992) as *gentle-slope systems* and further developed by Myers et al. (2000), each end-user programming system has an informal function showing how difficulty increases with capability. Systems typically display steps in these functions that correspond to the need to learn new programming constructs and ideas. Figure 4.14 shows the ideal of slowly increasing difficulty with capability; the typical situation in which difficulty becomes an insurmountable obstacle to progress; and a realistic goal in which simple programming features can be learned and used incrementally without removing the end-user programmer from his task.

Parametric modelers do have common cause with professional programmers. Software engineering is the body of knowledge and craft for making provable, reliable, reusable and maintainable programs. In recent years software engineers have paid considerable attention to so-called *agile methods* (Highsmith, 2002), in which programs and their specifications develop in tandem, and programmers work in continuous consultation with those who use (or will use) their work. The *Manifesto for Agile Software Development* (Beck et al., 2009) declares four core principles for agile methods:

> Individuals and interactions over processes and tools
>
> Working software over comprehensive documentation
>
> Customer collaboration over contract negotiation
>
> Responding to change over following a plan
>
> That is, while there is value in the items on the right,
>   we value the items on the left more.

These sound much like design. Clearly, the contingent, task-focused style of parametric work and agile methods share much common ground. At the time of writing though, there was little explicit connection between them.

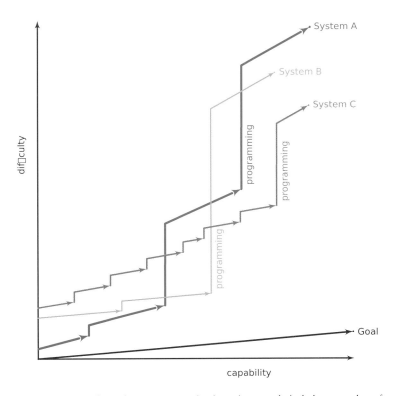

4.14: A good strategy for end-user programming is to aim at a relatively large number of small steps in the capability/difficulty function. Adopted from Myers et al. (2000) the diagram compares fictional but representative systems offering similar capabilities. The intent of the figure is to give a sense for the relative difficulty of using tools to achieve results. The specific shape of each curve can be only anecdotally explained. For instance, System A provides an initial low barrier to use, but has a confusing interface that makes it difficult to learn new features. It presents a significant incremental step when its key feature of constraints are used. Its scripting language is separate from the interface and is based on an old and inelegant language, making it hard to connect programs to the model. In comparison, System B s user interface has a high initial barrier as it is principle-based, but a low slope as its principles make it predictable. Programming in System B requires invocation of an integrated development environment, and this a barrier to its use. In System C, programming language constructs are available directly in the interface and are carefully factored so that they can be largely used independently. A typical end-user programer learns and uses these features in increments, seldom straying far from the task at hand. At some point, the end-user programming does need to take advantage of the full system capabilities. The jump to its full programming environment is reduced by prior practice with programming elements. Though these three systems are abstract, their basic structure can be found in several CAD systems that were on the market in 2010.

Chapter 5

The New Elephant House

Copenhagen, Denmark
Architect: Foster + Partners

by Brady Peters

5.1   Introduction

Copenhagen s New Elephant House opened in June 2008 replacing a structure
dating from 1914. The Copenhagen Zoo, set within a historic park, is one of
the largest cultural institutions in Denmark. The New Elephant House seeks
to create a close visual relationship between the zoo and the park, to provide
the elephants with a stimulating environment, and to create exciting spaces that
provide excellent views of the elephants. The House brings a sense of light and
openness to a traditionally closed building type. Two lightweight, glazed domes
cover the building and maintain a strong visual connection to the sky and the
changing patterns of daylight. The elephants can congregate under these glazed
domes or out in the connecting paddocks. In the wild, bull elephants have a
tendency to roam away from the main herd. The plan form therefore comprises
two separate enclosures, a large one for the main herd, and a smaller one for
the more aggressive bull elephants. Dug into the site, the building has minimal
visual impact on the landscape and excellent passive thermal performance. For
visitors, a ramped promenade leads down through the building looking into the
elephant enclosures along the way.

This chapter focuses on the design of the glazed domes of the New Elephant
House. The canopy design was explored in many ways, through sketching,
physical model making, and three-dimensional explorations using computer
modeling. The torus, a mathematical form, harnessed the complexity of the
design by providing a geometric logic to which the structural and glazing could
relate. A parametric computer model encoded this set-out and constructional
logic. This allowed for the generation and exploration of many different design
options. As the design comprised a collection of relationships and the computer

model could be updated instantaneously, the design remained uid until late in the design process. A series of opening panels and a varying fritting pattern on the glazing panels of the canopy formed the design s environmental strategy. The design of this system – the distribution of the different panel types and the creation of the bespoke fritting patterns – was explored using custom computer programming. A design emerged that incorporated a semi-random placement of leaf textures. This created an environment with different light levels simulating the elephants natural environs.

5.2   Capturing design intent

The architect s design studies suggested two canopy structures rising from the landscape, one larger than the other, with the bulk of the building built into the earth. The two canopies relate to the internal arrangement of the elephant spaces and to the landscape. The structure became an array of members defining quadrilaterals and covered by a fully glazed surface. Both canopies had double curvature and the glazing followed the quadrilateral structure geometry.

While these design studies used many media, physical model making played a crucial role. Both the architects and structural engineers made models to test spatial, formal and structural ideas allowing ideas of structure and of form to interweave. Specific model-making techniques and many different materials carry with them their own material logic. This inherent material logic can be explored to achieve families of similar options. Shown in Figure 5.1, canopy design concepts were developed and tested using many form-making techniques: grid shells made from wood and metal, form-found models in metal and fabric, sculpted vacuum-form models, cable net structures and bendable metal mesh each suggested exciting new formal compositions.

As the design rules developed, a more descriptive solution became necessary, and digital models became essential. The geometric logic of the New Elephant House was neither pre-rationalized nor post-rationalized; the construction system concepts developed with the design. When a design concept became both interesting and sufficiently clear, it was translated into a computer model. "Interpretation" is perhaps more apt than "translation". The digital medium usually suggests or even demands new geometric logic. The particulars of this new logic depend on the software tools and the skill of the person doing the modeling. In this project, one of the first tasks for computer modeling became templates for making detailed physical models of the canopy structure. Through sketch CAD models the design team resolved dimensional characteristics of the structure and its set-out. The geometric complexity of the canopies required exploring these digital sketches with three dimensional CAD models, not just simple two dimensional drawings. This was an important part of the design process, and computer modeling an essential tool throughout the project, not just a drafting and rationalization tool to be used at the end of the project.

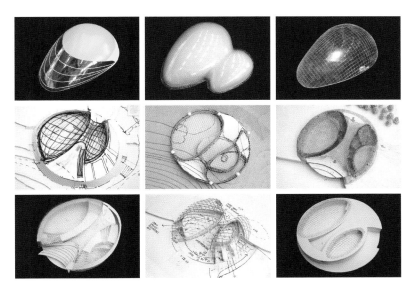

5.1: Physical sketch models.
Source: Foster + Partners / Buro Happold

5.3   The torus

The torus, colloquially known as a "donut", is a mathematically defined surface of revolution. It is generated by revolving a circle around an axis lying outside and in the plane of the circle. Useful defining parameters for this surface are the radius of the circle, and the distance of the circle from its rotational axis. The torus form has many benefits for architecture: the surface is constructed from a series of arcs; the arcs in the rotational direction are equal; the surface can be discretized into planar four-sided panels; those panels are identical when rotated about the torus s axis, but not along the defining circle; and the panels align with each other along their edges. The torus thus defines an array of planar faces suitable for manufacture. Project cost constraints put a high priority on using repeated identical panels. This geometric set-out is based on arcs, another very useful property as this allows for reliable solid and surface offsets, which helps to resolve many complex issues of design and production. Typically, a project uses only part of a torus surface, which is referred to as a *torus patch*.

Physical model making motivated the inital computer modeling. The structure was set-out on the computer, and then assembled by hand. While the torus is a very clear and practical form, it does not capture the playfulness that existed in many of the original physical study models. The early studies of the torus form produced canopies that did not relate well to each other or to the plan beneath. A more exible form was needed. Figure 5.3 demonstrates the key discovery: tilting the axes of two torii. Assymetric forms result by slicing these tilted torii by a horizontal plane By tilting each torus in opposite directions, the plan form

of both canopies defined a central area between the domes. By adjusting the parameters of the torus and angle of axis tilt, the form of the canopies came to both define and fit the New Elephant House plan.

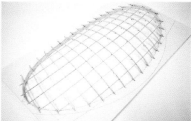

5.2: Study model of torus geometry
Source: Brady Peters / Buro Happold

As shown in an initial sketch model in Figure 5.2, the set-out for the structural and glazing systems follows the torus geometry. Structural centrelines, as well as beam and glazing elements, derive from the torus geometry. The structure and glazing systems of the canopy terminate at a structural ring beam. This ring beam lies on the horizontal plane intersecting the torus.

To arrive at the basic spatial composition, the design team employed a variety of media in sometimes unanticipated ways. The team started with sketches and physical models, worked through a stage of literal computer modeling and then used parametric modeling to discover and refine a simple underlying geometry giving a complex visual form. Ironically, once discovered, the form s geometric simplicity meant that designers could choose either computational or analogue tools in further work.

5.4   Structure generator

As with physical models, design ideas in digital models are often first developed in a manual fashion, however, as the geometric rules and construction details are established the case for investing in a parametric model grows.

With the two-torus geometric framework (though not its specific parameters) decided, the designers turned to structure and glazing. They quickly found their task to be designing a family of ideas and discovery of a specific solution, rather than simple detailing of a single sketch. The level of complexity and the sheer number of potential configurations necessitated a parametric approach. The team decided to work with an architectural designer possessing programming skills to write a custom program, called the *structure generator*. Programming freed the team from the limited command palette available in any particular CAD package. In use, it became like any other design tool – applied iteratively

5.3: Torus geometry set-out.
Source: Brady Peters,
based on Foster + Partners design

throughout the process. Instead of drawing with a pen, the designers sketched with code.

The careful creation (and naming!) of appropriate variables determines much of usefulness of a parametric system. For the New Elephant House structure generator, 26 variables controlled the number of elements, the size, spacing and type of the structural members, the different structural offsets, the primary and secondary radii of the torus, and extent of the structure generated. In turn, these numeric variables related to the torii axes expressed as coordinate systems. The structure generator produced all of the centrelines, primary, secondary, tertiary, quaternary structural members, glazing components, as well as tables of node points.

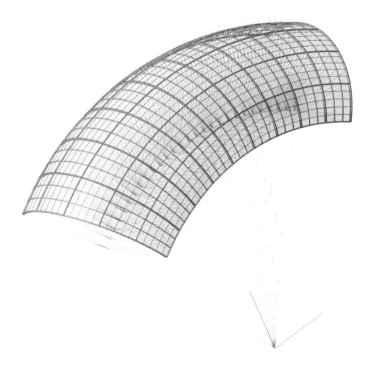

5.4: Structure generator interface and generated geometry.
Source: Brady Peters, based on Foster + Partners design

In this project phase, programming a parametric model enabled creating and testing many variations of structure and canopy within the two-torus form, itself a parametric model subject to change. Through the use of the structure generator many more options could be studied than if the canopies needed to be rebuilt with each new option. The speed of producing new options also allowed the canopy design to be changed late in the design process. Here computation became a refinement and optimization tool, resulting in the design shown in Figure 5.5.

The fabricator received the dome designs as a document called the *Geometry Method Statement*, rather than through a computer program or digital model. This simple, verifiable document assures reliable data transfer between CAD systems – fabricators must build their own digital models following its rules. As an educational and contractual strategy the Geometry Method Statement helps fabricators fully understand the geometric complexities of the project. This document describes the design in terms of simple geometric rules. For the New Elephant House project, it follows directly from the set-out logic of the torii and the structure generator computer program.

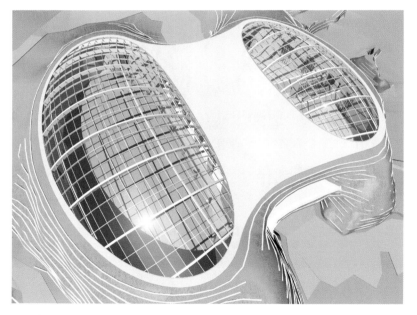

5.5: Elephant House canopy structure.
Source: Brady Peters, based on Foster + Partners design

5.5 Frit generator

The environmental strategy for the project was expressed both through a series of opening panels in the canopy, as well as a varying fritting pattern expressed on the glazing panels of the canopy. Through the use of a computer program, patterns emerged through a semi-random placement of leaf textures.

Environmental performance and occupant comfort were important design goals. The design team decided that glazing panels themselves should do as much environmental control work as possible. Through a series of opening panels in the canopy and a varying fritting panel it achieved ventilation, solar control and variable lighting simulating natural conditions. Variable openings in the glass canopy controlled natural air ow. Fritting patterns printed on the glass reduced solar radiation received and thus helped maintain a comfortable temperature. No other coatings were used on the glass so that the light within the elephant enclosures would be as natural as possible.

The solar control of the fritting depended on the local ratios of transparent to opaque areas. The environmental analysis defined the level of fritting and the number of panels of each type of fritting density. While the overall amount of fritting was critical, the distribution of these different panel types was not. A new distribution pattern for the different panel types was developed, dubbed the TREE SORT pattern and shown in Figure 5.6. As wild elephants gather at forest edges, the forest became a metaphor for distributing shading panels and fritting density. In the TREE SORT pattern, the opening panels are analogues of forest openings and therefore have no fritting. The pattern found a specified number of tree trunks (yellow panels) as far away from openings (red panels) as possible, and created a gradient of panel types radiating away from the tree trunk (See Figure 5.7). The dense areas of fritting centred around tree trunks, with decreasing density from the trunks towards the opening panels. The design team explored a range of results by adjusting the position of opening panels, the number of trees, the minimum distance between trees, the number of panel types and the number and distribution of each panel type.

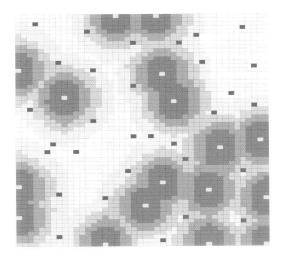

5.6: TREE SORT pattern
Source: Brady Peters

5.7: Panel Type Distribution on Canopies.
Source: Brady Peters, based on Foster + Partners design

Another computer program, called the *frit generator* and shown in Figure 5.8 was developed to create a custom frit pattern for the New Elephant House. The frit design started with a leaf pattern. A more standard micro-dot frit pattern did not work for this project as it would produce even internal light, suitable for an art gallery or office, but not for the elephant enclosure which needed areas of light and dark contrast. The intent is that this allows the elephants to seek out the area in which they would most like to stand.

The frit generator takes a series of shapes for the frit pattern, and a second series of shapes that the frit pattern will be created within. This last series of shapes represents the glazing panels. For each panel, the algorithm creates a unique fritting pattern as shown in Figure 5.10. A random frit shape from the first set is chosen and placed within the glazing panel. The frit shape can be randomly rotated, scaled, and its vertices subtly shifted. The algorithm continues to place these frit shapes until it reaches the desired frit area ratio. Figure 5.9 shows frit patterns at differing ratios.

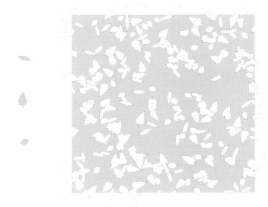

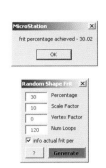

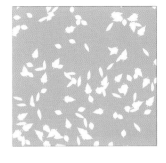

5.8: Frit generator with interface and generated frit shapes.
Source: Brady Peters, based on Foster + Partners design

5.10: Frit patterns distributed on canopies.
Source: Brady Peters, based on Foster + Partners design

5.9: 15%, 30%, 45%, 60% Frit patterns.
Source: Brady Peters, based on Foster + Partners design

5.6 Conclusions

The program for the New Elephant House in Copenhagen had both restrictive constraints and a complex and untested set of requirements. Its design process used many different media, both analogue and computational. Both physical and digital model making contributed to the design outcome. The mathematical form of the torus helped to achieve both an economy and a constructional logic for the project. A custom computer program enabled extensive exploration of the three-dimensional geometry of the digital model. This generation method helped to optimize building form and structure. The project s environmental performance was integrated into the design through new panel distribution patterns and semi-random fritting patterns. Figure 5.12 shows that the project incorporates patterns from nature, patterns from geometry and patterns from computation.

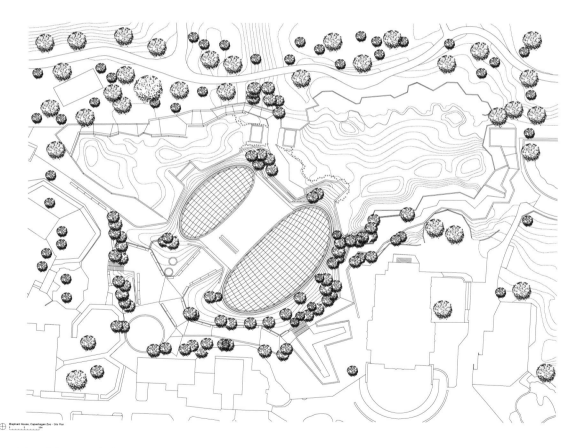

5.11: Plan of the New Elephant House.
Source: Foster + Partners

5.12: Interior of the main herd enclosure in the New Elephant House.
Source: Richard Davies / Foster + Partners

5.13: Detail of roof opening.
Source: Richard Davies /
Foster + Partners

5.14: Detail of frit pattern.
Source: Richard Davies /
Foster + Partners

Chapter 6

Geometry

Geometry is a very big topic. You can spend a lifetime learning it and master only a tiny fraction of the literature. It uses many mathematical concepts and formalisms, each of which takes time and effort to learn *before* you can begin to master the geometric ideas that use such concepts. Yet most of the objects made with parametric modeling systems are geometric. How can a designer ever learn anything like "enough"?

History shows that designers have always "learned enough" geometry in ways important to them. The master masons used Euclid s compass and straight-edge constructions to lay out Gothic cathedrals and their details (see Figures 6.1, 6.2 and 6.3). With a compass and straight-edge, a designer can reliably make many geometric figures, including straight lines and angles, divisions into two equal parts, isoceles triangles, and sequences of lengths in ratio to each other. Some constructions, like the trisection of an angle and the famous squaring of a circle (constructing a square of equal area to a given circle) are impossible with these tools.

The addition of rulers to the drawing toolbox allowed designers to work with scaled drawings and to make and transfer measurements within and between drawings.

In the Renaissance designers learned to construct perspectives explicitly. While the exact moment of the (re-)introduction of perspective into Western Art is a matter of debate, at its nexus were artists such as Masaccio and Masolino and painter-sculptor-architects such as Brunelleschi and Alberti. Notably, Alberti s book *On Painting* (1972) was key in disseminating the new perspective ideas. From these early beginnings, perspective became a tool for both depicting and creating architecture. Indeed, the practice of *trompe l oeil* murals quickly came to blur the boundary between depiction and design.

6.1: Stepwise construction of a Gothic tracery.

6.2: Gothic traceries were both drawn and constructed using compass and straightedge techniques. These simple media deeply in uenced the forms created. In effect, they left indelible marks on the geometry.
Source: Christopher Carlson.

Introduced by Gaspard Monge in 1795, and developed throughout the 19th Century, *descriptive geometry* is a body of techniques for constructing drawings of complex intersecting objects in multiple views. Such drawings enabled new designs for the increasingly complex machinery of the Industrial Revolution. Much of manual mechanical and architectural drawing is based on Monge s principles. In the first half of the 20th Century, it was taught extensively in schools of architecture and engineering. In the last half of the century, it largely faded from the curriculum, at least as an explicit subject.

6.4: The painting *Healing of the Cripple and Raising of Tabitha* by Masolino de Panicale (some attribute also to Masaccio) from 1424 in the Brancacci Chapel in Church of Santa Maria del Carmine in Florence, shows perspectives lines whose common intersection argues for understanding and deliberate use of perspective.
Source: The Yorck Project (2002).

6.3: Examples of Gothic traceries.
Source: Christopher Carlson (1993).

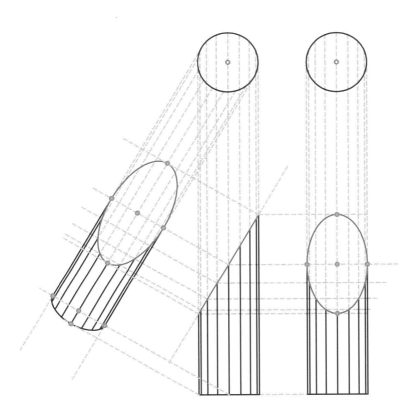

6.7: By 1428, Masaccio s *The Holy Trinity, with the Virgin and Saint John and Donors*, in the *Church of Santa Maria Novella* in Florence, showed explicit perspectival structuring of space and choice of view. Source: The Yorck Project (2002).

6.5: A simple example of descriptive geometry. Start with a drawing of a cut cylinder (centre) viewed along the edge of the cut. Produce a view showing the true size of the cut ellipse (left) and an orthogonal view at 90° to the original (right).

By the end of the 20th Century, CAD systems supported a wide variety of construction operations. Two principal ideas were *snapping* and *intersection*. Snapping, shown in Figure 6.8, is an interaction technique in which the system recognizes when a *source object* is moved sufficiently close to a *target object* and then places the source object coincident with the target object. If line midpoints are the target, then moving a polygon such that one of its vertices becomes close to a line midpoint will result in the system moving the polygon precisely so that the two points coincide. Intersection operators compute the precise location and result where objects intersect. The intersections produced can themselves take part in subsequent snap interactions. Combined with *global locators* such as grids, guides and reference planes, snaps and intersections play the role of the medieval compass and straight-edge construction system. Contemporary systems also provide the ability to enter numbers representing dimensions or positions, either explicitly by typing them into a dialogue box, or implicitly, through such interaction devices as *dimensions* and *rulers*.

6.6: Andrea Mantegna s oculus on the ceiling of the *Camera degli Sposi, Palazzo Ducale,* in Mantua (1471–74) is an early example of *trompe l oeil* perspective. Source: The Yorck Project (2002).

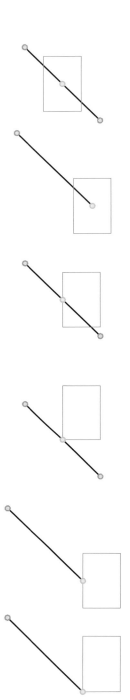

Geometry is at the core of all of these tools, and designers using them certainly became expert, if implicit, geometers within their domain. Using the "toolbox" available at the time, designers have always developed a suite of "tricks of the trade" by which they could reliably create their intended forms. Of course, the medium massaged the design. Traces of the compass and straight-edge show in the pointed arches, lancet windows and quatrefoil bosses of Gothic architecture. Many historians argue that the ability to create perspective changed the focus of Renaissance architecture from objects to expressing movement and views through space.

If you watch a designer using a contemporary CAD system, you are likely to see a combination of all of these techniques (explicit construction, perspective, descriptive geometry, snapping and intersection) and others at play. Designers do indeed use geometric tools in their work.

Parametric modeling is merely the newest toolbox for design work. At the risk of interpreting history as it happens, I ll argue that the tools in this box force a new and different relation to designers. One difference lies in persistence – once an object is placed parametrically, the operation placing it will continue to act every time the model is changed. This means that designers need to predict how the tool will work in the design as it develops. A second difference comes from diversity and abundance – there are simply more tools in the box. Each tool has a mathematical basis, which is open and available for designers to adapt. A third difference lies in the medium itself – however large the toolbox, designers will, at some point, be constrained by it. The solution here is to open the system, to allow designers to directly express new tools. Designers must explicitly translate of geometric "good sense" into precise mathematics and algorithms.

Mastering the new toolbox requires a different kind of geometric knowledge, one that enables designers to predict persistent effects, to understand (at least qualitatively) the diversity and structure of the mathematical toolbox, and to shuttle between intended effect and mathematical invention that models it. This chapter is my best guess at the set of key ideas designers need to master the new medium. Each idea may help in understanding an important group of the tools in the parametric box, as well as having a crisp mathematical and algorithmic structure.

Some ideas are more important than others, at least in practical use. In this chapter I cover a small set of important ideas. Actually, "cover" is a funny word. We usually mean it to treat a concept in detail. It means something different here – what is important is how the concept affects parametric modeling: how it helps predict effect, explain diversity and implement new ideas.

All of these concepts depend upon some basic mathematical ideas. It is these that are "covered" here in something like the traditional sense. These ideas are important because you, the parametric designer, will need them. They are the basis for much of what you do with a system and are the elements from which

6.8: Snapping has become essential in CAD systems and are part of a toolset that includes grids and numerical specification of location. An end point, midpoint or centre of the source (red rectangle) snaps to an endpoint or midpoint of the target (sloped line segment).

you construct new tools for the parametric box. They are necessary, but not sufficient. To become truly expert, you will need to grow beyond this basic starter set. Learning about parametric tools involves bringing together four distinct ways of understanding the mathematics of spatial objects: *geometric*, *visual*, *symbolic* and *algorithmic*. We call each of these a *view* onto the toolbox.

To think geometrically is to know and apply such ideas as the non-location of vectors, the existence of tangents and normals on curves, distance and angles between objects, and perpendicularity in general.

The visual realm comprises both static and dynamic displays. It is important to be able to draw and visualize the basic objects and their relationships. Many problems can be solved with an adroit choice of diagram. To draw a diagram is to choose to leave out certain information and to add other information that is not actually true. For instance, strictly speaking, vectors cannot be drawn – they have no location. We draw them anyway, putting them at specific places and then hopefully remembering not to form conclusions based on location. Drawings are static; our visual system evolved in a dynamic world. Parametric models enable us to take advantage of movement of objects to better understand how geometric relationships actually "work".

Algorithms are recipes. In parametric modeling they spell out the practical tasks of representing and manipulating design objects. They are specific, concrete lists of instructions, meant to be followed literally and in order. We write them with particular goals in mind: move along a curve, project a point, find an areea. The medium of spatial computing is the algorithm.

We live in a world culture with over 3000 years of collective experience using symbolic representation. Symbols allow us to join ways of understanding, and the symbolic realm is where we combine geometric, visual and algorithmic views. Symbols enable inference. They support precise reasoning beyond that practical in other views. The symbolic view is complex and we might well think of it as itself comprising several views. For instance, we can represent relations between points using symbols such as $\dot{p} - \dot{q}$, trigonometric relations such as $\cos(\dot{p}\dot{q}\dot{r}) = \sqrt{2}/2$ or coordinates such as

$$\begin{bmatrix} 3 & 2 & 5 \end{bmatrix}^T - \begin{bmatrix} 1 & -1 & 1 \end{bmatrix}^T = \begin{bmatrix} 2 & 3 & 4 \end{bmatrix}^T$$

Each way of using symbols supports different insights. A very common way of using symbols is to make explicit relations between different symbolic views. For instance, the two definitions of the scalar product developed in Section 6.1.9 relate geometric and coordinate-based symbolic views and, by that act, enable many insights and proofs.

To learn parametric modeling is to combine geometric, visual, symbolic and algorithmic representations of objects and especially to learn how these forms interrelate. We are in the very early days of this new medium and can predict neither the tools nor the techniques that will surely develop over time. That said, the geometric ideas of this chapter may be a beginning. They are certainly not an end. As you learn more about geometry, your bookshelf and hard disk will fill with geometry books and papers. There are classic texts, which you would do well to have. The surprisingly readable Euclid s *Elements*, *circa* 300BC (a recent version is (Euclid, 1956)), introduces basic geometric axioms and the process of proof by construction. Books on descriptive geometry entirely fill library shelves. Notable early books include the many editions of Gaspard Monge s (1827) seminal *Geométrié Descriptive*, Charles Davies (1859) text and Henry Miller s (1911) simply named *Descriptive Geometry* . The hand-illustrated *Natural Structure* (Williams, 1972) provides a visual introduction to symmetries in three-dimensional space, largely through polyhedra and their packings. The best mathematical textbooks are wonders of clarity. Math and proofs are presented with clear arguments, simple notation and compelling figures. But math is not done that way. It is an act of invention and discovery. *Proofs and Refutations* (Lakatos, 1991) is a fictional documentary of a seminar in mathematics. In it, a professor and his students model what really happens in mathematical work. It is surprisingly like design. The cleverly illlustrated *Architectural Geometry* (2007) explains geometric ideas particularly attuned to contemporary architectural design. It grounds its clear, visual explanations in actual design examples. Henderson s (1996) *Experiencing Geometry* gives many proofs and connects diverse topics such as symmetry and differential geometry in context of the plane, cone and sphere. The venerable *Mathematical Elements for Computer Graphics* (Rogers and Adams, 1976) constructs an early bridge from geometry to programming. More succinct is *A Programmer s Geometry* (Bowyer and Woodwark, 1983), which presents a selection of basic geometric structures and provides Fortan-like code to represent them. Twenty years later, with *Geometric Tools for Computer Graphics*, Schneider and Eberly (2003) gave the world a near-encyclopedia of algorithms for geometry. You must have this book if you are serious about geometry and computing. Vince (2005) provides hundreds of formulae, examples and proofs for fundamental geometric objects and relations. The slim volume *Interactive Curves and Surfaces* (Rockwood and Chambers 1996) may lack in depth, but it makes up for this in clarity, insight and fast pace. I especially treasure these few good books. There are hundreds of other useful ones out there.

6.1   Vectors and points

Vectors and points are the basic objects upon which three-dimensional spatial operations are performed. They form the foundation for parametric skill.

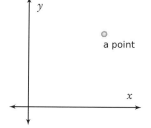

6.1.1   Points

Geometrically, a point is a position in space. Mathematics requires the space, so drawings of points usually include a *coordinate system* to define it.

Points are everywhere in a CAD system interface. Surprisingly, they mostly act as placeholders for the actual computational work. Almost all of the real work and concept is carried by vectors. Points mostly act to provide a spatial position the work done by vectors.

6.1.2   Vectors

Geometrically, a vector is a *direction* and *length* (other names for length are *norm* and *magnitude*). Mathematically, a vector is an abstract object that is part a of *vector space*, itself a mathematical object. We denote a vector space by the symbol V. The length of a vector $\vec{v}$ is denoted by $|\vec{v}|$.

a vector

Vectors carry most of the computational work in a parametric system. Yet, in most CAD, vectors are secondary objects. The representation and arithmetic of vectors is more complex than that of points, yet is nearly as simple and familiar as basic algebra.

We represent points and vectors as one-dimensional matrices. By convention, we make a choice of either column (the choice made here) or row matrices. It is often convenient to express a column vector as a row vector and vice versa; for this, the ^{T} operator specifies the matrix transpose.

We call the individual matrix elements the *components* of vectors and points.

6.1.3   Vectors and points are different

Since we represent vectors and points as identical matrices, it is easy to get them confused. Consider a tuple of three scalars x, y and z. Two interpretations are pertinent. The tuple

representing points

$$\dot{p} = \begin{bmatrix} x \\ y \\ z \end{bmatrix}$$

$$\dot{p} = \begin{bmatrix} x \\ y \\ z \end{bmatrix} = \begin{bmatrix} x & y & z \end{bmatrix}^T$$

specifies a point – a location in some coordinate system. Points are "bound" – they refer to a specific location with respect to some datum. The identical tuple

representing vectors

$$\vec{v} = \begin{bmatrix} x \\ y \\ z \end{bmatrix}$$

$$\vec{v} = \begin{bmatrix} x \\ y \\ z \end{bmatrix} = \begin{bmatrix} x & y & z \end{bmatrix}^T$$

specifies a vector – a direction and magnitude (but no fixed location). Vectors are "free" – having no position, they are meaningful at any position in space as simply a direction and magnitude.

Some texts (like this one) treat points and vectors as column vectors. Others use row vectors. Some texts even mix the two in different sections. They mean the same thing, but the notation and order of objects in equations differ. This is life. Get used to it. Consistency, though, is far from the last refuge of the mediocre. It makes a great deal of sense to use a uniform notation in your own work. Just don t expect it elsewhere.

Geometrically, we have different intuitions about points and vectors – we draw them differently, as shown in Figure 6.9. Not only do they look different when drawn, but they behave differently. We know that we can "move vectors around" without affecting them in any material way, but that the essence of a point is its position. However, we represent them with the same syntax – a row or column vector. From this notational convenience arises one of the principal obstacles in developing an intuitive grasp of the mathematics of computer graphics. Among other things, our intention here is to cement in place an understanding that makes explicit the difference between these two fundamental kinds of objects.

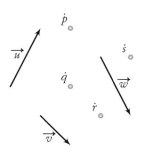

6.9: Vectors and points are not the same. We draw them with distinct glyphs. They obey their own mathematical rules. Yet, we represent them in very similar ways, which can (and does) cause confusion.

Later we add a fourth row to the vector and point representation. For vectors the value in this row will always be 0; for points it will be 1. Vectors and points so represented are said to be in *homogeneous coordinates*. An example vector is

$$\vec{v} = \begin{bmatrix} x \\ y \\ z \\ 0 \end{bmatrix} = \begin{bmatrix} x & y & z & 0 \end{bmatrix}^T$$

A point so represented is

$$\dot{p} = \begin{bmatrix} x \\ y \\ z \\ 1 \end{bmatrix} = \begin{bmatrix} x & y & z & 1 \end{bmatrix}^T$$

You will find more on homogenenous coordinates in almost every book on spatial computing – we introduce them here as you will see them elsewhere and as Section 6.5 uses them to represent coordinate systems.

6.1.4   The arithmetic of vectors

Basic mathematical literacy is founded on the arithmetic of numbers. Addition, subtraction, multiplication and division relate numbers to each other. Their combination into expressions with precedence rules (brackets before exponents before multiplication and division before addition and subtraction) are skills learned in grade school and used almost subconsciously in day-to-day work. Geometry is founded on arithmetic too: the arithmetic of vectors and points. This differs from number arithmetic in several ways.

Vectors (actually *vector spaces*) define two operations, *vector addition* and *scalar multiplication*.

Vector addition combines two vectors to create a third:

$$\vec{u} + \vec{v} = \vec{w}$$

vector addition

$$\begin{bmatrix} 1 \\ 2 \\ 5 \end{bmatrix} + \begin{bmatrix} 2 \\ -1 \\ 2 \end{bmatrix} = \begin{bmatrix} 3 \\ 1 \\ 7 \end{bmatrix}$$

Scalar multiplication ($a\,\vec{u}$ or $a \cdot \vec{u}$) combines a real number and a vector to produce a second vector with the identical direction, but a possibly different length:

$$a\,\vec{u} = \vec{v}$$
$$a = 2$$

scalar multiplication

$$2\begin{bmatrix} 2 \\ 1 \\ -3 \end{bmatrix} = \begin{bmatrix} 4 \\ 2 \\ -6 \end{bmatrix}$$

scalar multiplication
alternate notation

$$a\,\vec{u}$$
or
$$a \cdot \vec{u}$$

Vectors, together with vector addition and scalar multiplication, obey rules. These are the analogues of arithmetic over the familiar real numbers and are the basis for almost all other geometry in parametric modeling.

Closure of addition

$\vec{u} + \vec{v} \in \mathsf{V}$, the space of all vectors

Adding two vectors always produces a vector.

addition is closed

$$\begin{bmatrix} 1 \\ 2 \\ 3 \end{bmatrix} + \begin{bmatrix} 2 \\ -1 \\ 2 \end{bmatrix} = \begin{bmatrix} 3 \\ 1 \\ 5 \end{bmatrix}$$

Zero vector

$\vec{v} + \vec{0} = \vec{v}$

There is a unique *zero vector*. This plus any vector leaves the vector unchanged.

zero vector

$$\begin{bmatrix} 1 \\ -3 \\ 2 \end{bmatrix} + \begin{bmatrix} 0 \\ 0 \\ 0 \end{bmatrix} = \begin{bmatrix} 1 \\ -3 \\ 2 \end{bmatrix}$$

Inverse vector

inverse vector

$$\begin{bmatrix} 1 \\ -3 \\ 2 \end{bmatrix} + \begin{bmatrix} -1 \\ 3 \\ -2 \end{bmatrix} = \begin{bmatrix} 0 \\ 0 \\ 0 \end{bmatrix}$$

$$\vec{v} + -\vec{v} = \vec{0}$$

Every vector has an inverse. By convention, the inverse vector establishes the operation of subtraction as $\vec{v} - \vec{u} = \vec{v} + (-\vec{u})$.

Commutativity of addition

addition is commutative

$$\begin{bmatrix} 1 \\ 2 \\ 5 \end{bmatrix} + \begin{bmatrix} 2 \\ 1 \\ 2 \end{bmatrix} = \begin{bmatrix} 2 \\ 1 \\ 2 \end{bmatrix} + \begin{bmatrix} 1 \\ 2 \\ 5 \end{bmatrix}$$

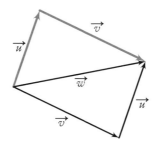 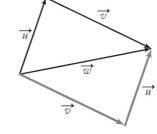

$$\vec{u} + \vec{v} = \vec{v} + \vec{u}$$

A given addition and its reverse order produce the same result.

Associativity of addition

addition is associative

$$\left(\begin{bmatrix} 1 \\ 2 \\ 3 \end{bmatrix} + \begin{bmatrix} 2 \\ 1 \\ 2 \end{bmatrix} \right) + \begin{bmatrix} 3 \\ 1 \\ 4 \end{bmatrix}$$

$$= \begin{bmatrix} 1 \\ 2 \\ 3 \end{bmatrix} + \left(\begin{bmatrix} 2 \\ 1 \\ 2 \end{bmatrix} + \begin{bmatrix} 3 \\ 1 \\ 4 \end{bmatrix} \right)$$

$$= \begin{bmatrix} 6 \\ 4 \\ 9 \end{bmatrix}$$

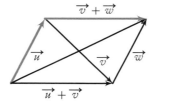 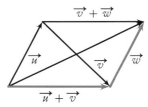

$$\vec{u} + (\vec{v} + \vec{w}) = (\vec{u} + \vec{v}) + \vec{w}$$

The order in which a given addition is done does not affect the outcome.

Closure of scalar multiplication

multiplication is closed

$$2 \begin{bmatrix} 2 \\ 1 \\ -3 \end{bmatrix} = \begin{bmatrix} 4 \\ 2 \\ -6 \end{bmatrix}$$

$$a\vec{v} \in V$$

Scalar multiplication always produces a result.

Identity element in scalar multiplication

$$1\overrightarrow{v} = \overrightarrow{v}$$

Multiplying a vector by 1 yields the original vector.

Associativity of scalar multiplication

$$(ab)\overrightarrow{v} = a(b\overrightarrow{v})$$

Scaling by a number or successively by its factors is the same.

Left distributivity of scalar multiplication

$$(a+b)\overrightarrow{v} = a\overrightarrow{v} + b\overrightarrow{v}$$

Multiplying a vector by a sum of scaling factors is the same as adding vectors scaled by each factor. You can add scaling factors then multiply or vice versa.

Right distributivity of scalar multiplication

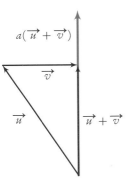

$$a(\overrightarrow{u} + \overrightarrow{v}) = a\overrightarrow{u} + a\overrightarrow{v}$$

Scaling a vector sum or summing the scaled components gives the same result. You can add vectors and then multiply, or vice versa.

multiplicative identity

$$1\begin{bmatrix} 2 \\ 1 \\ -3 \end{bmatrix} = \begin{bmatrix} 2 \\ 1 \\ -3 \end{bmatrix}$$

multiplication is associative

$$(3 \times 2)\begin{bmatrix} 2 \\ 1 \\ -3 \end{bmatrix} = 3\left(2\begin{bmatrix} 2 \\ 1 \\ -3 \end{bmatrix}\right)$$

left distributivity

$$(3 \times 2)\begin{bmatrix} 2 \\ 1 \\ -3 \end{bmatrix}$$
$$= 3\begin{bmatrix} 2 \\ 1 \\ -3 \end{bmatrix} + 2\begin{bmatrix} 2 \\ 1 \\ -3 \end{bmatrix}$$

right distributivity

$$3\left(\begin{bmatrix} 1 \\ 2 \\ 5 \end{bmatrix} + \begin{bmatrix} 2 \\ -1 \\ 2 \end{bmatrix}\right)$$
$$= 3\begin{bmatrix} 1 \\ 2 \\ 5 \end{bmatrix} + 3\begin{bmatrix} 2 \\ -1 \\ 2 \end{bmatrix}$$

6.1.5 The arithmetic of points

In sharp comparison to vectors, points have only a single operation. *Subtracting* two points yields a vector.

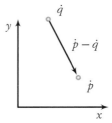

Points and vectors combine with a single operation. The *addition* of a point and vector produces a point.

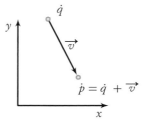

The overall structure of a typical arithmetic calculation in space is to start with points, use point–point subtraction to convert to vectors, do the serious work with vectors and convert back to points with point–vector addition.

6.1.6 Combining vectors

The operations of vector addition and scalar multiplication act on vectors to produce other vectors. Several terms describe the vectors so produced.

Linear combinations

A linear combination of a set of vectors is a sum arbitrarily scaling each of the vectors. Formally, a combination of vectors $\vec{u}_i, i = 0 \dots n$ generating $\vec{v}$ is linear if it can be expressed in the following form, where a_i are arbitrary reals and are called the *coef cients* of the linear combination.

$$\vec{v} = a_0 \vec{u}_0 + \cdots + a_n \vec{u}_n$$

Linear dependence and independence

Two vectors are *linearly independent* if one is not a scalar multiple of the other. A set of vectors $\vec{u}_i, i = 0\ldots n$ is linearly independent if no vector is a linear combination of the others.

Formally, linear independence occurs if $a_0 = \cdots = a_n = 0$ is the only solution to $a_0\vec{u}_0 + \cdots + a_n\vec{u}_n = \vec{0}$.

Span of a set of vectors

The span S of a set of vectors B is the set generatable by a linear combination of the vectors in B.

Vector basis

A set of vectors B is a basis for a vector space V if it is linearly independent and spans V.

The symbolic idea of a vector basis captures the geometric idea that a coordinate system has three vectors. The three vectors of a 3D coordinate system are basis vectors for that system.

Uniqueness of a linear combination

Given a basis B, every vector in the space spanned by B can be expressed as a unique linear combination of the vectors in B.

There are two powerful ideas here. First, basis vectors combine to represent any other vector in the space. Second, such representation is unique: there is only one combination of the basis vectors that will do the job.

Bases for 2D and 3D

Any two linearly independent vectors form a 2D basis, which can express all 2D vectors through their linear combinations. Similarly, three linearly independent vectors form a 3D basis.

Natural basis

The *natural basis* is the most simple form. Each of its unit vectors has precisely one non-zero component. So the natural basis for $\mathbb{R}^3$ comprises three vectors.

natural basis

$$i = \begin{bmatrix} 1 & 0 & 0 \end{bmatrix}^T$$
$$j = \begin{bmatrix} 0 & 1 & 0 \end{bmatrix}^T$$
$$k = \begin{bmatrix} 0 & 0 & 1 \end{bmatrix}^T$$

6.1.7   Length and distance

The *norm* (or *length*) of a vector $\vec{v} = \langle v_0, \ldots, v_n \rangle$, denoted $|\vec{v}|$ is defined as the square root of the sum of squares of its components, that is,

$$|\vec{v}| = \sqrt{{v_0}^2 + \cdots + {v_n}^2}$$

Note that, in two dimensions, this is simply a statement of Pythagoras s Law. So, for two-dimensional vectors the length of a vector $\vec{v}$ is

$$|\vec{v}| = \sqrt{{\vec{v}_x}^2 + {\vec{v}_y}^2}$$

For three-dimensional vectors

$$|\vec{v}| = \sqrt{{\vec{v}_x}^2 + {\vec{v}_y}^2 + {\vec{v}_z}^2}$$

The *distance* between two points is the length of the vector that results from their subtraction.

$$|\vec{pq}| = |\dot{q} - \dot{p}| = \sqrt{(\dot{q}_0 - \dot{p}_0)^2 + \cdots + (\dot{q}_n - \dot{p}_n)^2}$$

The direction of a vector $\vec{v}$ is another vector $\vec{dir}$ (called a *direction vector*) such that

$$\vec{dir}_{\vec{v}} = \frac{\vec{v}}{|\vec{v}|}$$

Any direction vector $\vec{dir}$ is of length 1 (aka *unit length*).

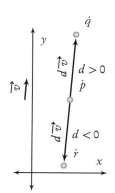

When dealing with vectors, it is useful to have a concept of *signed distance*. Given an initial point $\dot{p}$, a direction vector $\vec{dir}$, and a scaling factor d the point $\dot{q}$ is the signed distance d from $\dot{p}$ along $\vec{dir}$. A positive signed distance means that distance is measured "along" the vector; a negative signed distance means that distance is measured in the opposite direction. Signed distances do not translate well into drawings – dimension lines convey unsigned distances by convention. When drawn using a dimension line, a signed distance d reduces to its absolute value $|d|$.

Signed distances are comparable to our perceptions of subtraction along a real number line: $8 - 5 = 3$ is the signed distance from 5 to 8; whereas $5 - 8 = -3$ is the signed distance from 8 to 5.

6.1.8   Bound and free vectors

We usually think of vectors as being *free* or having no position in space: they give only length and direction, no matter where they are "located". Another interpretation is to treat vectors as *bound*, that is, beginning at a common point, usually the origin, which by convention is labeled $\dot{O}$. *Position vector* is another phrase for *bound vector.* A set of bound vectors with the origin as the common point identifies a set of points, one for each bound vector.

Bound vectors require a common point. When they are specified as matrices, they require an entire *coordinate system*. One has to know to where and in which direction to apply the components of the vector. The solution is to always have in mind three vectors, called $\vec{i}$, $\vec{j}$ and $\vec{k}$ representing the x-axis, y-axis and z-axis respectively. Thus a bound vector $\vec{v} = \begin{bmatrix} x & y & z \end{bmatrix}^T$ is actually the vector sum

$$x\,\vec{i} + y\,\vec{j} + z\,\vec{k}$$

and the point with which it is associated is

$$\dot{p} = \dot{O} + \vec{v}$$

6.1.9 The scalar product

The *scalar product* of two vectors is a number that can be used in several ways. It provides a test for perpendicularity, a measure of the angle between two vectors, a tool for projecting one vector onto another and a measure of the length of a vector. Informally, the scalar product is also known as the *dot product.*

The scalar product of two vectors $\vec{u} \bullet \vec{v}$ is

$$\vec{u} \bullet \vec{v} = \sum_{i=0}^{n} \vec{u}_i \cdot \vec{v}_i$$

For example, let $\vec{u} = \begin{bmatrix} \vec{u}_x & \vec{u}_y & \vec{u}_z \end{bmatrix}^T$ and $\vec{v} = \begin{bmatrix} \vec{v}_x & \vec{v}_y & \vec{v}_z \end{bmatrix}^T$ be two 3D vectors. The scalar product $\vec{u} \bullet \vec{v}$ is

$$\vec{u} \bullet \vec{v} = \vec{u}_x \vec{v}_x + \vec{u}_y \vec{v}_y + \vec{u}_z \vec{v}_z$$

The scalar product is defined on vectors only. By convention, it can be applied to points. When a point $\dot{p}$ is used in a scalar product, the meaning is that the vector involved is that from the origin $\dot{O}$ to the point $\dot{p}$.

The scalar product has several properties. These are useful when working with constructions and derivations involving the scalar product.

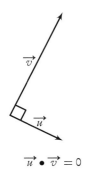

$$\vec{u} \bullet \vec{v} = 0$$

$$\vec{u} \bullet \vec{v} \text{ is a number}$$
$$\vec{u} \bullet \vec{v} = \vec{v} \bullet \vec{u}$$
$$\vec{u} \bullet \vec{0} = 0 = \vec{0} \bullet \vec{u}$$
$$\vec{u} \bullet \vec{u} = |\vec{u}|^2$$
$$(a\vec{u}) \bullet \vec{v} = a(\vec{v} \bullet \vec{u}) = \vec{v} \bullet (a\vec{u})$$
$$\vec{u} \bullet (\vec{v} + \vec{w}) = \vec{u} \bullet \vec{v} + \vec{u} \bullet \vec{w}$$

Perpendicularity of vectors

If $\vec{u}$ and $\vec{v}$ are two non-zero vectors, they are perpendicular if and only if *(iff)* their scalar product is equal to 0.

The angle between two vectors

If $\vec{u}$ and $\vec{v}$ are two non-zero vectors, then they determine a unique angle α, $0 \le \alpha \le 180°$. It can be shown that another way of stating the scalar product includes α.

$$\vec{u} \bullet \vec{v} = |\vec{u}||\vec{v}|\cos\alpha$$

If $\vec{u}$ and $\vec{v}$ are both unit vectors then

$$\vec{u} \bullet \vec{v} = \cos\alpha$$
$$\alpha = \arccos(\vec{u} \bullet \vec{v})$$

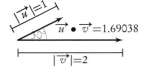

6.1.10 Projecting one vector onto another

Algebraically the scalar product is the sum of products of the components of its arguments.

Geometrically, the scalar product is a measure of the projection of one vector onto another. First, consider the case in which both $\vec{u}$ and $\vec{v}$ are unit vectors. Then the scalar product is simply $\cos\alpha$ or the projection of $\vec{v}$ onto $\vec{u}$ or vice versa.

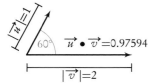

When either $\vec{u}$ or $\vec{v}$ are non-unit, the scalar product is simply scaled by their lengths. Thus, in general, the projection length $l_{\vec{u},\vec{v}}$ of a vector $\vec{u}$ onto a vector $\vec{v}$ is given by

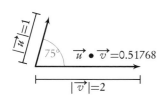

$$l_{\vec{u},\vec{v}} = |\vec{u}|\cos\theta = \frac{|\vec{u}||\vec{v}|\cos\theta}{|\vec{v}|} = \frac{\vec{u} \bullet \vec{v}}{|\vec{v}|}$$

Note carefully that $l_{\vec{u},\vec{v}}$ is a measure of the length of the vector $\vec{u}$ projected onto the vector $\vec{v}$. Often, what is needed is the actual projected vector. There is no universal notation for such vectors. Here we modify the notation used in Schneider and Eberly (2003, p. 87). The projection of a vector u onto a vector v is given by

$$\vec{u}_{\parallel\vec{v}} = l_{\vec{u},\vec{v}} \, \frac{\vec{v}}{|\vec{v}|} = \frac{\vec{u} \bullet \vec{v}}{|\vec{v}|} \, \frac{\vec{v}}{|\vec{v}|} = \frac{\vec{u} \bullet \vec{v}}{\vec{v} \bullet \vec{v}} \, \vec{v} \tag{6.1}$$

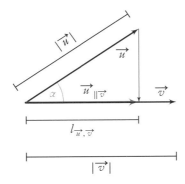

6.10: The projection of vector $\vec{u}$ onto $\vec{v}$.

6.1.11   Converse projection

Sometimes the projection of a vector perpendicular to itself and onto another vector is useful.

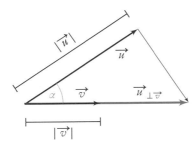

6.11: The converse projection of vector $\vec{u}$ onto $\vec{v}$.

The converse projection $\vec{u}_{\perp\vec{v}}$ is given by

$$\vec{u}_{\perp\vec{v}} = \frac{\vec{u} \bullet \vec{u}}{\vec{u} \bullet \vec{v}} \, \vec{v}$$

6.2 Lines in 2D

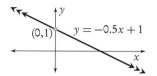

6.12: Explicit equations are simple to plot. Place a point $\dot{b}$ at $(0, b)$ on the y-axis. Draw a line with slope m through $\dot{b}$.

After vectors and points, lines are the most basic spatial objects. Lines in two-dimensional space (2D) are almost exactly analogous to planes in three-dimensional space. In 2D, lines can be represented in several ways. Each representation makes some mathematical inferences and/or algorithm steps easier than others.

From a geometric perspective there are several objects from which a line can be built. For instance, a point known to be on a line, the direction of the line, the point at which the line crosses a principal axis, the slope of the line and a direction normal to the line can all be used as part of a line representation. Each of the four equations below appeal to one or more of these geometric ideas.

6.2.1 Explicit equation

The *explicit equation* is also called the *slope y-intercept equation*.

$$y = mx + b$$

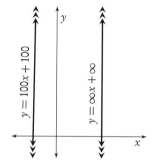

6.13: Lines of near vertical slope have high coefficients. Lines with vertical slope have infinite coefficients. Designers frequently want to use such lines.

In this equation, m is the slope of the line (the rise over the run) and b is the y-intercept. This is, perhaps, the most familiar equation. But it isn t a very good one for computing. Vertical lines have an infinite slope, so cannot be represented with the equation. Lines that are nearly vertical have slopes that approach or exceed the practical numerical precision of computation.

6.2.2 Implicit equation

The *implicit* equation is a simple linear equation.

$$ax + by + d = 0$$

Note: we use d in the equation rather than the more common c in order to make the corresponding line and plane equations (Section 6.4.2) cohere. The character d is also a reminder that of the role this variable plays in the equation – it carries information about distance – see below.

The implicit equation provides an easy test to determine if a given point is on a line. Simply substitute the point s coordinates for x and y in the equation. If the equation is satisfied, the point is on the line. In contrast, constructing a point on the line is less direct.

When $d = 0$ the line passes through the origin, as can be seen by assigning $x = 0$, $y = 0$ and $d = 0$ to the equation.

The vector $\overrightarrow{v} = \begin{bmatrix} a & b \end{bmatrix}$ is normal (perpendicular) to the line.

When $|\overrightarrow{v}| = 1$ the implicit equation is *normalized*. In this form, it has a simple geometric interpretation, in which the vector components relate directly to the angles α and β and d is a signed distance. The values $a = \cos\alpha$ and $b = \cos\beta$ are the *direction cosines* of the vector $\overrightarrow{v}$, and $-d$ is the distance along $\overrightarrow{v}$ from the origin to the line. If d is negative, the line is located in the direction pointed to by $\overrightarrow{v}$. If d is positive, the line lies at the distance d from the base of $\overrightarrow{v}$ in the opposite direction.

When $\overrightarrow{v}$ is not normalized, things are more complex. The vector $\overrightarrow{v}$ remains perpendicular to the line. The direction cosines can no longer be read directly from $\overrightarrow{v}$; they can be computed by scaling the vector by its length $1/\sqrt{a^2 + b^2}$. The quantity d becomes the negative of the distance to the line multiplied by the length of $\overrightarrow{v}$, that is, $\sqrt{a^2 + b^2}$. The actual signed distance from the origin to the line along $\overrightarrow{v}$ is $-d/|\overrightarrow{v}|$. When $|\overrightarrow{v}| = 1$, $-d$ is the signed distance!

Changing the sign of d creates a parallel line equidistant from the origin, but along the opposite vector direction.

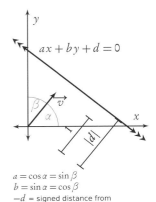

$a = \cos\alpha = \sin\beta$
$b = \sin\alpha = \cos\beta$
$-d$ = signed distance from origin to line

6.2.3 Line operator

The implicit equation gives a very tidy matrix form for representing lines called the *line operator*. A line is a row vector $\gamma = \begin{bmatrix} a & b & d \end{bmatrix}$ such that a point $\dot{p} = \begin{bmatrix} x & y & 1 \end{bmatrix}^T$ is on the line γ if and only if

$$\gamma\dot{p} = \begin{bmatrix} a & b & d \end{bmatrix} \begin{bmatrix} x \\ y \\ 1 \end{bmatrix} = 0$$
$$ax + by + d = 0$$

This test has all of the properties of the implicit line equation above. Its form as a matrix makes it easy to visualize other properties. It is useful to break the line operator into two parts: $\gamma_{\overrightarrow{v}}$ and γ_d, representing the vector and distance components respectively.

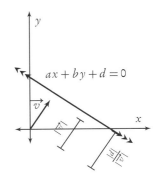

$$\gamma = \begin{bmatrix} \gamma_{\overrightarrow{v}} & | & \gamma_d \end{bmatrix}$$

where

$$\gamma_{\overrightarrow{v}} = \begin{bmatrix} a & b \end{bmatrix}, \text{ and } \gamma_d = \begin{bmatrix} d \end{bmatrix}$$

In spite of the simplicity of the line operator, much can be inferred from it. The first inference is its effect on vectors. We define the result of applying the line operator to a vector as

$$\gamma \overrightarrow{v} = \begin{bmatrix} a & b & d \end{bmatrix} \begin{bmatrix} x \\ y \\ 0 \end{bmatrix}$$

$$= ax + by + 0d$$
$$= ax + by$$

Consider any vector $\overrightarrow{v} = \begin{bmatrix} x & y & 0 \end{bmatrix}^{T}$. Since the third vector element is zero, the effect of $\gamma \dot{p}$ is to compute the scalar product of the first two elements of the line operator and the vector. We know that vectors are perpendicular when their scalar product is zero. Since $\gamma_{\overrightarrow{v}}$ is perpendicular to the line, $\gamma \overrightarrow{v} = 0$ for any vector parallel to the line.

The line operator can be multiplied by any real number r (except 0) without changing the line. This is equivalent to scaling both the vector $\gamma_{\overrightarrow{v}}$ and the value γ_d by r. Of course, the result of scaling the line operator by zero is undefined.

Lines are sided. The vector $\overrightarrow{v} = \begin{bmatrix} a & b \end{bmatrix}$ points towards the positive side. When the result of applying the line operator is positive, the point so tested lies on the positive side of the line. When the result is negative, the point lies on the negative side: the side away from which $\overrightarrow{v}$ points. Multiplying the operator by a negative number reverses line sidedness. Further, when the line operator is normalized ($\gamma_{|\overrightarrow{v}|} = 1$), it produces the signed distance from a point to the line; $\gamma \dot{p}$ = distance from $\dot{p}$ to γ along $\gamma_{\overrightarrow{v}}$. Sidedness is often used to represent where solid material lies in a design.

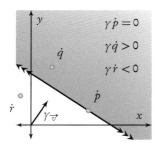

6.2.4   Normal-point equation

The *normal-point* equation of a line is defined through a point $\dot{q}$ and a non-zero vector $\overrightarrow{n}$ normal to the line. Since $\dot{q}$ is on the line, any vector between it and another point on the line must be perpendicular to the line normal $\overrightarrow{n}$ and therefore have a zero scalar product with $\overrightarrow{n}$.

$$\overrightarrow{n} \bullet (\dot{p} - \dot{q}) = 0$$

This equation provides a simple test using vectors and points as entire entities to determine if $\dot{p}$ is on the line. It is thus useful in parametric modelers that provide basic vector operations – no conversion to other equation forms or unpacking of vector and point components is needed.

6.2.5   Parametric equation

The *parametric* equation is perhaps the most widely used form. This is because it works in both 2D and 3D and because it is *constructive*, that is, it can be used to generate points on the line. In contrast, the implicit line equation is good for testing whether a point lies on a line.

A line is uniquely defined by a point and a vector. Given a point $\dot{p}$ and a vector $\overrightarrow{v}$, any point $\dot{p}(t)$ on the line has the functional equation

$$\dot{p}(t) = \dot{p} + t\,\overrightarrow{v}$$

where t is a real value that scales the vector $\overrightarrow{v}$. Each value of t picks out a distinct point on the line.

Let the point $\dot{p}_1$ be the sum of $\dot{p}_0$ and $\overrightarrow{v}$. Then

$$\begin{aligned} \dot{p}(t) &= \dot{p}_0 + t(\dot{p}_1 - \dot{p}_0) \\ &= (1-t)\dot{p}_0 + t\,\dot{p}_1 \end{aligned} \tag{6.2}$$

or alternatively (in vector form)

$$\dot{p}(t) = \dot{p}_0 + t(\overrightarrow{\dot{p}_0\dot{p}_1})$$

Each of the forms above is called a *parametric line equation* with parameter t.

Equation 6.2 can be rewritten as

$$\begin{aligned} \dot{p}(t) &= \dot{p}_0 + t(\dot{p}_1 - \dot{p}_0) \\ &= (1-t)\dot{p}_0 + t\,\dot{p}_1 \\ &= t_0\dot{p}_0 + t_1\dot{p}_1, \quad \text{where} \quad (t_0 + t_1 = 1) \end{aligned}$$

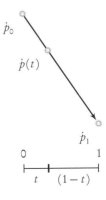

Even though they involve points, parametric line equations are drawn without coordinate systems, because the point produced $\dot{p}(t)$ depends only upon the points $\dot{p}_0$ and $\dot{p}_1$ – it is independent of where the points are located in space.

Changing the parameter t moves the point $\dot{p}(t)$ along the line. Specifically, it moves $\dot{p}(t)$ *in proportion* to t. For example, if $t = 0.4$, $\dot{p}(t)$ is 4/10ths of the distance along the line from $\dot{p}_0$ to $\dot{p}_1$. This *linear* relationship between t and $\dot{p}(t)$ holds only for lines. Section 6.9.5 shows that it does not hold for curves.

If $t = 0$ then $\dot{p}(t) = \dot{p}_0$

If $t = 1$ then $\dot{p}(t) = \dot{p}_1$

If $0 < t < 1$ then $\dot{p}(t)$ is between $\dot{p}_0$ and $\dot{p}_1$

If $t < 0$ then $\dot{p}(t)$ is to the left of $\dot{p}_0$

If $t > 1$ then $\dot{p}(t)$ is to the right of $\dot{p}_1$

6.2.6 Projecting a point to a line

Projecting a point $\dot{p}$ onto a line $\overline{L}$ means finding the point $\dot{q}$ that on the line that is closest to $\dot{p}$. Alternatively it means finding $\dot{q}$ such that the line between $\dot{p}$ and $\dot{q}$ is perpendicular to the line $\overline{L}$.

Projection is most easily expressed when the line is in normalized line operator form, where $\gamma\dot{p}$ is the signed distance from the point to the line. The projection of $\dot{p}$ to the line is the sum of $\dot{p}$ and the normal vector to the line $\gamma_{\overrightarrow{v}}$ scaled by the result of the line operator $\gamma\dot{p}$.

$$\dot{p}_{proj} = \dot{p} + (\gamma\dot{p})\gamma_{\overrightarrow{v}}$$

Often though, it is useful to have the parametric coordinate of the projected point. Using the parametric line equation, one way to compute the projection is to appeal to Equation 6.1 on page 97 for vector projection. Given point $\dot{q}$ to project onto the parametric line at $\dot{p}(t) = \dot{p}_o + t(\dot{p}_1 - \dot{p}_0)$, simply add the projection of of $\overrightarrow{\dot{p}_0\dot{q}}$ onto $\overrightarrow{\dot{p}_0\dot{p}_1}$ to the point $\dot{p}_0$. The projected point $\dot{p}(t)$ on line $\overline{L}$ is thus:

$$\dot{p}(t) = \dot{p}_0 + \frac{\overrightarrow{\dot{p}_0\dot{q}} \bullet \overrightarrow{\dot{p}_0\dot{p}_1}}{\overrightarrow{\dot{p}_0\dot{p}_1} \bullet \overrightarrow{\dot{p}_0\dot{p}_1}} \overrightarrow{\dot{p}_0\dot{p}_1} \tag{6.3}$$

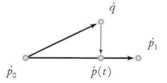

$$t = \frac{\overrightarrow{\dot{p}_0\dot{q}} \bullet \overrightarrow{\dot{p}_0\dot{p}_1}}{\overrightarrow{\dot{p}_0\dot{p}_1} \bullet \overrightarrow{\dot{p}_0\dot{p}_1}} \tag{6.4}$$

6.14: The projection of point $\dot{q}$ onto parametric line $\overline{L}$ at $\dot{p}(t)$.

The parameter t in Equation 6.4 is exactly the same as the scale factor for the vector in Equation 6.3.

6.3   Lines in 3D

In three dimensions, lines have neither an explicit nor an implicit equation. For almost all practical purposes, the parametric equation dominates. In it, a point and a vector defines a line. Its form is exactly the same as in two dimensions – given a point $\dot{p}_1$ and a vector $\overrightarrow{v}$, any point $\dot{p}(t)$ on the line has the equation

$$\dot{p}(t) = \dot{p}_1 + t\,\overrightarrow{v}$$

The only difference is that the points and vectors have three components rather than two.

6.4   Planes

Planes in 3D are the natural counterpart to lines in 2D. The implicit and parametric line equations easily expand to represent planes.

6.4.1   Normal vector

There are several ways to define a plane: three non-collinear points; a vector normal to the plane plus a point on the plane; and two non-collinear vectors parallel to the plane plus a point on the plane all suffice.

Given a vector $\overrightarrow{n}$ normal to the plane, and a point $\dot{p}$ on the plane, any vector parallel to the plane will be perpendicular to the plane normal $\overrightarrow{n}$. The scalar product provides an easy test for parallelism. The known point $\dot{p}$ on the plane defines a vector to any other point $\dot{q}$ in space. If this vector is perpendicular to $\overrightarrow{n}$, then $\dot{q}$ is on the plane.

Without any loss of generality, exactly the same drawings explain both planes and lines. The third dimension is simply suppressed by using an orthogonal drawing along one of the principal spatial axes. The only information that this fails to reveal concerns the angles that vectors make with the principal axes.

6.4.2   Implicit equation

The implicit equation for a plane is

$$ax + by + cz + d = 0$$

Just as for a two-dimensional line, all but the last term describes a vector. When the vector is of unit-length, the equation is normalized. $a = \cos\alpha$, $b = \cos\beta$ and $c = \cos\gamma$ are the *direction cosines* of the vector $\overrightarrow{v}$, and $-d$ is the signed distance along $\overrightarrow{v}$ from the origin to the line.

$ax + by + cz + d = 0$

$a = \cos\alpha$
$b = \cos\beta$
$c = \cos\gamma$
$-d$ = signed distance from
     origin to line

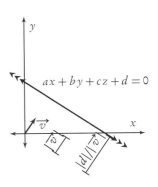

$ax + by + cz + d = 0$

6.4.3   Normal-point equation

The *normal-point* equation of a plane takes a point $\dot{q}$ and a non-zero vector $\overrightarrow{n}$ normal to the plane. The equation is exactly the same as for lines; the objects involved simply have a z-component.

$$\overrightarrow{n} \bullet (\dot{p} - \dot{q}) = 0$$

6.4.4   Plane operator

Just as for 2D lines, the implicit equation gives a tidy matrix form to represent planes.

A plane is represented as a row vector $\gamma = \begin{bmatrix} a & b & c & d \end{bmatrix}$ such that a point $\dot{p} = \begin{bmatrix} x & y & z & 1 \end{bmatrix}^T$ is on the plane γ if and only if

$$\gamma \dot{p} = \begin{bmatrix} a & b & c & d \end{bmatrix} \begin{bmatrix} x \\ y \\ z \\ 1 \end{bmatrix} = 0 \tag{6.5}$$

$$ax + by + cz + d = 0$$

This test, which is a matrix representation of the implicit plane equation, is known as the *plane operator*. It has all of the properties of the implicit plane equation above.

The direction cosines of the normalized plane operator are the cosines of the angles α, β and γ between the vector $\overrightarrow{v}$ and the x-, y- and z-axes respectively.

For vectors parallel to the plane, the plane operator is equal to 0.

$$\gamma \overrightarrow{v} = \begin{bmatrix} a & b & c & d \end{bmatrix} \begin{bmatrix} x \\ y \\ z \\ 0 \end{bmatrix}$$

$$= ax + by + cz + 0d$$
$$= ax + by + cz$$
$$= 0, \text{ iff } \overrightarrow{v} \text{ is parallel to the plane.}$$

The plane operator can be multiplied by any real number r (except 0) without changing the plane.

Plane have sides. As for lines, the vector $\overrightarrow{v} = \begin{bmatrix} a & b & c \end{bmatrix}$ points towards the positive side. When the plane operator is normalized, the number $\gamma \dot{p}$ itself gives the signed distance of $\dot{p}$ to the plane.

6.4.5   Parametric equation

A plane is defined by two vectors and a point $\dot{p}$ known to be on the plane. The plane comprises all points that can be reached by binding a linear combination of the two vectors to the point $\dot{p}$.

The parametric equation of a plane takes two parameters; each acts as a scaling factor for one of two vectors defining the plane.

$$\dot{p}(u,v) = \dot{p} + (u \cdot \overrightarrow{u} + v \cdot \overrightarrow{v})$$

Typically, the vectors $\overrightarrow{u}$ and $\overrightarrow{v}$ are chosen to be mutually perpendicular and of unit length. Such a choice establishes a two-dimensional coordinate system on the plane. Points can then be represented locally with respect to the plane.

The parametric plane equation is easily derived from three points defining a plane. Given three non-collinear points $\dot{p}_0$, $\dot{p}_1$ and $\dot{p}_2$.

$$\dot{p}_{(u,v)} = \dot{p}_0 + (u \cdot \overrightarrow{\dot{p}_0\dot{p}_1}) + (v \cdot \overrightarrow{\dot{p}_0\dot{p}_2})$$

6.4.6   Projecting a point onto a plane

Projecting a point $\dot{q}$ onto a plane means finding the closest point on the plane to $\dot{q}$. Equivalently, it means finding the point on the plane that intersects the line given by $\dot{q}$ and the normal vector to the plane. The latter definition gives a strong hint for using the plane operator.

Just as for lines, in the normalized plane operator, the signed distance between a point $\dot{q}$ and the plane γ is given by $\gamma \dot{q}$. So, the projection of $\dot{q}$ to the plane is the sum of $\dot{q}$ and the normal vector to the plane $\gamma_{\overrightarrow{v}}$ scaled by the result of the plane operator $\gamma \dot{q}$.

$$\dot{q}_{proj} = \dot{q} + (\gamma \dot{q}) \cdot \gamma_{\overrightarrow{v}}$$

If the parameters of the projected point are needed use the parametric plane equation. It is best if the plane vectors are mutually perpendicular and of unit length. Then the scalar products of the vector $\overrightarrow{\dot{p}\dot{q}}$ and each of $\overrightarrow{u}$ and $\overrightarrow{v}$ give the parameters u and v of the projected point on the plane.

$$\dot{q}(u,v) = \dot{p} + (\overrightarrow{\dot{p}\dot{q}} \bullet \overrightarrow{u}) \cdot \overrightarrow{u} + (\overrightarrow{\dot{p}\dot{q}} \bullet \overrightarrow{v}) \cdot \overrightarrow{v}$$

6.5   Coordinate systems ≡ frames

What is a coordinate system?

You likely know the answer informally. Coordinate systems define the axes of a space. The x- and y-axes on a graph define the dimensions of a two-dimensional coordinate system. Add a z-axis to get a three-dimensional system. Systems are located in space – they move and the objects in them move along. A coordinate system carries exactly and all of the information needed to place a rigid body in space. Thus the coordinate system, not the point, is the quintessential concept of location.

Hopefully you will not be surprised that, taking a geometric view, we represent the coordinate system axes as vectors and the location as a point. Formally, a coordinate system in 3D is three vectors and a point. In 2D, it is two vectors and a point. The vectors must be linearly independent. Collectively, they form a *basis* for the space – all vectors in the space can be expressed as a unique linear combination of these basis vectors.

Much of the literature uses the term *frame* instead of *coordinate system*. It is shorter, so we use it here too.

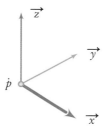

6.15: The x-, y- and z-axes of a frame have colours *red, green* and *blue* respectively. Point $\dot{p}$ locates the frame in space.

By putting constraints on a frame s vectors and point we can create special kinds of frames. For instance, a frame in which the vectors form a *natural basis*, that is, they are unit length and oriented to the principal global directions can be thought of as representing a simple translation of amount given by the frame s point.

You might have noticed something. Phrases such as "principal global directions" imply that frames are relative to other frames. Geometrically, there is no master frame, no universal frame of reference. Practically, choosing a particular frame and relating all points to it creates an effective master frame for a particular computation.

By convention we consider only *right-handed frames*. We refer to the three frame vectors either as $\begin{bmatrix} \overrightarrow{x} & \overrightarrow{y} & \overrightarrow{z} \end{bmatrix}$ or as $\begin{bmatrix} \overrightarrow{n} & \overrightarrow{o} & \overrightarrow{a} \end{bmatrix}$. The former is in reference to the x-, y-, and z-axes of Euclidean space, the latter to the words $\overrightarrow{n}ormal$, $\overrightarrow{o}rientation$ and $\overrightarrow{a}pproach$. To see the relevance of these words, extend your right hand in front of you with the index finger pointing at something, the thumb at right angles to the index finger and parallel to the line between your eyes, and the middle finger vertically at right angles to both index finger and thumb. You count the $\overrightarrow{x}$(or $\overrightarrow{n}$), $\overrightarrow{y}$(or $\overrightarrow{o}$) and $\overrightarrow{z}$(or $\overrightarrow{a}$) axes from thumb to middle finger: thumb $= \overrightarrow{x}$(or $\overrightarrow{n}$), index finger $= \overrightarrow{y}$(or $\overrightarrow{o}$) and middle finger $= \overrightarrow{z}$(or $\overrightarrow{a}$). The terms *normal, orientation* and *approach* relate to robotics where they are used to describe the position of a right-handed frame at the effector end of a robotic arm. Why have two ways of describing the axes? In some situations, x, y and z makes sense, for instance when you are indexing a named frame. Other times, for instance, when describing a frame s internal components, expressions such as $\overrightarrow{x}_x$ (the x-component of the $\overrightarrow{x}$ vector) are confusing and the $\overrightarrow{n}$, $\overrightarrow{o}$ and $\overrightarrow{a}$ notation is better.

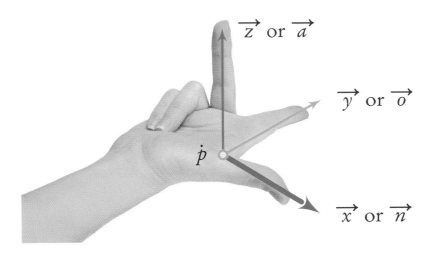

6.16: The $\overrightarrow{x}$ *($\overrightarrow{n}ormal$)*, $\overrightarrow{y}$ *($\overrightarrow{o}rientation$)* and $\overrightarrow{z}$ *($\overrightarrow{a}pproach$)* vectors of a right-handed frame superimposed on a person s right hand.

A second convention takes a counterclockwise rotation about a coordinate axis to have a positive rotation angle if we look along the positive axis toward the coordinate origin. This is well-known as the *right-hand rule*. A way to stamp it indelibly into memory is to thumb your nose with your right hand (Go ahead! Do it! I do in Figure 6.17) and curl your fingers. If you are looking at the origin, your fingers show the direction of positive rotation. *Right-handed frames* and the *right-hand rule* cohere together well. You use the same hand to understand both.

6.17: An unforgettable way of remembering the right-hand rule for rotation.

There are three really important things to know about frames: how to generate them, how to represent them and how to compose them.

6.5.1   Generating frames: the cross product

The *cross product* constructs one of two unique vectors given any two linearly independent vectors.

Taking a geometric view, let $\vec{u}$ and $\vec{v}$ be two linearly independent vectors. Figure 6.18 shows the cross product $\vec{u} \otimes \vec{v}$ as a third vector perpendicular to both. Its length is the area of the parallelogram spanned by the two vectors. The cross product forms the z-axis of a *right-handed frame* formed with $\vec{u}$ as the x-axis and $\vec{v}$ as the y-axis. Thus $\vec{u} \otimes \vec{v} \neq \vec{v} \otimes \vec{u}$. In fact, the two cross products are vector inverses $\vec{u} \otimes \vec{v} = -1\,\vec{v} \otimes \vec{u}$.

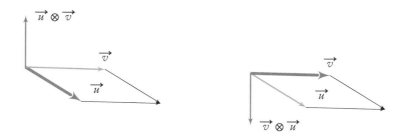

6.18: The cross product of two linearly independent vectors. Since the cross product always produces a right-handed frame, changing the order of the arguments to the cross product simply inverts the result vector: $\vec{u} \otimes \vec{v} = -1\,\vec{v} \otimes \vec{u}$.

The length of the cross product is the area of the parallelogram defined by $\vec{u}$ and $\vec{v}$. The area of a parallelogram is the base times the height. Taking $\vec{u}$ as the base, then basic trigonometry (Figure 6.19) shows that the height is $|\vec{v}|\sin\theta$ where θ is the angle between $\vec{u}$ and $\vec{v}$. Thus the area is $|\vec{u}||\vec{v}|\sin\theta$, and $|\vec{u}\otimes\vec{v}| = |\vec{u}||\vec{v}|\sin\theta$.

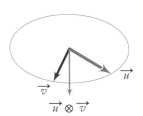

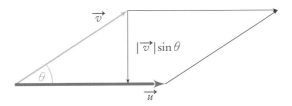

6.19: The area of a parallelogram.

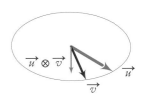

If the argument vectors $\vec{u}$ and $\vec{v}$ are unit-length, the cross product s length is the sine of the angle between $\vec{u}$ and $\vec{v}$. If the vectors are mutually perpendicular, then the parallelogram is a square with unit-length sides and area 1. The cross product vector thus has a length of 1. Frames having mutually orthogonal and unit length vectors are called *orthonormal*. If the vectors form a basis for the space they occupy, they are collectively an *orthonormal basis* for the space. Orthonormal bases have several nice mathematical properties (such as the scalar product of any arbitrary vector $\vec{u}$ with a basis vector being the length of the projection of the vector $\vec{u}$ onto the basis vector) that make them the main form for representing vector bases.

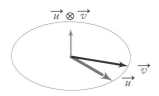

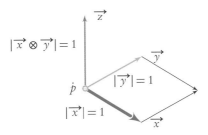

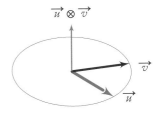

6.20: An orthonormal basis. Each axis is perpendicular to the others and is of unit length. The area of the parallelogram defined by the x- and y-axes is 1.

In terms of the components of $\vec{u}$ and $\vec{v}$, the cross product $\vec{w} = \vec{u}\otimes\vec{v}$ is given by the formulae

$$\vec{w}_x = \vec{u}_y\vec{v}_z - \vec{u}_z\vec{v}_y$$
$$\vec{w}_y = \vec{u}_z\vec{v}_x - \vec{u}_x\vec{v}_z$$
$$\vec{w}_z = \vec{u}_x\vec{v}_y - \vec{u}_y\vec{v}_x$$

(6.6)

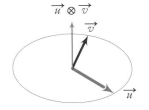

6.21: The length of the cross product of two unit vectors is the sine of the angle between them $|\vec{u}\otimes\vec{v}| = \sin\theta$. In this figure, both $\vec{u}$ and $\vec{v}$ are located on a circle of unit radius.

The cross product and plane equations

The cross product of the two vectors defining a plane is normal to the plane. This gives a way to compute the implicit plane equation from a point and two vectors (or from three points on the plane). Given a point $\dot{p}$ on the plane and two non-collinear vectors $\overrightarrow{u}$ and $\overrightarrow{v}$ in the plane, the implicit equation of the plane is as follows. Given

$$\overrightarrow{w} = \overrightarrow{u} \otimes \overrightarrow{v} \tag{6.7}$$

then the implicit equation is

$$\overrightarrow{w}_x \dot{p}_x + \overrightarrow{w}_y \dot{p}_y + \overrightarrow{w}_z \dot{p}_z - (\overrightarrow{w}_x \dot{p}_x + \overrightarrow{w}_y \dot{p}_y + \overrightarrow{w}_z \dot{p}_z) = 0$$

and the plane operator is

$$\begin{bmatrix} \overrightarrow{w}_x & \overrightarrow{w}_y & \overrightarrow{w}_z & -(\overrightarrow{w}_x \dot{p}_x + \overrightarrow{w}_y \dot{p}_y + \overrightarrow{w}_z \dot{p}_z) \end{bmatrix} \tag{6.8}$$

Using the cross product

It is extremely common to need a frame somewhere when defining a model. If the model is to be reused, or moved without restriction in space, such a frame should be *internal* to the model. If it is external, then the model can depend on its position, and sometimes in surprising ways. Whenever a model has three non-collinear points, or a single plane in parametric form, it is easy to construct such a frame. Vector bases (and therefore frames) are best when orthonormal – remember the discussion on page 109.

The process above produces a result equivalent to what is called the *Gram–Schmit orthonormalization process*. Given three linearly independent vectors $\overrightarrow{u}$, $\overrightarrow{v}$ and $\overrightarrow{w}$, the orthonormal frame with vectors $\overrightarrow{x}$, $\overrightarrow{y}$ and $\overrightarrow{z}$ is computed as follows:

$$\overrightarrow{x} = \frac{\overrightarrow{u}}{|\overrightarrow{u}|}$$

$$\overrightarrow{y_{pre}} = \overrightarrow{v} - (\overrightarrow{v} \bullet \overrightarrow{x}) \overrightarrow{x}$$

$$\overrightarrow{y} = \frac{\overrightarrow{y_{pre}}}{|\overrightarrow{y_{pre}}|}$$

$$\overrightarrow{z_{pre}} = w - (\overrightarrow{w} \bullet \overrightarrow{x}) \overrightarrow{x} - (\overrightarrow{w} \bullet \overrightarrow{y}) \overrightarrow{y}$$

$$\overrightarrow{z} = \frac{\overrightarrow{z_{pre}}}{|\overrightarrow{z_{pre}}|}$$

6.5.2   Representing frames

Up until now, we have treated objects as if they are located in some universal space. While all geometry can be represented this way, modeling, mathematics and programming quickly become cumbersome and tedious. Frames provide an essential practical tool for organizing objects in space.

There are several modeling tasks that all require the ability to represent objects locally and to relate local representations to each other.

- We want to refer to things in differing frames of reference. A bicycle wheel is most easily described if we think of it as being located at the origin of some frame with the centreline of its axle coincident with one of the primary axes.

- We want to move things around. Positioning the bicycle wheel with respect to its frame can be achieved more easily by moving its frame than by moving all of its points. Rotating the bicycle wheel is simply done by rotating its frame.

- We want to be able to draw images of three-dimensional objects on a two-dimensional screen. This involves creating a sequence of frames: the world, the camera and the screen.

To represent frames is to go from the geometric idea of a frame as three vectors (a basis) and a point to a notation for representing vectors and vector bases as matrices. Representation of and operations on frames are largely a matter of structuring information to apply vector operations in appropriate ways. It is usually a very good idea to understand everything about frames by constructing representations from vectors on up. In other words, do not treat operations and transformations as black boxes – understand the ideas.

The first structuring step is to use a matrix to represent the vectors of a frame – its vector basis. Given that every vector basis over vectors of n elements has n vectors there exists a natural representation of a vector basis as an $n \times n$ matrix as shown for the two-dimensional case in Equation 6.9.

$$\left[\begin{array}{cc} \vec{u} & \vec{v} \end{array} \right] = \left[\begin{array}{cc} \left[\begin{array}{c} u_1 \\ u_2 \end{array} \right] & \left[\begin{array}{c} v_1 \\ v_2 \end{array} \right] \end{array} \right] = \left[\begin{array}{cc} u_1 & v_1 \\ u_2 & v_2 \end{array} \right] \qquad (6.9)$$

By convention, the columns of the matrix are the basis vectors. Representing a basis as a matrix is thus simple: take each basis vector as the column of a matrix. For two dimensions the array is 2×2; for three dimensions it is 3×3.

The well-known identity matrix from linear algebra represents the natural basis.

$$\left[\begin{array}{ccc} \vec{x} & \vec{y} & \vec{z} \end{array}\right] = \left[\begin{array}{ccc} \begin{bmatrix} 1 \\ 0 \\ 0 \end{bmatrix} & \begin{bmatrix} 0 \\ 1 \\ 0 \end{bmatrix} & \begin{bmatrix} 0 \\ 0 \\ 1 \end{bmatrix} \end{array}\right] = \left[\begin{array}{ccc} 1 & 0 & 0 \\ 0 & 1 & 0 \\ 0 & 0 & 1 \end{array}\right]$$

Using the interpretation of the column vectors being the basis vectors simply read off the natural basis vectors.

The three vectors that represent a space give us everything but the location of the vector basis. Remember? A frame is three vectors and a point – its location. The location gets added as a fourth column in the matrix. A frame matrix thus has two components. The first records the vector basis of the frame, the second the point of origin. Using the $\vec{n}$, $\vec{o}$ and $\vec{a}$ notation for the frame vectors (so the x, y and z coordinates do not get mixed up with the vectors), this gives

$$\left[\begin{array}{ccc|c} \vec{n} & \vec{o} & \vec{a} & \dot{p} \end{array}\right] = \left[\begin{array}{ccc|c} \vec{n}_x & \vec{o}_x & \vec{a}_x & \dot{p}_x \\ \vec{n}_y & \vec{o}_y & \vec{a}_y & \dot{p}_y \\ \vec{n}_z & \vec{o}_z & \vec{a}_z & \dot{p}_z \end{array}\right]$$

where $\vec{n}_x$ represents the x coordinate of the n basis vector of the frame and $\dot{p}_x$ represents the x coordinate of the point of origin of the frame.

This matrix is not square, and square matrices are "nice" in the sense that they enter into algebraic formulae with less dimension checking, have determinants (a very useful number that describes matrix properties) and potentially inverses. To recover the useful property of squareness, we add a row to the bottom of the matrix.

We now distinguish vectors and points by augmenting their representation with a single number: 0 for vectors and 1 for points. Vectors become $\left[\begin{array}{cccc} x & y & z & 0 \end{array}\right]^T$ and points become $\left[\begin{array}{cccc} x & y & z & 1 \end{array}\right]^T$.

The non-square matrix suffers this augmentation to become

$$\left[\begin{array}{ccc|c} \vec{n}_x & \vec{n}_y & \vec{n}_z & \dot{p}_x \\ \vec{o}_x & \vec{o}_y & \vec{o}_z & \dot{p}_y \\ \vec{a}_x & \vec{a}_y & \vec{a}_z & \dot{p}_z \\ \hline 0 & 0 & 0 & 1 \end{array}\right]$$

The first three columns can be read off as vectors (signaled by the fourth row being 0) and the fourth column is a point (signaled by its fourth row being 1). The vectors and points actually mean something. In fact, they mean three things. A matrix holding them can be seen as either a *representation*, a *mapping operator* between frames, or a *transformation operator* that changes objects.

6.5.3 Matrices as representations

The first interpretation is that a matrix specifies a frame in terms of another frame. In this interpretation, the first three column vectors of a matrix are the vectors of its corresponding basis, written in terms of the vectors of some other frame. The fourth vector is the location of the frame, again written in terms of the other frame. This idea can be represented with perfect correspondence as both drawing and matrix.

If you have a drawing (or physical model) you can make a matrix representing a frame. The vectors of the frame are columns in the upper left block of the matrix. The frame location is the upper right block. If you have a matrix you can make a drawing of the corresponding frame. Simply use the columns of the upper left block matrix as the x-, y- and z- coordinates of the vectors in the drawing. Use the column in the upper right block as the frame location.

The relation between matrix and drawing is one of the very rare perfect correspondences between mathematics and diagrams. Usually drawings both remove information (they abstract) and introduce extraneous information. In this case even the fiction that the vectors are bound to a point has significance. Projecting a vector from the frame origin to a point $\dot{p}$ onto the frame vectors and dividing by the length of the frame vectors yields coordinates in the frame.

Frame:

$$\begin{bmatrix} -0.3 & -0.3 & 0.9 \end{bmatrix} \qquad \begin{bmatrix} -0.6 & 0.8 & 0.1 \end{bmatrix}$$

$$\begin{bmatrix} 0 & 0 & 0 \end{bmatrix} \qquad \begin{bmatrix} 0.8 & 0.6 & 0.1 \end{bmatrix}$$

Matrix:

$$\begin{bmatrix} \begin{array}{ccc|c} 0.8 & -0.6 & -0.3 & 0 \\ 0.6 & 0.8 & -0.3 & 0 \\ 0.1 & 0.1 & 0.9 & 0 \\ \hline 0 & 0 & 0 & 1 \end{array} \end{bmatrix}$$

6.22: The correspondence between a frame drawing and its matrix is perfect and literal. The dashed frame is the reference in which the frame is drawn and in which the matrix is defined. (Careful reading of this frame shows that it is not perfectly orthonormal – here accuracy is sacrificed to gain short numbers.)

6.5.4   Matrices as mappings

Representing frames as matrices suggests matrix multiplication might be useful. Remember that points and vectors are column matrices so must appear *after* the matrix in any matrix multiplication (the basic rule of matrix multiplication conformality is a matrix of dimension $m \times n$ can only be multiplied by a matrix of dimension $n \times p$).

If T is a matrix representation of a frame, then

$$\vec{v}\,' = \mathsf{T}\,\vec{v}$$

means that some new vector $\vec{v}\,'$ is produced by the expression $\mathsf{T}\,\vec{v}$.

A useful interpretation is that $\vec{v}\,'$ represents a vector in a *reference frame* A, that $\vec{v}$ represents the same vector in a *represented frame* B and that T represents the represented frame in terms of the reference frame. A notation that makes this clear can really help. Write ${}^{A}_{B}\mathsf{T}$ to denote the represention of frame B in terms of the frame A and ${}^{A}\vec{v}$ to denote the representation of vector $\vec{v}$ in terms of frame A. To complete the picture write ${}^{B}\vec{v}$ as the representation of $\vec{v}$ in terms of the frame B.

$${}^{A}\vec{v} = {}^{A}_{B}\mathsf{T}\,{}^{B}\vec{v} \tag{6.10}$$

Figure 6.23 shows that both ${}^{A}\vec{v}$ and ${}^{B}\vec{v}$ represent the same geometric vector $\vec{v}$ – they differ numerically because they are representations of this vector in their respective frames.

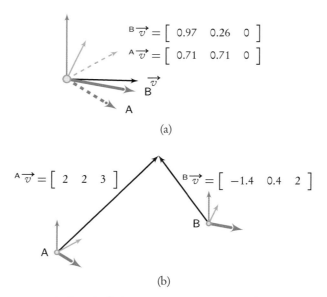

6.23: The equation ${}^{A}\vec{v} = {}^{A}_{B}\mathsf{T}\,{}^{B}\vec{v}$ maps the geometric vector $\vec{v}$ from its representation as ${}^{B}\vec{v}$ in frame B to its representation as ${}^{A}\vec{v}$ in frame A. In (a) the two frames share an origin and differ by a z-axis rotation. In (b) the two frames also differ by a translation.

Geometrically this means that every point represented within a frame B has at least two sets of coordinates: those in frame B itself and those in the frame A that "holds" B. This explains the usual representation in a parametric modeling system in which a point has X, Y and Z properties as well as XLocal, YLocal and ZLocal properties [1]. Of course, every point has an implicit representation in terms of every frame specified in a model. Usually a system computes these only if needed.

A frame B that holds another frame C might itself be held in a third frame A.

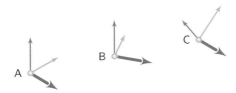

The frame notation above conveys an advantage in reading chains of mappings. For example, the following chain

$$
{}^A\vec{v} = {}^A_BT\,{}^B_CT\,{}^C_DT\,{}^D_ET\,{}^E_FT\,{}^F_GT\,{}^G\vec{v}
$$

can be checked for consistency by "canceling" any mapping that represents a frame G if it is to the left of another mapping whose representation is written in terms of G.

$$
{}^A\vec{v} = {}^A_{\not B}T\,{}^{\not B}_{\not C}T\,{}^{\not C}_{\not D}T\,{}^{\not D}_{\not E}T\,{}^{\not E}_{\not F}T\,{}^{\not F}_{\not G}T\,{}^{\not G}\vec{v}
$$

Of course, the canceling is a notational trick with no mathematical significance in and of itself. It does allow us to check if a chain is well-formed. If cancellation does not work, we cannot multiply the matrices and expect a sensible result.

Equation 6.10 gives a second meaning to the matrix representation of a vector frame: as a mapping between frames. We use matrices as both a representation of frames and as a mapping between them.

---

[1] The conventions on these names vary widely. For instance, global and local names might respectively be X:XLocal, XGlobal:X, XGlobal:XLocal, X:XTranslation or use another convention. You have to get used to the system you use.

6.5.5　Matrices as transformations

There is yet a third meaning to the matrix representation of a frame. This is as an operation that produces a new vector in the same frame as the original vector. We say that the new vector is a transformation of the old. The operation differs not in mathematical form, but in interpretation.

Write $\vec{v}' = \mathsf{T}\,\vec{v}$ to denote that both vectors are defined within a single frame. Figure 6.24 shows vectors $\vec{v}$ and $\vec{v}'$ as being on the xy-plane of a reference frame and $\vec{v}'$ being rotated about the z-axis by 30° from $\vec{v}$. The matrix gives just this 30° rotation about the z-axis.

$$
\left[
\begin{array}{ccc|c}
\cos 30 & -\sin 30 & 0 & 0 \\
\sin 30 & \cos 30 & 0 & 0 \\
0 & 0 & 1 & 0 \\
\hline
0 & 0 & 0 & 1
\end{array}
\right]
$$

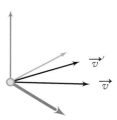

6.24: Vector $\vec{v}'$ is the result of rotating vector $\vec{v}$ around the z-axis with both vectors represented in the same frame.

Figure 6.25 shows a mental trick that helps in understanding transformation. Think about the mapping equation ${}^{A}\vec{v} = {}^{A}_{B}\mathsf{T}\,{}^{B}\vec{v}$ and then move frame B to coincide with frame A, bringing the vector $\vec{v}'$ along with it. When the frames coincide, that is B becomes A, the vector $\vec{v}$ will have moved into the correct position. In essence, transformation is the same as mapping, except that the original vector is assigned to frame A from the outset, not frame B.

6.6　Geometrically significant vector bases

Typically, a frame is composed by expressing it as a sequence of more simple frames. For example, a rotation around the z-axis of a translated frame A in space can be thought of a translation that takes A to the global origin, then a rotation about the global origin and finally a translation back to the original

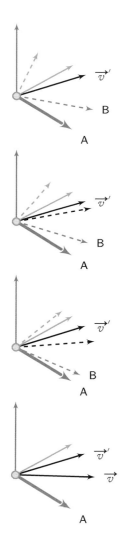

6.25: When frame B rotates, it brings its representation of the vector with it. When it coincides with frame A, its vector coincides with vector $\vec{v}$ of the equation $\vec{v}' = \mathsf{T}\,\vec{v}$.

location of A. The simple frames involved in such compositions are *rotation, scaling, shearing* and *translation.*

The three primitive rotations are about the x-, y- and z-axes. Composition of rotation about a single axis is commutative. Composition of rotations about multiple axes is not commutative.

Rotation about the x-axis

Frame: **Matrix:**

$$\text{Rot}_x(\theta) = \left[\begin{array}{ccc|c} 1 & 0 & 0 & 0 \\ 0 & \cos\theta & -\sin\theta & 0 \\ 0 & \sin\theta & \cos\theta & 0 \\ \hline 0 & 0 & 0 & 1 \end{array} \right]$$

Rotation about the y-axis

Frame: **Matrix:**

$$\text{Rot}_y(\theta) = \left[\begin{array}{ccc|c} \cos\theta & 0 & \sin\theta & 0 \\ 0 & 1 & 0 & 0 \\ -\sin\theta & 0 & \cos\theta & 0 \\ \hline 0 & 0 & 0 & 1 \end{array} \right]$$

Rotation about the z-axis

Frame: **Matrix:**

$$\text{Rot}_z(\theta) = \left[\begin{array}{ccc|c} \cos\theta & -\sin\theta & 0 & 0 \\ \sin\theta & \cos\theta & 0 & 0 \\ 0 & 0 & 1 & 0 \\ \hline 0 & 0 & 0 & 1 \end{array} \right]$$

Why is rotation about the y-axis different in form from rotation about the x- or z-axis? Look at the figures and imagine looking down the respective axes. The

117

y-axis rotation presents a different geometry than the other two – the x- and z-axes are comparatively in a different order than the other cases.

Uniform scaling

Uniform scaling increases the "size" of a frame. Composition of uniform scaling is commutative.

Frame: **Matrix:**

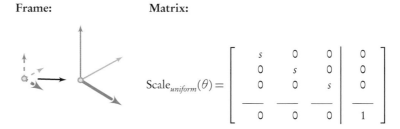

$$\text{Scale}_{uniform}(\theta) = \left[\begin{array}{ccc|c} s & 0 & 0 & 0 \\ 0 & s & 0 & 0 \\ 0 & 0 & s & 0 \\ \hline 0 & 0 & 0 & 1 \end{array} \right]$$

6.26: Uniform scaling of a frame **B** about the origin of another frame **A**. Note that the reference frame and the represented frame are not coincident in the drawing – visual coincidence would be confusing. No translation is implied.

Scaling along one axis

Scaling along one axis is also known as *non-uniform scaling*. Such scaling on all three axes can be combined in a single matrix. Each of the axes is scaled by the corresponding factor. Composition of non-uniform scaling is commutative.

Composition of scaling in general is commutative.

$$\text{Scale}_{x,y,z}(s_x, s_y, s_z) = \left[\begin{array}{ccc|c} s_x & 0 & 0 & 0 \\ 0 & s_y & 0 & 0 \\ 0 & 0 & s_z & 0 \\ \hline 0 & 0 & 0 & 1 \end{array} \right]$$

Frame: **Matrix:**

$$\text{Scale}_{x}(\theta) = \left[\begin{array}{ccc|c} s & 0 & 0 & 0 \\ 0 & 1 & 0 & 0 \\ 0 & 0 & 1 & 0 \\ \hline 0 & 0 & 0 & 1 \end{array} \right]$$

6.27: Scaling of a frame **B** about the origin and along the x-axis of another frame **A**. Note that the reference frame and the represented frame are not coincident in the drawing – visual coincidence would be confusing. No translation is implied.

Shear

The shearing factor gives the amount of shear along the shearing coordinate per unit of distance from the origin along the sheared coordinate. This is the definition of the tangent of the angle between the old and new sheared axes.

Frame: **Matrix:**

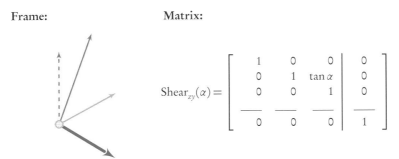

$$\text{Shear}_{zy}(\alpha) = \left[\begin{array}{ccc|c} 1 & 0 & 0 & 0 \\ 0 & 1 & \tan\alpha & 0 \\ 0 & 0 & 1 & 0 \\ \hline 0 & 0 & 0 & 1 \end{array} \right]$$

6.28: Shearing of the z-axis along the y-axis of a frame B. The original z-axis is said to be the *sheared coordinate* and the original y-axis the *shearing coordinate*. The shearing factor is the tangent of the angle between the old and new z-axes.

There are six possible primitive shears, corresponding to the six zero values off the diagonal of the basis identity matrix.

$$\left[\begin{array}{ccc|c} 1 & Sh_{yx} & Sh_{zx} & 0 \\ Sh_{xy} & 1 & Sh_{zy} & 0 \\ Sh_{xz} & Sh_{yz} & 1 & 0 \\ \hline 0 & 0 & 0 & 1 \end{array} \right]$$

To model a primitive shear only one of these may be non-zero. To compose shears combine primitive shears with matrix multiplication. In general, the composition of primitive shears is not the simple setting of two values in a single shear matrix. Equation 6.11 (showing just the basis components of the frames) shows that the composition of a 45° zx shear with a 45° xz shear yields a matrix with non-unit values on the diagonal.

In general, composition of shears is not commutative.

$$\left[\begin{array}{ccc} 1 & 0 & 1 \\ 0 & 1 & 0 \\ 0 & 0 & 1 \end{array} \right] \left[\begin{array}{ccc} 1 & 0 & 0 \\ 0 & 1 & 0 \\ 1 & 0 & 1 \end{array} \right] = \left[\begin{array}{ccc} 2 & 0 & 1 \\ 0 & 1 & 0 \\ 1 & 0 & 1 \end{array} \right] \tag{6.11}$$

However, two axes can be sheared parallel to the third axis, and this combination is straightforward.

Frame: **Matrix:**

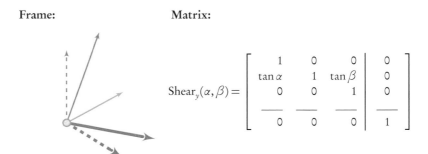

$$\text{Shear}_y(\alpha, \beta) = \left[\begin{array}{ccc|c} 1 & 0 & 0 & 0 \\ \tan\alpha & 1 & \tan\beta & 0 \\ 0 & 0 & 1 & 0 \\ \hline 0 & 0 & 0 & 1 \end{array}\right]$$

6.29: Shearing of the x- and z-axes along the y-axis of a frame **B**. The original x- and z-axes are said to be the *sheared coordinates* and the original y-axis the *shearing coordinate*. The shearing factors are the tangent of the angle between the old and new x- and z-axes.

Translation

Translation represents the position of one coordinate system with respect to another, by distances along the x-, y- and z-axes. Composing translations is commutative.

Frame: **Matrix:**

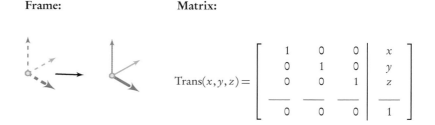

$$\text{Trans}(x, y, z) = \left[\begin{array}{ccc|c} 1 & 0 & 0 & x \\ 0 & 1 & 0 & y \\ 0 & 0 & 1 & z \\ \hline 0 & 0 & 0 & 1 \end{array}\right]$$

6.7   Composing vector bases

All of the primitive geometrically significant vector bases can be composed to model more complex geometry and there is a general mental technique for doing this. First, imagine that the geometry is located in a universal, global frame. Second, use a sequence of geometric operations to bring the geometry into alignment with the global frame. Third, model the appropriate geometry. Fourth, use the inverse of the sequence of geometric operations from the second step to restore the geometry to its original location with the modeled change.

Matrices representing vector bases compose from *RIGHT* to *LEFT*. Why is this so? Consider a series of matrices each implementing an operation on vectors as follows:

$$R_0 \ R_1 \ldots R_{n-1} \ R_n$$

Any vector $\overrightarrow{v}$ that is operated on by this sequence is placed at the end of the sequence. Thus,

$$\overrightarrow{v}' = R_0 \ R_1 \ldots R_{n-1} \ R_n \ \overrightarrow{v}$$

Since matrix multiplication is associative, this can be rewritten as

$$\overrightarrow{v}' = (R_0 \ (R_1 \ldots (R_{n-1} \ (R_n \ \overrightarrow{v}))))$$

Each successive operation, reading from right to left, produces another vector that has been transformed with respect to the global frame that is implied by the operator view of matrix representation of vector bases. Thus, reading from right to left, apply operator R_n, then R_{n-1} ... then R_1 then finally R_0.

Matrices representing vector bases compose from *RIGHT* to *LEFT*. Reading from the right, each successive transformation changes the relationship between itself and the frame to its left. Thinking about matrices as operations this has the effect of moving the frame and everything to its right. As you add bases on the left, each effects a movement with respect to the global origin.

6.7.1   Which comes first? Translation or rotation?

Frames combine three vectors and a point. Consider these two parts as motions; then a frame might combine, say, a rotation and a translation. Which comes first? The answer reveals itself in both geometric and matrix views.

First geometry. As in frame representation, a matrix is a direct representation of the frame it implements. So Figure 6.30 represents the frame given by the matrix

$$\begin{bmatrix} \cos 30 & -\sin 30 & 0 & 2 \\ \sin 30 & \cos 30 & 0 & 2 \\ 0 & 0 & 1 & 1 \\ \hline 0 & 0 & 0 & 1 \end{bmatrix}$$

Remember that successive matrix operations taken right-to-left model motions with respect to the global origin. Thus, if we want to think of the rotation and the translation acting separately, the frame must be generated by first a rotation of 30° about the z-axis, followed by a translation of $\begin{bmatrix} 2 & 2 & 1 \end{bmatrix}^T$. The vector component acts first in a frame representation!

121

Frame:

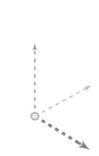

Matrix:

$$\text{Trans}_{x,y,z}(\theta) = \left[\begin{array}{ccc|c} \cos 30 & -\sin 30 & 0 & 2 \\ \sin 30 & \cos 30 & 0 & 2 \\ 0 & 0 & 1 & 1 \\ \hline 0 & 0 & 0 & 1 \end{array}\right]$$

6.30: The frame represesenting a rotation of 30° about the z-axis followed by a translation of $[2\,2\,1]^T$.

A second view using matrix multiplication confirms this geometric insight.

$$\left[\begin{array}{ccc|c} 1 & 0 & 0 & 2 \\ 0 & 1 & 0 & 2 \\ 0 & 0 & 1 & 1 \\ \hline 0 & 0 & 0 & 1 \end{array}\right] \left[\begin{array}{ccc|c} \cos 30 & -\sin 30 & 0 & 0 \\ \sin 30 & \cos 30 & 0 & 0 \\ 0 & 0 & 1 & 0 \\ \hline 0 & 0 & 0 & 1 \end{array}\right] = \left[\begin{array}{ccc|c} \cos 30 & -\sin 30 & 0 & 2 \\ \sin 30 & \cos 30 & 0 & 2 \\ 0 & 0 & 1 & 1 \\ \hline 0 & 0 & 0 & 1 \end{array}\right]$$

whereas

$$\left[\begin{array}{ccc|c} \cos 30 & -\sin 30 & 0 & 0 \\ \sin 30 & \cos 30 & 0 & 0 \\ 0 & 0 & 1 & 0 \\ \hline 0 & 0 & 0 & 1 \end{array}\right] \left[\begin{array}{ccc|c} 1 & 0 & 0 & 2 \\ 0 & 1 & 0 & 2 \\ 0 & 0 & 1 & 1 \\ \hline 0 & 0 & 0 & 1 \end{array}\right] = \left[\begin{array}{ccc|c} \cos 30 & -\sin 30 & 0 & 2(\cos 30 - \sin 30) \\ \sin 30 & \cos 30 & 0 & 2(\sin 30 + \cos 30) \\ 0 & 0 & 1 & 1 \\ \hline 0 & 0 & 0 & 1 \end{array}\right]$$

6.8   Intersections

The intersection of geometric primitives is a fundamental construct in many computer graphics and modeling applications. Its most simple form involves the linear elements *points* (1D), *lines* (2D) and *planes* (3D). In general, two elements may intersect (or not) as elements of equal or one lesser dimension than the lowest dimension of the elements involved. Thus two planes may intersect at a plane or a line (but not at a point), lines may intersect at a line or a point, and points may intersect at a point (this is point identity). With mixed elements, a line may intersect a plane at either a line or a point.

The number of intersection conditions is large, and the mathematics is, in cases, complex. Most parametric modeling systems provide a large set of intersection operators. Most of the time, these suffice. Note the phrase "most of the time". The rest of the time it helps to be able to reason through intersection problems. This section presents a small suite of intersection problems and their solutions. The intent is to demonstrate approaches to framing and solving some simple problems. In more complex cases it really helps to have a good text at hand, for example, Schneider and Eberly (2003).

Recall the available three-dimensional representations for points, lines and planes. Geometrically, a point is a point. A line is defined parametrically as a point and a vector (or alternatively two points). A plane has many definitions occurring in two families, one related to the normal vector (implicit, plane operator) and the other parametric to a point and two linearly independent vectors (point–vector and three–point).

There are several kinds of intersection-related questions.

- Determine if two objects intersect, without actually generating the intersection.

- Generate an object (point, line, plane) that lies on another object.

- Determine the object of intersection of two other objects, if it exists.

- Determine the kind of intersection (point, line or plane) at which two objects intersect.

- Determine the object that most closely joins two objects, for example, the line between a point and a line or the line between two lines.

All require similar thinking and similar mathematics to solve. The previous secions cover the needed mathematical basics. This section presents problems and discussion of how to go about solving each one. It takes a constructive approach, that is, it presents a solution as a series of steps, each geometric and visual. Such solutions are seldom the most efficient and often have cases in which they may not be as stable as possible. Indeed, when intersections (and other problems) are professionally programmed in CAD systems, developers go to great lengths to ensure the code is robust, accurate and efficient. Amateur programmers do not and generally cannot program this way. They usually work by imagining a series of steps, each using simple constructs, that solve the immediate geometric problem.

6.8.1   Do two objects intersect?

Point on line $\equiv$ point collinearity

Are three points $\dot{p}$, $\dot{q}$ and $\dot{r}$ collinear?
Are $\dot{p}(5,2,4)$, $\dot{q}(2,-4,1)$ and $\dot{r}(4,0,3)$ collinear?
Are $\dot{p}(5,2,4)$, $\dot{q}(2,-4,1)$ and $\dot{r}(3,-1,2)$ collinear?

Discussion. Three points are collinear if the triangle they form has zero area. The cross product is twice the area of the triangle defined by two vectors. If $|\overrightarrow{pq} \otimes \overrightarrow{pr}| = 0$, $\dot{p}$, $\dot{q}$ and $\dot{r}$ are collinear. In English, if the cross product produces the zero vector, the points are collinear.

Using Equation 6.6 on page 109

$$\overrightarrow{pq} \otimes \overrightarrow{pr} = \begin{bmatrix} \overrightarrow{u}_y \overrightarrow{v}_z - \overrightarrow{u}_z \overrightarrow{v}_y & \overrightarrow{u}_z \overrightarrow{v}_x - \overrightarrow{u}_x \overrightarrow{v}_z & \overrightarrow{u}_x \overrightarrow{v}_y - \overrightarrow{u}_y \overrightarrow{v}_x \end{bmatrix}^T$$

For $\dot{r}(4,0,3)$, $\overrightarrow{u} = \overrightarrow{pq} = \begin{bmatrix} 3 & 6 & 3 \end{bmatrix}^T$, $\overrightarrow{v} = \overrightarrow{pr} = \begin{bmatrix} 1 & 2 & 1 \end{bmatrix}^T$

$$\overrightarrow{pq} \otimes \overrightarrow{pr} = \begin{bmatrix} 6 \cdot 1 - 3 \cdot 2 & 3 \cdot 1 - 3 \cdot 1 & 3 \cdot 2 - 6 \cdot 1 \end{bmatrix}^T = \begin{bmatrix} 0 & 0 & 0 \end{bmatrix}^T$$

The points $\dot{p}$, $\dot{q}$ and $\dot{r}$ are collinear.

For $\dot{r}(3,-1,2)$, $\overrightarrow{u} = \overrightarrow{pq} = \begin{bmatrix} 3 & 6 & 3 \end{bmatrix}^T$, $\overrightarrow{v} = \overrightarrow{pr} = \begin{bmatrix} 2 & 3 & 2 \end{bmatrix}^T$

$$\overrightarrow{pq} \otimes \overrightarrow{pr} = \begin{bmatrix} 6 \cdot 2 - 3 \cdot 3 & 3 \cdot 2 - 3 \cdot 2 & 3 \cdot 3 - 6 \cdot 2 \end{bmatrix}^T = \begin{bmatrix} 3 & 0 & -3 \end{bmatrix}^T$$

The points $\dot{p}$, $\dot{q}$ and $\dot{r}$ are not collinear.

Point in plane

Does the plane $2x - 3y + z = 11$ contain the point $\dot{p}(1,-2,3)$?
The point $\dot{q}(5,-6,0)$?

Discussion. This is easily solved if the plane is represented in any form related to the implicit, as it is here. Simply plug the point values into the equation.

For $\dot{p}(1,-2,3)$, $2 \cdot 1 - 3 \cdot (-2) + 3 = 11$, so $\dot{p}$ is on the plane.

For $\dot{q}(5,-6,0)$, $2 \cdot 5 - 3 \cdot (-6) + 0 = 28$, so $\dot{q}$ is not on the plane.

Computationally, a result "close enough" to zero means that the point is on the plane. We gloss over what "close enough" means. Geometry uses real numbers, which are only approximately represented in computers. A simple threshold δ, where $-\delta < a < \delta \implies a = 0$, suffices for most design applications.

Line in plane

Determine if a line lies in a plane.

Line through $\dot{p}_{start}(1,3,1)$

with direction vector $\vec{d} = \begin{bmatrix} 2 \\ 3 \\ 1 \end{bmatrix}$

Plane through $\dot{q}(0,1,0)$ with normal vector $\vec{n} = \begin{bmatrix} 1 \\ -1 \\ 1 \end{bmatrix}$

Discussion. It suffices here to check each of the end points of the line. These are $\dot{p}_{start}(1,3,1)$ and $\dot{p}_{end}(3,6,2)$. If they are both in the plane then the line is in the plane. A point is in a plane if its product with the plane s operator is zero.

The plane operator is $\gamma = \begin{bmatrix} \vec{n}^T & | & d \end{bmatrix} = \begin{bmatrix} 1 & -1 & 1 & d \end{bmatrix}$. Since Q is in the plane $\gamma Q = 0$, therefore,

$$\begin{bmatrix} 1 & -1 & 1 & d \end{bmatrix} \begin{bmatrix} 0 \\ 1 \\ 0 \\ 1 \end{bmatrix} = 0 \implies d = 1$$

For $\dot{p}_{start}$

$$\begin{bmatrix} 1 & -1 & 1 & 1 \end{bmatrix} \begin{bmatrix} 1 \\ 3 \\ 1 \\ 1 \end{bmatrix} = 0 \implies \dot{p}_{start} \text{ is in the plane}$$

For $\dot{p}_{end}$

$$\begin{bmatrix} 1 & -1 & 1 & 1 \end{bmatrix} \begin{bmatrix} 3 \\ 6 \\ 2 \\ 1 \end{bmatrix} = 0 \implies \dot{p}_{end} \text{ is in the plane}$$

Therefore the line is in the plane.

Line in plane

Determine if a line lies in a plane.

$$\text{Line} \begin{bmatrix} x \\ y \\ z \end{bmatrix} = (1-t) \begin{bmatrix} 1 \\ 3 \\ 1 \end{bmatrix} + t \begin{bmatrix} 3 \\ 6 \\ 2 \end{bmatrix}$$

Plane $x - y + z + 1 = 0$

Discussion. The only difference with the previous problem is that the line is expressed in parametric form and the plane in implicit form. The start and end points can be read directly from the line equation. The plane operator is simply the coefficients of the plane equation, that is, $\begin{bmatrix} 1 & -1 & 1 & 1 \end{bmatrix}$.

Intersecting lines

Determine if the lines $\overline{L}$ and $\overline{K}$ intersect.

$$\text{Line } \overline{K}(s) = \begin{bmatrix} 2 \\ 1 \\ 7 \end{bmatrix} + s \begin{bmatrix} -4 \\ 4 \\ -8 \end{bmatrix}$$

$$\text{Line } \overline{L}(t) = \begin{bmatrix} 3 \\ 5 \\ 2 \end{bmatrix} + s \begin{bmatrix} 6 \\ -3 \\ -3 \end{bmatrix}$$

Discussion. Infinite lines intersect if the lines are not parallel and their four defining points are co-planar.

Instead of the cross product, use the scalar product to test for parallelism. If the vectors of the two lines are parallel so are the lines. The angle between parallel vectors is 0° or 180°, and the cosine of the angle is 1 or −1. Thus for parallel vectors

$$\vec{u} \bullet \vec{v} = |\vec{u}||\vec{v}| \cos \alpha$$
$$= \pm |\vec{u}||\vec{v}|$$

Squaring both sides removes the effect of a 180° rotation.

$$(\vec{u} \bullet \vec{v})^2 = |\vec{u}|^2 |\vec{v}|^2$$

Expanded this is

$$(\vec{u}_x\vec{v}_x + \vec{u}_y\vec{v}_y + \vec{u}_z\vec{v}_z)^2 = (\vec{u}_x^2 + \vec{u}_y^2 + \vec{u}_z^2)(\vec{v}_x^2 + \vec{v}_y^2 + \vec{v}_z^2)$$

In this case

$$\begin{aligned}
(\vec{u} \bullet \vec{v})^2 &= ((-4)(6) + (4)(-3) + (-8)(-3))^2 \\
&= ((-24) + (-12) + (24))^2 \\
&= (-12)^2 \\
&= 144
\end{aligned}$$

and

$$\begin{aligned}
|\vec{u}|^2|\vec{v}|^2 &= ((-4)^2 + 4^2 + (-8)^2)(6^2 + (-3)^2 + (-3)^2) \\
&= (16 + 16 + 64)(36 + 9 + 9) \\
&= (96)(54) \\
&= 5184
\end{aligned}$$

The example lines are not parallel.

With non-parallelism established, use both points of one line and the start point of the other to determine a plane. Use Equation 6.6 on page 109 to determine if the three points are collinear – all three components of the cross product must be equal to zero. If so, the lines intersect.

Collinearity of $\overline{K}_{start}, \overline{K}_{end}$ and $\overline{L}_{start}$

$$\begin{aligned}
\overline{K}_{\vec{u}} = \vec{u} &= \begin{bmatrix} -4 & 4 & -8 \end{bmatrix}^T \\
\overrightarrow{K_{start}L_{start}} = \vec{w} &= \begin{bmatrix} -5 & 4 & -5 \end{bmatrix}^T
\end{aligned}$$

$$\begin{aligned}
\vec{n} = \vec{u} \otimes \vec{w} \\
= \begin{bmatrix} 4(-5)-(-8)4 & (-8)(-5)-(-4)(-5) & (-4)4-4(-5) \end{bmatrix}^T \\
= \begin{bmatrix} 12 & 20 & 4 \end{bmatrix}^T
\end{aligned}$$

The cross product vector is not zero, so the points are not collinear. The cross product $\vec{n}$ is normal to the plane formed by the three points.

With non-collinearity now known, use Equation 6.8 on page 110, the normal vector $\vec{n}$ and any of the three points, say, $\overline{K}_{start}$, to determine a plane operator. Test the end point of the second line with the plane operator.

The plane operator $\lambda = \begin{bmatrix} \overrightarrow{n} & | & d \end{bmatrix} = \begin{bmatrix} 12 & 20 & 4 & -72 \end{bmatrix}$

$$d = -(122 + 201 + 47)$$
$$= -(24 + 20 + 28)$$
$$= -72$$

Test $\overline{L}_{end}$ against λ.

$$\begin{bmatrix} 12 & 20 & 4 & -72 \end{bmatrix} \begin{bmatrix} 3 \\ 2 \\ -1 \\ 1 \end{bmatrix} = 36 + 40 - 4 - 72 = 0$$

Since all four points are co-planar and the two lines are not parallel, the lines intersect.

Since the lines are in parametric form, they define both infinite lines and line segments. These segments intersect if the infinite lines intersect and the point of intersection has parameter values s and t on each line between zero and one, $0 \leq s \leq 1$ and $0 \leq t \leq 1$. This latter test requires that the actual parameters and therefore point of intersection be computed. See Section 6.8.3 below.

6.8.2 Generate an object lying on another object

Plane through point

Find the equation of a plane λ through $\dot{m}(2, -1, 5)$ and parallel to the plane γ through the points $\dot{a}(3, -7, 1)$, $\dot{b}(2, 0, -1)$, $\dot{c}(1, 3, 0)$.

Discussion. The plane γ is expressed as three points. Use Equation 6.7 on page 110 to determine a vector normal and a d value for the plane.

Find the plane normal using the cross product on vectors between pairs of points.

$$\begin{array}{rclcl} \overrightarrow{ab} & = & \begin{bmatrix} 2 & 0 & -1 \end{bmatrix} - \begin{bmatrix} 3 & -7 & 1 \end{bmatrix} & = & \begin{bmatrix} -1 & -7 & -2 \end{bmatrix} \\ \overrightarrow{ac} & = & \begin{bmatrix} 1 & 3 & 0 \end{bmatrix} - \begin{bmatrix} 3 & -7 & 1 \end{bmatrix} & = & \begin{bmatrix} -2 & 10 & -1 \end{bmatrix} \end{array}$$

$$\begin{aligned} \overrightarrow{n} &= \overrightarrow{ab} \otimes \overrightarrow{ac} \\ &= \begin{bmatrix} 10(-2) - (-1)7 & (-1)(-1) - (-2)(-2) & (-2)7 - 10(-1) \end{bmatrix}^T \\ &= \begin{bmatrix} 13 & 5 & -4 \end{bmatrix}^T \end{aligned}$$

Use this normal and the given point $\dot{m}$ in the plane operator of Equation 6.5 on page 104 yielding an equation in the single unknown d. Solve for d.

$$d = -(132 + 5(-1) + (-4)5)$$
$$= -(26 - 5 - 20)$$
$$= -1$$

The plane λ is then $\begin{bmatrix} \overrightarrow{n} & | & d \end{bmatrix} = \begin{bmatrix} 13 & 5 & -4 & -1 \end{bmatrix}$.

Plane through point

Find the equation of the plane λ through $\dot{q}(6,1,0)$ and perpendicular to the line

$$\overline{L}: \begin{bmatrix} x \\ y \\ z \end{bmatrix} = \begin{bmatrix} 5 \\ 5 \\ 5 \end{bmatrix} + s \begin{bmatrix} 8 \\ -2 \\ 0 \end{bmatrix}$$

Discussion. The line s direction vector is $\overrightarrow{n} = \begin{bmatrix} 8 & -2 & 0 \end{bmatrix}^T$.

The plane λ is then

$$\lambda: \overrightarrow{n} \bullet (\dot{p} - \dot{q}) = 0$$

For the given points the equation is

$$\begin{bmatrix} 8 \\ -2 \\ 0 \end{bmatrix} \bullet \left(\dot{p} - \begin{bmatrix} 6 \\ 1 \\ 0 \end{bmatrix} \right) = 0$$

6.8.3 Intersect two objects

Line and plane

Consider the line $\overline{L}$ given by point $\dot{p}$ and vector $\overrightarrow{d}$.

$$\dot{p}(t) = \dot{p} + t\overrightarrow{d}.$$

Also, consider a plane λ determined by a point $\dot{q}$ and a normal vector $\overrightarrow{n}$. Determine the intersection of the line and the plane.

Discussion. Convert the plane description to the *plane operator* form, that is,

$$\lambda = \left[\ \vec{n}_x \quad \vec{n}_y \quad \vec{n}_z \quad d \ \right]$$

where

$$d = -\vec{n} \bullet \dot{q}$$

Test each of the line s endpoints against the plane operator.

$$\text{Let } \dot{p}_{start} = \dot{p}$$

$$\dot{p}_{end} = \dot{p} + \vec{d}$$

$$\lambda_{start} = \lambda \bullet \dot{p}_{start}$$

$$\lambda_{end} = \lambda \bullet \dot{p}_{start}$$

If $\lambda_{start} = 0$ and $\lambda_{end} = 0$, the line is on the plane, else

If $\lambda_{start} = \lambda_{end}$, the line is parallel to the plane, else

If $\text{sign}(\lambda_{start}) = \text{sign}(\lambda_{end})$, the segment is on one side of the plane, else

If $\text{sign}(\lambda_{start}) \neq \text{sign}(\lambda_{end})$, the segment intersects the plane.

The actual intersection occurs at the point with parameter

$$\frac{-\lambda_{start}}{\lambda_{end} - \lambda_{start}}$$

Figure 6.31 shows why this is so.

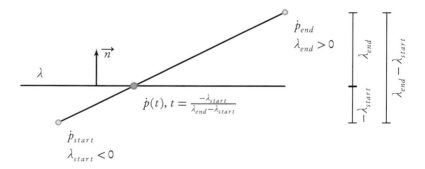

6.31: Computing the parameter value for the intersection point of a plane and a line. The plane is viewed "on edge", that is, the plane s normal vector is perpendicular to the view vector. The values λ_{start} and λ_{end} are proportional measures of the signed distance of their respective points to the plane (they are actually scaled by the length of the normal vector). The ratio of λ_{start} to $(\lambda_{end} - \lambda_{start})$ is the parameter value sought. This occurs because the domain λ_{start} to λ_{end} maps linearly onto the range 0 to 1.

Plane and plane

Consider two planes, λ and γ defined in normal-point form.

$$\lambda : \overrightarrow{n}_\lambda \bullet (\dot{p} - \dot{q}_\lambda) = 0$$
$$\gamma : \overrightarrow{n}_\gamma \bullet (\dot{p} - \dot{q}_\gamma) = 0$$

The locus of points $\dot{p}$ defines either a plane, a line or is null. Determine the intersection of the two planes.

Discussion. If $\overrightarrow{n}_\lambda \otimes \overrightarrow{n}_\gamma = \overrightarrow{0}$ the planes are parallel and the intersection is either null or the planes are the same.

If the planes are parallel and the point of one plane is on the other, the planes are coincident and the intersection can be specified simply as either plane.

$$\overrightarrow{n}_\lambda \bullet (\dot{q}_\gamma - \dot{q}_\lambda) = 0$$

Otherwise the planes intersect on the line $\overline{L}$. A normalized direction vector of the line is the normalized cross product of the two plane vectors.

$$\overrightarrow{dir}_{\overline{L}} = \frac{\overrightarrow{n}_\lambda \otimes \overrightarrow{n}_\gamma}{|\overrightarrow{n}_\lambda \otimes \overrightarrow{n}_\gamma|}$$

A point on the two planes completes a point-vector equation for the line. Clearly, there is an infinity of such points. A suitable one is the point on the line that is closest to the origin. This point is found as the solution of the following three linear equations ($\dot{o}$ is the origin).

$$\lambda : \overrightarrow{n}_\lambda \bullet (\dot{p} - \dot{q}_\lambda) = 0 \qquad \dot{p} \text{ is on } \lambda$$
$$\gamma : \overrightarrow{n}_\gamma \bullet (\dot{p} - \dot{q}_\gamma) = 0 \qquad \dot{p} \text{ is on } \gamma$$
$$\overrightarrow{dir}_{\overline{L}} \bullet \overrightarrow{\dot{o}\dot{p}} = 0 \qquad \overrightarrow{\dot{o}\dot{p}} \text{ is perpendicular to } \overline{L}$$

Plane and plane

Determine the intersection of the following two planes.

$$\begin{aligned} \lambda \quad &: 2x - 3y + 5z \quad = 2 \\ \gamma \quad &: 3x - y + z \quad = 4 \end{aligned}$$

Discussion. This problem is the same as the prior problem, except that the first two equations are in implicit form – the respective plane vectors are simply the coefficients of the x, y and z terms in the equations.

Like the previous example, finding the point needed to define the result line requires three equations. The first two are the implicit plane equations. The third results from taking the cross product of the normal vectors to the planes.

$$\begin{bmatrix} 2 \\ -3 \\ 5 \end{bmatrix} \otimes \begin{bmatrix} 3 \\ -1 \\ 1 \end{bmatrix} = \begin{bmatrix} 2 \\ 13 \\ 7 \end{bmatrix}$$

The three needed equations are thus as follows:

$$2x - 3y + 5z = 2 \qquad\qquad \dot{p} \text{ is on } \lambda$$
$$3x - y + z = 4 \qquad\qquad \dot{p} \text{ is on } \gamma$$
$$\overrightarrow{OP} \bullet \begin{bmatrix} 2 \\ 13 \\ 7 \end{bmatrix} = 0 \qquad\qquad \overrightarrow{OP} \text{ is perpendicular to } \overline{L}$$

6.8.4   Closest fitting object

Line between two lines

Given two lines in space, determine the shortest line segment joining the two lines. If the lines are parallel there is an infinity of shortest lines, all themselves mutually parallel. If the lines intersect, the line has zero length but still exists. If the lines do not intersect and are not parallel, they are said to be *skew*. Many CAD systems provide this function, either separately or as a special condition of intersection. It can also be computed efficiently. The point of including it here is to demonstrate how simple geometric constructions can produce needed answers. Sometimes direct geometric reasoning is faster; certainly it is more designerly than equation solving.

Discussion. The solution combines a cross product, two vector projections, a converse vector projection and a few miscellaneous operations such as point–vector sums. Each can be visualized as a step in a geometric construction.

Geometrically, when the two lines are parallel, the solution is indeterminate as there is an infinity of lines perpendicular to both and of identical length. In this case the cross product of the two lines is the zero vector.

When the cross product is not the zero vector, the two lines either intersect directly or are skew. In this case, the cross product produces a vector partially defining the line. What remains is to find a point on the line and to scale the vector so that its length is equal to the shortest distance between the two lines.

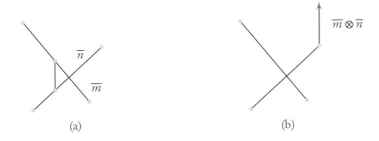

(a)   (b)

6.32: (a) Two skew lines $\overline{m}$ and $\overline{n}$ and the shortest line between them.
(b) Compute the cross product of the vectors of $\overline{m}$ and $\overline{n}$ and place at the end of line $\overline{n}$.
This vector defines the direction of the shortest line between the two lines $\overline{m}$ and $\overline{n}$.

(c)   (d)

6.33: (c) Project a point from line $\overline{m}$ onto the cross product vector. Since the cross product vector is located, this produces a point $\dot{p}$. The length of the vector $\vec{v}$ between the end point of the line $\overline{m}$ and this point is the length of the shortest line.
(d) Project point $\dot{p}$ back onto line $\overline{m}$. This gives a point $\dot{q}$ and a vector $\overrightarrow{pq}$ perpendicular to $\overline{m}$.

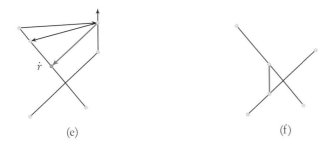

(e)   (f)

6.34: (e) Conversely project $\overrightarrow{pq}$ onto the vector of $\overline{n}$. Add the resulting vector to point $\dot{p}$ on the cross product. This produces the point $\dot{r}$ as one end of the shortest line.
(f) Project point $\dot{r}$ onto the line $\overline{n}$. Alternatively, subtract the vector $\vec{v}$ from the point $\dot{r}$ just found.

133

6.9   Curves

Lines and planes are convenient. They are simple to represent and objects based on them are simple to construct. Look around you though. Unless you are on a wilderness survival trip, you are most likely surrounded by artifacts – things people have created, manufactured or built. When practical, for example, in paper sizes and window glass, straight lines and at surfaces dominate. Most artifacts though have curved outlines and surfaces. Look carefully at a few of the artifacts around you and ask yourself the question "What determined the curve used in this design?" In a physically constrained environment, function typically dominates. For example, a sailing dinghy operates in the boundary between water and wind. Its form is deeply constrained by the complex forces acting upon it. Hull, centreboard, rudder and sails are all designed to convert force efficiently into forward motion and take whatever form is needed to meet that end. In an environment constrained by fabrication, the tools used impose geometry on the design. For example, in building construction, the relative lower cost of straight elements puts a premium on straight lines, at surfaces and curves that can directly develop from them. In less constrained situations, representational tools impose geometry. As I write, I am sitting at a desk with a computer, a digital camera, a printer, an MP3 player, a telephone, a mobile telephone, a calculator and a set of speakers in my immediate view. Each has circular curves in its design that seem neither functional, nor constructional in origin. I would guess that they arise simply because it is easy for a designer to make a circle in a drawing or model. Function, fabrication and representational convenience all seem to in uence the forms we make. CAD systems introduce computation as a fourth determinant. Especially with curves and surfaces, the tools CAD systems provide are formed more by computational tractability than functionality, constructional affordances or representational appropriateness. Indeed, the history of curves and surfaces in CAD systems can be well-read as the progressive development of representations guaranteeing increasing levels of computational capability. There is amazingly little in this literature about intended function or constructional constraint!

This section introduces curves, especially the so-called *free-form curves,* paying particular attention to the computational properties that they provide. This book is about parametric modeling, not mathematics, so why go into depth here? One answer is that curves are exemplary parametric objects. They can be defined clearly and elegantly using simple parametric structures. Understanding how this is done may well help in making your own structures. Another answer is that the architectural literature contains much nonsense about how curves and surfaces relate to architecture (I could cite some of the guilty parties here, but this would not be fair – there are too many to name them all). By showing the mathematics of curves in a largely qualitative (and hopefully readable) form, perhaps I can remove some of the mystery around these very common design objects and help writers avoid future embarrassment.

Designers describe curves by specifying a small set of objects (often points) that form an abstract representation of the curve. An algorithm then computes the curve from these objects. For example, a circle can be described as a centre, a radius and a plane to which the circle is parallel.

6.9.1   Conic sections

The *conic sections* curves are the circle, parabola, hyperbola and ellipse. Each is described by an equation with a maximum exponent of two. Each is relatively simple to draw and physically construct. Designers, being sensible and frugal, use these curves frequently. The key issue is connecting them smoothly. For joining circle segments, the French curves of manual drawing are a mature and stable technology. Repeating use of conic sections through a design can aid visual composition. Conic sections do present problems. While they can be joined without obvious kinks (this is called first-order continuity), they cannot achieve any higher smoothness.

In contemporary CAD, both conventional and parametric, designers use these curves less than they might. The so-called *free-form curves* are easy to use and give the immediate appearance of uid control.

6.9.2   When conic sections are not enough

Sometimes conic sections are truly not sufficient for design. Figure 6.37 shows a boat hull (the International Finn Dinghy). Its design is in uenced, nay driven, by narrow considerations of stability, speed and volume and by the designer s eye for a fair and sleek form. In its constrained world, conics hinder rather than help. Other domains feel similar forces, for instance, airplanes, automobiles and hand-held tools. In the 1990 s and 2000 s there was certainly great interest in non-conic sections in architectural design. Whatever the specific motivation, it was seldom comparable to the necessity experienced in other domains.

In CAD, *free-form* curves have come to dominate the toolbox, most likely due to the wide range of forms they encompass and their relative ease of editing. Some parametric modelers do not even support the full range of conic sections! Mathematically, free-form curves are hardly free. Rather, they are a constrained and specific means of expressing parametric polynomial curves. A polynomial is a sum of non-negative integer powers of one or more variables. Each variable may be multiplied by a real coefficient. A polynomial of one variable (called a *univariate* polynomial) has the general form $a_n x^n + a_{n-1} x^{n-1} + \cdots + a_1 x + a_0$. The equation $3.1x^2 - 2x$ is a polynomial, while $4x^{2.2} + 7x - 4$ is not, as it has a real-valued power. Free-form curves were initially motivated by the process of laying out complex forms using physical splines on a lofting oor and by the reality of World War II. Mathematics could be copied and thus was much less

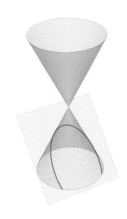

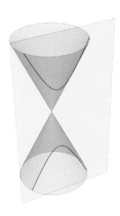

6.35: The four conic section curves and how they are derived from a cone. The circle s plane is perpendicular to the cone axis. The parabola s is parallel to a cone side. The hyperbola s is parallel to the cone axis. All other planes produce an ellipse.

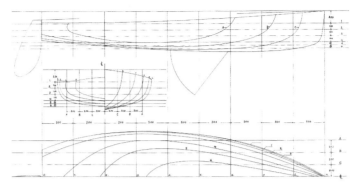

Source: International Finn Association

(a)

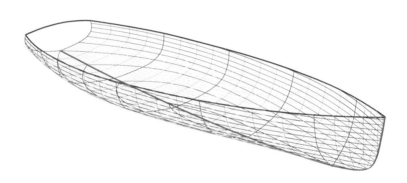

Source: Gilbert Lamboley

(b)

6.36: Finn dimensions persist, but technology advances. The wooden boats of the 1950s had wooden masts and cotton sails. Current fibreglass boats have carbon fibre masts and Mylar sails.

Source: International Finn Association

6.37: The lines for the Internatial Finn Class sailboat (designed by Rickard Sarby), which has been in the Olympics since 1952. (a) A drawing of unknown provenance, but believed to be that sent to competing countries as they prepared for the 1952 Helsinki Olympic Games. (b) A digital model of the Finn hull. The history of measurement records for the Finn Class demonstrates the practical need for accurate mathematical representation. Until 1964, the International Finn Association had only tables of offsets sourced from the Scandinavian Yacht Racing Union. The drawings from which those offsets were issued are believed to have disappeared in a fire. Charles Currey (at Fairey Marine) carved a physical template of full size Finn lines (together with transverse template lines) onto sheets of aluminium alloy in 1964. These sheets were treated to neutralize residual stress and so be dimensionally stable. The template was made according to the earlier offsets, obvious mistakes being ignored. Mylar copies taken from the aluminium templates were later found to be dimensionally unstable. Aluminum transverse section templates fabricated for field use themselves deformed over time by being dropped or otherwise impacted. In turn, the orignal template sheets were lost in the late 1990s. In 2003, working from the spotty historical record, Gilbert Lamboley reconstructed the tables of offsets and prepared the first digital Finn models.

likely to be bombed out of existence than was a factory oor. The boat hull in
Figure 6.37 provides an actual case of such need as the original drawings were
lost in a fire! Prior to having these mathematical and ultimately computer-based
representations, the principal design media were drawings and half-models of
the hull lines in four orthogonal projections (see Figure 6.37 (a)). Building a
boat started by consturcting stations along a strongback. The lines were then
faired by physical splines through the stations. In abstracting to mathematics,
the constraints of physical splines largely disappeared, leaving only metaphors
such as *poles* and the word "spline" itself in the new toolbox. Free-form curves
have their own logic, divorced from their physical origins and largely aimed at
achieving mathematically and computationally well-behaved curves that can
be used in design. In turn, CAD developers and designers have adopted and
adapted these curves into their modeling toolboxes. In this process of cultural
co-evolution, mathematics enables design, but is constrained by the possible,
and design poses new questions to mathematicians based on the realities of the
design profession and its marketplace.

The following sections provide an introduction to curves, applicable in both
two and three dimensions. They form the mathematically most involved part
of this book. Why spend so many pages on such detail? The answer is simple.
Curves are exemplary parametric objects. Understanding how they work gives
insight into both the form-making possibilities of curves and into parametric
modeling in general. With few exceptions, everything learned about curves
translates to surfaces, so the chapter on surfaces is brief, introducing only key
new concepts needed for effective modeling and design.

6.9.3   Interpolation versus approximation

Figure 6.38 shows that some curve algorithms *interpolate:* they compute curves
that go through the input points. Others *approximate:* they place curves that
are, in some sense, "near" the input points. We call the input points the *control
points* and the (possibly open) polygon they define the curve s *control polygon*.

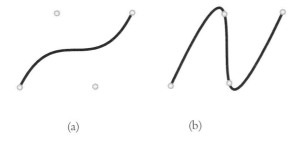

(a)   (b)

6.38: (a) An interpolating curve and (b) an approximating curve.

In most design systems, the dominant mode is approximation. This may seem surprising: having a curve go through known locations seems a useful idea. The reason is that approximating curves tend to be geometrically more predictable and "well-behaved", and are mathematically more simple.

6.9.4   Linear interpolation ≡ tweening

The fundamental constructor for many kinds of curves employs the concept of *linear interpolation* or *tweening*. Informally, interpolation moves a value "within" a set of other values. Linear interpolation moves it smoothly and in constant proportion. You have seen this concept before in the mathematics of the parametric line and plane equations. Parametric curves result from linearly interpolating a parameter in an equation to generate the points on the curve. In a parametric line, the point and the parameter have a direct relationship: equal increments between parameter values produce corresponding equal increments between points on the line. In curves, this relation becomes indirect. Identical parameter changes can yield unequal spacing between points – the implications deeply affect the form-making process.

Figure 6.39 shows a useful diagram, called a *systolic array*, for representing a parametric line equation, that is, the relationship between $\dot{p}(t)$, $\dot{p}_0$, $\dot{p}_1$ and t. The coordinate values from $\dot{p}_0$ and $\dot{p}_1$ ow into $\dot{p}(t)$ where they combine in the equation $\dot{p}(t) = \dot{p}_0 + t(\dot{p}_1 - \dot{p}_0)$.

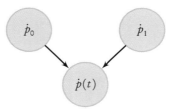

6.39: This *systolic array* comprises three points where the lower point is determined by the upper points and the *systolic array parameter* t. It is the basic (primitive) structure from which systolic arrays representing curves can be constructed.

6.9.5   Parametric curve representations

Like parametric lines, parametric curves are defined by a point that moves with a parameter t.

Unlike lines, the movement is not linear; the distance along a curve between $\dot{p}(t)$ and $\dot{p}(t + \delta t)$ is not necessarily the same as that between $\dot{p}(t + \delta t)$ and $\dot{p}(t + 2 * \delta t)$, where δt is a number expressing a very slight change relative to t.

Points can be placed at uniform increments by distance along the curve – except that the last point may not be at the given distance from the end of the curve. Points can also be placed at uniform spacing given a specified number of points.

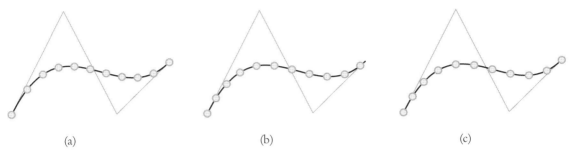

(a) (b) (c)

6.40: Points can be distributed along a parametric curve in several ways: (a) shows points at equal parameter intervals of 0.1, that is $t = \{0, 0.1, 0.2, \ldots, 1\}$. Note that the distance along the curve between points varies. (b) shows equal spacing at a given distance. Note that the rightmost point is not at the end of the curve, leaving a gap less than the chosen distance between it and the curve end. (c) shows equal spacing given a specified number of points on the line.

The very big lesson here is that parametric and geometric space are different. It is easy to work in parametric space, but designs are built in geometric space. The difference between the two bedevils much work.

6.9.6 Relating objects to curves

In design, curves relate to other objects and complex relationships are built from simple ones. Two basic relationships involve vectors: tangent and normal.

Tangent vector

Every (well, almost every) point $\dot{p}(t)$ on a curve has a family of vectors tangent to it. The sole exceptions occur when the *rst derivative* (from calculus) is not defined or is the zero vector.

Of the infinitely many vectors tangent at a parametric point $\dot{p}(t)$, only one is the *tangent vector*. The reason is that the length of the tangent vector captures the rate at which $\dot{p}(t)$ moves along the curve as t changes. In calculus terms, the tangent vector is the first derivative of the parametric curve at point $\dot{p}(t)$. The tangent vectors vary in length along the curve. When all are bound to one point, it is easy to see that their lengths differ. Figure 6.41 shows points along the curve at equal parameter spacing. The relative geometric distance between points approximates the relative tangent vector lengths. When successive points are close together, the tangent vectors are commensurately short. Normalizing the tangent vector gives the *unit tangent vector*, which is useful, for example, when constructing coordinate systems on curves. See Figure 6.42.

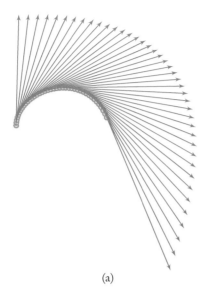

(a)

(b)

6.41: (a) The tangent vectors at example points along a curve. (b) A set of vectors each of the length of its corresponding tangent vector but sharing the same direction. Notice that the variation in length. This depends on the specific equation representing the curve. In particular the tangent vector is the first derivative of the curve.

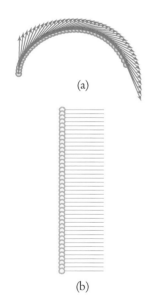

(a)

(b)

Normal vector

In the case of a two-dimensional curve there is (in almost every case) a unique direction vector normal to the curve. Of the two such vectors, one pointing to each side of the curve, by convention, we choose the one that points "into the curve". Of course, it lies in the plane of the curve.

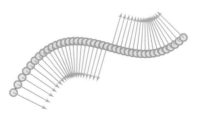

6.42: 6.4(a) Unit tangent vectors arrayed along a curve.
(b) Corresponding vectors, of identical direction and each of length of of the respective unit tangent vector shows that all such vectors share the same length.

6.43: Almost every point on a two-dimensional curve has a unique unit normal vector.

For three-dimensional curves, things are more complex. A point on the curve and its tangent vector define a plane normal to the curve at that point. Every vector in this plane is normal to the curve.

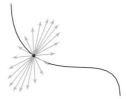

6.44: A sample from the infinite family of co-planar unit vectors normal to the tangent vector at three points on a curve.

However, there is a distinguished vector in that plane. It is called the *normal vector* of the curve at $\dot{p}(t)$. The normal vector is of unit length and lies in what is called the *osculating plane* of the curve at $\dot{p}(t)$. Its direction is approximated by the second derivative. This is the plane that most closely approximates the curve at $\dot{p}(t)$. Lying in this plane is the *osculating circle*, which is the circle that is both tangent to and has the same curvature as the curve at $\dot{p}(t)$. The centre points of the osculating circles at each point along the curve define another curve called the *evolute*.

Binormal vector

The binormal vector is the cross product of the unit tangent vector and the normal vector.

The unit tangent, normal and binormal vectors can be combined into a structure that, with a few exceptions, provides a sensible coordinate system at every point on the curve. This is the *Frenet frame*.

Frenet frames

The Frenet frame is an orthonormal frame defined at (almost) every point on a 3D curve. It comprises the unit tangent, normal and binormal vectors as the x-, y- and z-axes of the frame.

Frenet frames have some problems as design tools. At singular and in ection points they are not defined. When a point crosses an in ection point, the Frenet frame seems to invert or " ip", that is, it instantaneously rotates 180° around the tangent vector. This is not a good thing if, for instance, you are using a Frenet frame to orient windows on a curved façade and the frame inverts twice at each inward curve of the façade. Geometrically the osculating circle has an infinite radius at an in ection point.

When a curve is confined to a plane, such in ection points are frequent, indeed they are to be expected. Figure 6.47 shows one such curve.

Frenet frames are not defined on straight lines. A straight line is essentially an infinite in ection point.

6.45: The unit tangent vector; the normal vector; the osculating circle for three points on a 3D curve; and the curve evolute, the collection of all osculating circle centres.

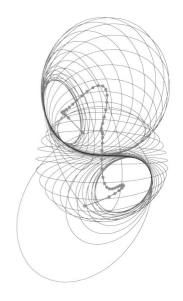

6.46: A collection of 50 osculating circles distributed uniformly along a curve. The circle centres trace the curve evolute.

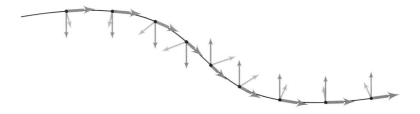

6.47: Frenet frames on a curve that has an in ection point. Note that the Frenet frame inverts on each side of the in ection point. At the in ection point itself, the frame is not defined.

In ection points seldom occur in 3D curves. In their place comes something worse: high torsion. Even though a curve may appear to contain an in ection point, it usually avoids in ection narrowly by, in effect, twisting around the point. This results in the Frenet frame rotating nearly or exactly 180° within a short parametric range.

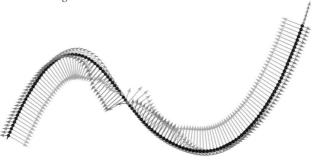

6.48: A curve that comes close to an in ection condition results in its Frenet frame rapidly rotating around the curve. This makes it difficult to orient objects along the curve.

A common remedy for these situations is to adopt a reference direction that does not depend on the local context of the point $\dot{p}(t)$ on the curve. Then place a frame on the curve with its x vector set to be the x vector of the Frenet frame and its z vector at right angles to the x vector and co-planar with the x vector and the reference vector. The frame will be on the curve and its x vector will have the same direction as the curve tangent vector. There are many ways to make the choice, for example, the z vector of the global coordinate system. But such a frame is not a Frenet frame; it no longer holds information on curvature or torsion. Its y vector will not always point towards the centre of curvature. The choice of a reference direction external to the curve will sometimes result in a strange orientation for the new frame. A better choice is to compute a local reference based on three non-collinear points in the curve control polygon or, better, on the average plane of the curve control polygon. This approach will fail less frequently, for example, when the curve is a straight line.

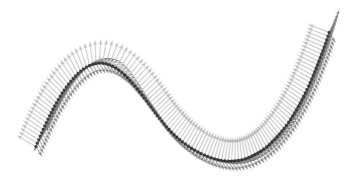

6.49: This is the same curve as in Figure 6.48. The coordinate system on the curve has its *x* vector tangent to the curve and its *z* vector approximating a reference vector.

Almost any point...

Several times above, I have stated that a property exists at "almost any point" on a parametric curve. The four exceptions occur where first or second derivatives are either undefined or zero. In practice, curves almost always have defined first derivatives, so this case is rare. Unfortunately, the other three cases are quite common, or at least common enough to cause trouble. Actually, I lied; they are really common. For instance, a line is a curve, but has a constant first derivative and a zero second derivative everywhere, so the Frenet frame is not defined at any point on a line.

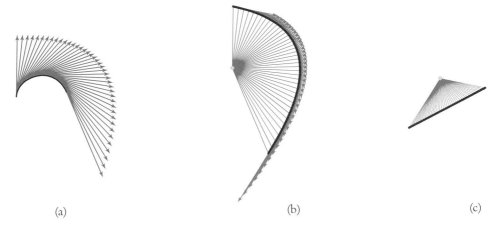

(a)   (b)   (c)

6.50: The (red) tangent vectors at example points along a curve, (a) placed on the curve and (b) collected at a single point into the hodograph and thus displaying the first derivative of the curve. (c) The hodograph of the hodograph collects the (blue) tangent vectors of the first derivative and locates them at the origin. This is the second derivative of the original function. In this and the following two figures, the second derivative vectors are scaled to 20% of their actual length, otherwise the figures become too large. In all three cases the second derivative is a straight line. Foreshadowing Section 6.9.9, this occurs because the example curves are of order 4 and degree 3.

Locating the tangent vectors of a curve at the origin produces the *hodograph*, a curve defined by the ends of the vectors and a good device for illustrating when exceptional points arise. The hodograph is the first derivative of the curve. The hodograph of the hodograph is the second derivative. Using the curve from Figure 6.41 above, Figure 6.50 shows the first and second hodographs.

An exceptional point on the curve occurs when either hodograph goes through zero or the two become locally collinear. The first hodograph goes through zero at a *cusp* and the two hodographs align at in ection points. For example, see the curves in Figures 6.51 and 6.52 below.

6.9.7   Continuity: when curves join

With parametric functions, continuity is trick as it comes in two avours, one with respect to parametric space and one with respect to geometric space. These are called C and G continuity respectively.

If a curve is connected, it has C_0 continuity. If its first derivative is continuous, the original curve has C_1 continuity. If the nth derivative is continuous, the original curve has C_n continuity. The curves in Figures 6.50, 6.51 and 6.52 are all C_2 continuous.

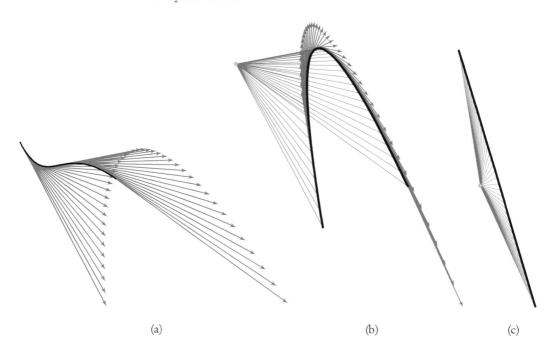

(a)   (b)   (c)

6.51: The two hodographs of an in ected curve are collinear at the in ection point, resulting in an undefined Frenet frame.

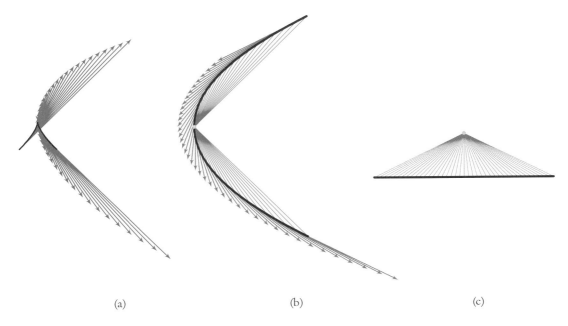

(a)   (b)   (c)

6.52: The hodograph (b) of a cusped curve (a) goes through zero, thus the Frenet frame is undefined at the cusp.

However, C continuity does not mean that a curve is geometrically smooth. For example, the cusped curve in Figure 6.52 above has a geometric kink, but is parametrically smooth. This is because C continuity is measured in parameter space not geometric space.

The notion of G continuity captures geometric smoothness.

If a curve is C_0 continuous, it is G_0 continuous. It is connected and this means the same thing in both parameter and geometric space.

If a curve is G_0 continuous and its tangent direction varies continuously, the curve is G_1 continuous. An example of a curve with C_1 continuity but not G_1 continuity is any curve whose hodograph goes through the origin, as shown in Figure 6.52 above. Coming into the origin, the tangent has one direction – leaving the origin, the tangent jumps to a different direction. Mathematically, G_1 continuity exists if the normalized tangent vector of a curve is continuous.

Most parametric modelers implement C continuity and leave control of G continuity to the user.

The next sections move from generic properties that apply to all curves to representation of specific curve types.

6.9.8   Bézier curves – the most simple kind of free-form curve

The most simple free-form curve is the Bézier curve, which is named after its inventor, Pierre Bézier. The cubic form (more on the *cubic* label later) of the Bézier curve is recursively defined on a control polygon of four points.

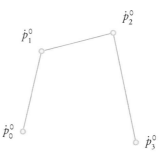

6.53: Bézier curve control points. In the notation $\dot{p}_j^0$, j stands for the jth control point and 0 stands for the ith *level* of the control polygon. This is the outer or 0th level.

Then a parametric point is placed on each line. Each of the lines in the control polygon holds a parametric point with a given parametric value, say, $t = 0.5$. These are the control points of the level 1 control polygon, which joins the level 1 control points in order.

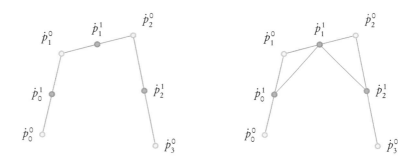

6.54: The level 1 control points $\dot{p}_0^1, \dot{p}_1^1, \dot{p}_2^1$. Each has the same parameter t, in this case, $t = 0.5$. The level 1 control polygon joins these points.

Parametric points with the same $t = 0.5$ value form the level 2 control points, which define the level 2 control polygon comprising a single line.

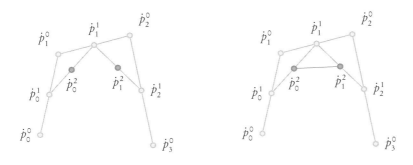

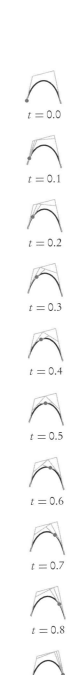

$t = 0.0$

$t = 0.1$

$t = 0.2$

$t = 0.3$

$t = 0.4$

$t = 0.5$

$t = 0.6$

$t = 0.7$

$t = 0.8$

$t = 0.9$

$t = 1.0$

6.55: The level 2 control points $\dot{p}_0^2, \dot{p}_1^2$. Again, each has the same $t = 0.5$ parameter. The level 2 control polygon is a single line.

The level 3 control point $\dot{p}(t) = \dot{p}_0^3$ is on the Bézier curve at parameter $t = 0.5$. Figure 6.57 show that, as t varies from 0 to 1, $\dot{p}(t)$ traces out the Bézier curve.

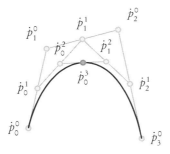

6.56: The level 3 control point $\dot{p}_0^3$. This is the defining point of the Bézier curve.

A Bézier curve can be represented symbolically by combining *primitive systolic arrays* (Figure 6.58) into a *composite systolic array* (or just a *systolic array*), shown in (Figure 6.59) that defines the entire Bézier curve. The systolic array suggests a clear convention for labeling the intermediate points of the array. In the point $\dot{p}_j^i$, i refers to the level in the systolic array (starting with the zeroth level) and j refers to the index of the point (the point s place in a sequence) at its particular level. In the systolic array data ows downwards along arcs from higher nodes to lower nodes. The *top* nodes in the systolic array receive no data; they are the inputs to the system. The *internal* nodes of the array receive inputs from those above and connected to them. The arcs denote data ow from an upstream to a downstream node. The nodes in this particular systolic array combine the inputs by a parametric line equation. (An expression could be added to each node to determine how inputs are handled, but that is not necessary here as all nodes use the same simple operation: a sum of a point and a vector scaled by t.)

6.57: As t varies between 0 and 1, $\dot{p}(t)$ travels along, indeed it defines, the curve.

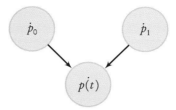

6.58: A *primitive systolic array* records the parametric line equation with the line end-points as the upstream nodes and the parametric point as the sole downstream node.

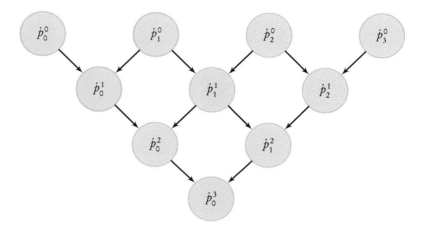

6.59: This *systolic array* combines six primitive systolic arrays (the first is shown in blue), each representing a line, to define the parametric point $p(t) = \dot{p}_0^3$.

The definition of each point (other than the control points) in the systolic array is simply a parametric line equation using the two points above the point being computed.

The systolic array is used to define what is called the deCasteljau algorithm for computing a point $\dot{p}(t)$ on a Bézier curve for a given value of t. In essence, the algorithm can be stated as:

> Start with a set of control points $\dot{p}_i^0$ and a parameter t.
>
> Create the systolic array
>
> Compute the values of any nodes for which you have the values of the upstream nodes.
>
> Stop when you cannot compute anything more.

Geometrically, the algorithm steps down through levels in the geometric structure, finding points with the same parameter values at every level.

6.9.9 Order and degree

Bézier curves belong to a very useful class of curves made from polynomials. A polynomial is a sum of monomials. A monomial is a product of constants and variables raised to exponents that are positive integers. For instance, $3x^7$ is a monomial and $4x^2 - 2x + 1$ is a polynomial.

Monomials and polynomials have two descriptors: order n and degree d, with $n = d + 1$. The term *degree* refers to the maximum exponent in the polynomial. *Order* equals $d + 1$. So $4x^2 + 2x + 1$ has degree $d = 2$ and order $n = 3$.

Bézier curves take their order (and thus degree) from the number of vertices in the control polygon. An order 4 Bézier curve has a four-point control polygon, an order 3 curve a three-point control polygon and an order 2 curve a two-point control polygon. Figure 6.60 shows that the two-point case defines a straight line segment. The simple parametric line equation is, in fact, a trivial Bézier curve.

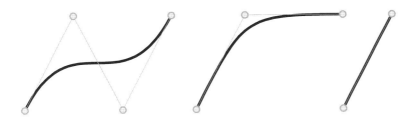

6.60: Order 4, 3 and 2 Bézier curves (in black) and their control polygons (in grey).

6.9.10 Bézier curve properties

Bézier curves have several useful properties that help us to understand the curves and to write algorithms that use them.

Convex hull. Intuitively, the convex hull of a set of points can be described by thinking of a rubber band stretched around the points. Some of the points will form vertices of a convex polygon; others will be on the interior of the polygon. Such a polygon is called the *convex hull*. It a useful approximation of the region occupied by the points. Algorithms over convex hulls can use the property of convexity. For example, testing if a point lies in a convex hull is a simple matter of checking that the point is on the same side of each hull line (or plane if 3D).

A Bézier curve is entirely contained in the convex hull of its control polygon.

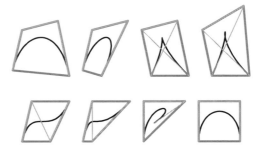

Symmetry. For a Bézier curve it does not matter whether we label the control points $\dot{p}_0, \dots, \dot{p}_d$ or $\dot{p}_d, \dots, \dot{p}_0$. The curves corresponding to the two orderings look the same, they only differ by their direction of parametric traversal.

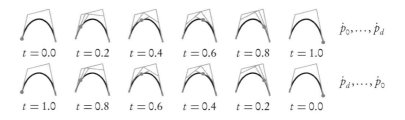

$$t = 0.0 \qquad t = 0.2 \qquad t = 0.4 \qquad t = 0.6 \qquad t = 0.8 \qquad t = 1.0 \qquad \dot{p}_0, \dots, \dot{p}_d$$

$$t = 1.0 \qquad t = 0.8 \qquad t = 0.6 \qquad t = 0.4 \qquad t = 0.2 \qquad t = 0.0 \qquad \dot{p}_d, \dots, \dot{p}_0$$

Endpoint interpolation. A Bézier curve of degree d passes through $\dot{p}_0$ and $\dot{p}_d$. In a design situation, having control over the starting and ending points of a curve is very important.

This can be seen directly from the systolic array by labeling each of the arcs with the factor that each source point contributes the result point. Remember that a parametric line equation is written as $\dot{p}(t) = (1-t)\dot{p}_0 + t\dot{p}_1$. Encoded into a primitive systolic array (as in Figure 6.61), the left arc carries the factor $1-t$ and the right arc t. The equation in each internal node of the systolic array takes the sum of the upstream points, weighted by the arc factors.

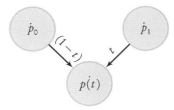

6.61: A primitive systolic array with arcs labeled with the scale factors defined in the parametric line equation.

Labeling the entire systolic array (Figure 6.62) shows that, when $t = 0$, all right branches of the systolic array contribute nothing, meaning that $\dot{p}_0^0$ is the sole contributor to the final point $\dot{p}_0^3$. Thus $\dot{p}(0) = \dot{p}_0^0$. When $t = 1$, $\dot{p}_0^0$ is the sole contributor to $\dot{p}_0^3$. Thus $\dot{p}(1) = \dot{p}_3^0$.

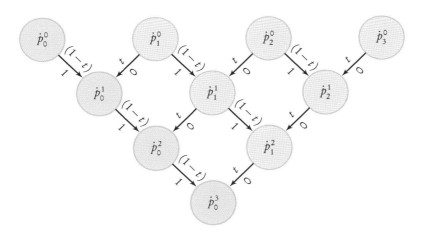

6.62: An entire systolic array labeled with scale factors for the parametric line equation.

Affine invariance. Bézier curves are invariant under affine maps. This means that the following two processes yield the same result: (1) first calculate $\dot{p}(t)$ and then apply an affine map to it; (2) first apply an affine map to the control polygon and then evaluate the image at t.

Affine invariance comes in handy when, say, we want to plot a rotated cubic curve $\dot{p}(t)$ by evaluating it at 100 points. Instead of rotating each of the 100 computed points and then plotting them, we can rotate the four control points, then evaluate 100 times and plot. Instead of 100 matrix multiplications we can do only four.

A big disadvantage of Bézier curves is that they are not projectively invariant, that is, they change in perspective. Of course, all CAD systems use perspective. Section 6.9.13 outlines *Non-Uniform Rational B-Splines* (NURBs), the main purpose of which is to ensure projective invariance.

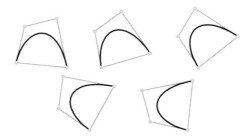

Invariance under affine parameter transformations. We usually consider Bézier curves defined on the interval $[0, 1]$. However, we can also think of a Bézier curve as being defined on any interval $[p, q]$ with parameter s since by taking $t = \frac{s-p}{q-p}, p \leq s \leq q$, we convert the interval $[p, q]$ into $[0, 1]$. In essence this means that any interval on the real number line can be used to control the parameter t. It just takes a little work.

Linear precision. When the Bézier control points are collinear, the Bézier curve is a straight line.

Variation diminishing. Any line intersects the control polygon of a Bézier curve at least as many times as it intersects the Bézier curve.

Pseudo-local control. The principle of local control means that moving any control point should move only the part of the curve "near" the control point. Local control is good – as counterpoint, think about editing a single point at the corner of a stadium roof and having the entire roof change as a consequence. Bézier curves fail to meet this principle, as all points (except for the endpoints) are affected by the movement of any given control point. They do implement local control in a partial sense: the "closer" to a control point that part of the curve lies, the more it is affected by movement of the control point. The quotes around the words "near" and "closer" signal their mathematical informality.

6.63: Moving an internal point on the control polygon moves all points except for the endpoints. Points parametrically closer to the control point move more than points further away, demonstrating the informal notion of pseudo-local control.

6.64: Moving an endpoint of the control polygon similarly moves all points on the curve, except the other endpoint.

6.9.11 Joining Bézier curves

A *spline* is a composite curve in which the parts connect. Bézier curves can be joined together to make splines. Doing so reveals why Bézier curves are not normally used in applications where splines are required.

We are interested in joining together curves with various levels of *continuity* or *smoothness,* which two terms we treat qualitatively here. Recall that Section 6.9.7 introduces some of the basic ideas of continuity and smoothness.

Joining together two Bézier curves can be done in sequence of methods, with each member of the sequence increasing the smoothness of the result.

If two curves share the last and first control points respectively, they will join, since Bézier curves interpolate their endpoints, two connected control polygons will produce curves sharing endpoints, but there may be a "kink" where they join. Such splines have both C_0 and G_0 continuity.

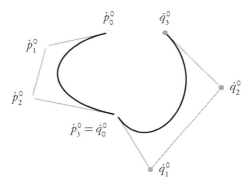

6.65: In C_0 continuity the control polygons of two Bézier curves share a single control point. Points $\dot{q}_1^0$, $\dot{q}_2^0$ and $\dot{q}_3^0$ (shown in eopdRed) can be freely moved.

If curves share the last and first control points and if the next control point on each control polygon and the joined point are collinear and equidistant from the joint, the Bézier spline will be C_1 continuous. It will be smooth across the join, but the distance between equal parametric points may suddenly change. A consequence is that, if you are joining one curve to another, two points are pre-determined.

In addition to the constraints of C_1 continuity, C_2 continuity requires that the second derivatives of the two Bézier curves be the same at the joining point. For the Bézier curves we have used so far, this condition has a surprising geometric result, as shown in Figure 6.67.

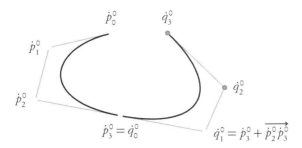

6.66: C_1 continuity constrains two points on each control polygon. Two points $\dot{q}_2^0$ and $\dot{q}_3^0$ (in red) remain free.

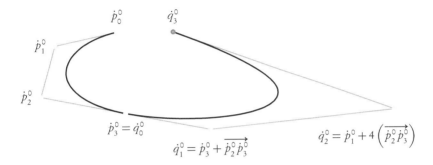

6.67: To join two curves $\dot{p}(t)$ and $\dot{q}(t)$ with C_2 continuity, the second derivative of their endpoints and startpoints must be equal. That is, $\dot{p}''(1.0) = \dot{q}''(0.0)$. This determines $\dot{q}_1^0$ and $\dot{q}_2^0$. Three of the four points on a degree 3 Bézier curve are determined when splining to C_2 continuity, leaving only $\dot{q}_3^0$ free (in red).

6.9.12   B-Spline curves

Bézier curves are geometrically and mathematically simple, but they have deep (and related) problems: control is only pseudo-local, and the order of a Bézier curve is the number of points in the control polygon. Pseudo-local control means that all points in a curve change when any control point is changed: it would be good to adjust the bow of a boat hull without affecting the stern. The link between order and control points means that a complex design must be done with high-order curves and this creates problems in interactive editing: it is easy to introduce local bumps and hard to make a curve visually fair. The curve also may lie far from the control polygon, making it hard to predict how an editing action might affect the curve. All of these problems can be remedied by connecting a series of curves into a composite curve, that is, a *spline curve*. Unfortunately, Bézier curves do not spline gracefully.

B-Spline curves address all of these problems. Like Bézier curves, B-Splines are defined on a control polygon. Unlike Bézier curves, they can be easily splined. In fact, splining is so natural that often no distinction is made between a curve (one spline segment) and a spline (multiple segments). The only constraint on the order of the curve is that it must be less than or equal to the number of points in the control polygon.

There are beautiful mathematical and computational ways to describe B-Splines (Rockwood and Chambers, 1996; Piegl and Tiller, 1997; Rogers, 2000; Farin, 2002) that provide great insight on how and why the curves work. But using B-Splines is the important thing here, and B-Splines provide two new modeling controls to the control points of Bézier curves: choice of *knots* and independent specification of order. The following explanation expands on the treatment of Bézier curves above to demonstrate B-Splines and their controls.

In essence, B-Spline curves are a framework for constructing Bézier curves – the B-Spline control polygon is just a new way to specify a Bézier control polygon that, in turn, defines the intended curve. This has profound implications for design – B-Splines and Béziers can model exactly the same possibilities; they just do it differently; see Figure 6.68.

6.68: A B-Spline control polygon (in grey), the derived Bézier control polgyon (in red) and the resulting B-Spline (and Bézier) curve.

The data needed for an order n B-Spline curve are the same as those for a Bézier curve, with the addition of a *knot vector* comprising a non-decreasing sequence of real values. The knot vector not only determines the parameter values over which the curve is defined, but also affects the shape of the curve. Depending on the specific mathematical explanation, a knot vector of length k for an order n curve with p control points has either $k = p + n$ or $k = p + n - 2$ elements. The technique shown here uses the shorter knot vector, that is, having length $k = p + n - 2$; see Rogers (2000) for the longer form.

We demonstrate the B-Spline construction method (the deBoor algorithm) for an order 4 curve with four control points. This yields a single B-Spline curve segment.

In essence, B-Splines generalize the deCasteljau algorithm to produce both the new Bézier control points and the curve from these new points. The first of two key ideas, shown in Figure 6.69, is that the parameter used at each level in the algorithm can be different. Instead of a single t, use a collection t_0, t_1, t_2. Thus, a point produced by the algorithm has not one parameter, but three: $\dot{p}(t_0, t_1, t_2)$.

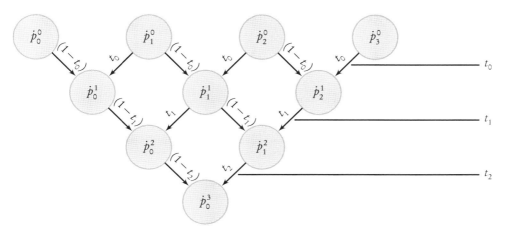

6.69: The first step in generalizing the deCasteljau algorithm defines a different parameter t_i at each level of the systolic array.

Clearly, the point produced by the algorithm is freer than before.

Taken together, the t-values are called the *blossom values* of the point $\dot{p}(t_0, t_1, t_2)$ and are written as $\langle t_0, t_1, t_2 \rangle$. Thus the input to the algorithm is a blossom value $\langle t_0, t_1, t_2 \rangle$ and the output is a *blossom point* with the input blossom value $\langle t_0, t_1, t_2 \rangle$. Strangely, the order of the blossom values does not matter: $\langle 0, 1, 2 \rangle$ produces the same output as $\langle 2, 0, 1 \rangle$, or any other permutation of the values! To make it easy to distinguish blossom values producing different results, we make a canonical notation by sorting blossom values in non-decreasing order (numeric order for numbers and alphabetic order for variables).

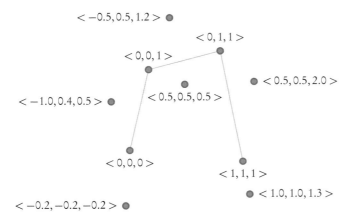

6.70: The location of blossom points $\langle a, b, c \rangle$ depends on the values given to a, b and c. Blossoms $\langle 0, 0, 0 \rangle$, $\langle 0, 0, 1 \rangle$, $\langle 0, 1, 1 \rangle$ and $\langle 1, 1, 1 \rangle$ correspond to the control points.

If two points share all but one blossom value in common, they can be combined to form a new point. Two points with blossom values $\dot{p}\langle a,b,c\rangle$ and $\dot{q}\langle b,c,d\rangle$ produce a third point $\dot{r}\langle b,c,e\rangle$ through a parametric line equation with an affine parameter transformation, as shown below.

$$\dot{r}\langle b,c,e\rangle = \dot{p} + \frac{e-a}{d-a}(\dot{p}-\dot{q}) = \frac{d-e}{d-a}\dot{p} + \frac{e-a}{d-a}\dot{q}$$

The point $\dot{r}$ lies on the line between $\dot{p}$ and $\dot{w}$.

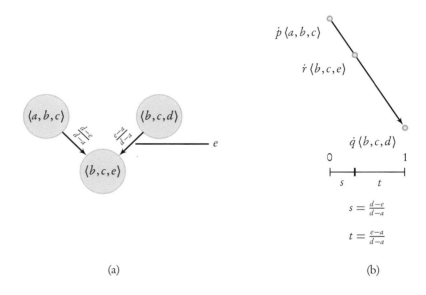

6.71: Computing a point from blossoms that share two common values. (a) The labels on the nodes are blossom values. The labels on the arcs give the coefficients for each input point in computing the resulting point. (b) The resulting point lies on the line between $\dot{p}$ and $\dot{q}$.

The second key idea generalizes the algorithm one step further by assigning each of the points in the systolic array its own blossom value, and using those blossom values to determine how linear interpolation works between points. Here is where the main new control of the B-Spline comes into the picture. The *knot vector* is a non-decreasing sequence of real values, the most simple being $\langle 0,1,2,3,4,5\rangle$. Such a *uniform* knot vector has identical increments between each successive knot.

To use a knot vector, distribute three of its successive elements over each control point. To control point $\dot{p}_0^0$ assign knot vector elements $\langle 0,1,2\rangle$; to control point $\dot{p}_1^0$ assign elements $\langle 1,2,3\rangle$, and so on. In the general case, using knot vector k, assign $\langle k_i, k_{i+1}, k_{i+2}\rangle$ to control point $\dot{p}_i^0$. These are the *blossom values* of the control points. Note well that each pair of adjacent control points share two blossom values – *they can be combined using the above logic, and their result will share two blossom values with the original points as well!*

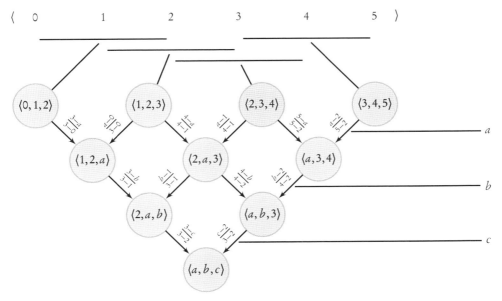

6.72: The blossom values $\langle a, b, c \rangle$ enter the algorithm, one at each level as the parameter in an affine parameter transformation using the unsharede blossom values as the bounds of the transformation. The blossoms, in turn, are defined by the knot vector.

At each layer in the graph, the algorithm uses the corresponding element from the input blossom value to compute the points and their blossom values at the next step. The algorithm is completed by building this equation into every primitive element of the systolic array. The output of the algorithm is a point with blossom value $\langle t_0, t_1, t_2 \rangle$ given parameters t_0, t_1 and t_2.

The middle two elements $\langle 2, 3 \rangle$ of the knot vector $\langle 0, 1, \mathbf{2}, \mathbf{3}, 4, 5 \rangle$ determine the parametric interval over which the implied Bézier curve will be defined. The Bézier control points are the blossom points with values $\langle 2, 2, 2 \rangle$, $\langle 2, 2, 3 \rangle$, $\langle 2, 3, 3 \rangle$ and $\langle 3, 3, 3 \rangle$.

Using the control points and their respective blossoms, the deBoor algorithm computes points on the curve by equating its three input arguments. That is, $\dot{p}(t) = \text{deBoor}(t, t, t), 2 <= t <= 3$. Of course, using a knot vector other than $\langle 0, 1, 2, 3, 4, 5 \rangle$ will change these bounds. For a single B-Spline segment the order is given by the number of control points, so the length of the knot vector is twice the curve degree $k = 2d$ or twice the curve order minus two, that is, $k = 2n - 2$. The nth and $(n + 1)^{th}$ elements of the knot vector determine the lower and upper curve parameters respectively.

Any point $\dot{p}(t)$ on the derived Bézier curve can be computed with either the deCasteljau algorithm over the derived control polygon or by using the deBoor algorithm with uniform knots: the result is the same. In turn, the deCasteljau algorithm over the derived control polygon is a special and simple case of the deBoor algorithm over these same points with blossom values $\langle 2, 2, 2 \rangle$, $\langle 2, 2, 3 \rangle$, $\langle 2, 3, 3 \rangle$ and $\langle 3, 3, 3 \rangle$ and bounds $\langle 2, 3 \rangle$.

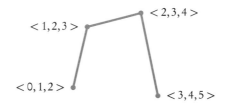

6.73: A B-Spline control polygon labeled with blossom values. This is the 0th level of the deBoor algorithm.

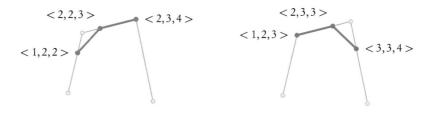

6.74: The level 1 control points for $\langle 2,2,2 \rangle$ (on the left) and $\langle 3,3,3 \rangle$ (on the right). Each has its respective blossom values as computed by the first level of the deBoor algorithm.

6.75: The level 2 control points for $\langle 2,2,2 \rangle$ (on the left) and $\langle 3,3,3 \rangle$ (on the right). Each has its respective blossom values as computed by the second level of the deBoor algorithm. The level 3 points are already computed at this stage as one of the level 2 control points.

6.76: A B-Spline control polygon, curve and the derived Bézier control polgyon.

A look at the above figures and the deBoor algorithm shows more work being done than is strictly necessary to compute the internal Bézier control points. For instance, with inputs $\langle 2,2,2 \rangle$, $\dot{p}\langle 2,2,3 \rangle$ is computed at the first level of the algorithm, and $\dot{p}\langle 2,2,2 \rangle$ at the second level. The algorithm though is general: it works to compute all control points, any blossom value and any point on the B-Spline curve.

160

An elegant shorthand for determining the Bézier control points and thus the B-Spline curve segment for the standard knot vector uses coefficients of the affine parameter transformation at each level of the deBoor algorithm. (The standard knot vector is $\langle 0, 1, 2, 3 \rangle$ for order 3, and $\langle 0, 1, 2, 3, 4, 5 \rangle$ for order 4 curve segments.) For example, when computing the point $p \langle 2, 2, 2 \rangle$ for an order 4 curve, the deBoor algorithm uses fractions $\frac{1}{3}$ and $\frac{2}{3}$ at the first level, and $\frac{1}{2}$ at the second level, as shown in Figure 6.77 below.

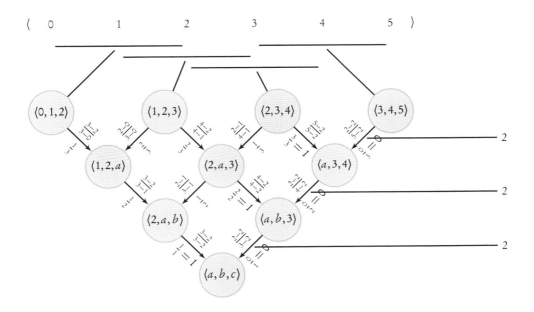

6.77: Computing the Bézier control points $p \langle 2, 2, 2 \rangle$, $p \langle 2, 2, 3 \rangle$, $p \langle 2, 3, 3 \rangle$ and $p \langle 3, 3, 3 \rangle$ with knot vector $\langle 0, 1, 2, 3, 4, 5 \rangle$ produces simple fractions at each level of the deBoor algorithm. Shown here is computation for $p \langle 2, 2, 2 \rangle$.

The Bézier control points can be directly drawn using these fractions as follows.

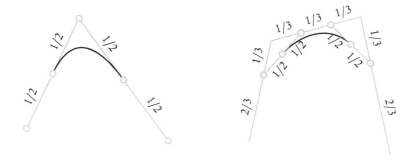

6.78: The Bézier control points for order 3 and order 4 B-Spline curve segments, drawn using fractional proportions from the deBoor algorithm.

< 0, 1, 2, 3, 4, 5 >

< 0, 0, 1, 2, 3, 3 >

< 0, 0, 0, 1, 1, 1 >

< 0, 0, 0, 1, 2, 3 >

6.79: Repeating knots at the end of a knot vector pulls the curve towards the endpoints of the control polygon.

The knot vector itself provides a control for B-Splines. Using it, B-Splines can be forced to interpolate their control polygon endpoints, moved and changed within the control polygon and joined with different degrees of continuity.

When values are repeated at the ends of a knot vector, as in Figure 6.79, the curve is "pulled towards" the ends of the control polygon. For a single curve segment (the number of control polygon vertices k and the curve order n are the same), when the knot vector repeats $n-1$ values at both beginning and end, a B-Spline becomes a Bézier curve. In the contemporary curve literature such curves are described as being *clamped*. A very confusing historical fact is that they were called *open* curves by Rogers (2000) but now *open* generally means the opposite of clamped! Repeating values at one end and not the other leaves the other endpoint of the curve unchanged.

Figure 6.80 shows that "spreading" knot vector values in the centre of the vector moves the curve towards the bottom of the control polygon (and vice versa).

At first glance, B-Splines seem a rather awkward way to compute the Bézier curves of which they are composed. After all, Bézier curves interpolate their endpoints, the first and last control polygon segments directly give the endpoint tangents, and the curve is closer to the control polygon than for the B-Spline. The benefit becomes clear when curves spline together. B-Splines connect easily and maintain continuity through the connection. They join curve pieces into an entire spline with the control points being shared by adjacent curves. This is more easily drawn than written.

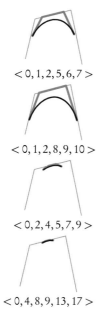

< 0, 1, 2, 5, 6, 7 >

< 0, 1, 2, 8, 9, 10 >

< 0, 2, 4, 5, 7, 9 >

< 0, 4, 8, 9, 13, 17 >

6.80: Increasing the relative spread between central knot values pulls the curve towards the control points.

6.81: A B-Spline control polygon; its Bézier structures; and the B-Spline curve.

The order (and thus degree) of the curve simply determines how many points of the control polygon to use for each segment. For example, an order 4 B-Spline uses four control points per piecewise curve. Each of the points contributes to the location of every point on each curve segment in which it participates, but has no effect on segments in which it does not participate. Figure 6.83 shows successive B-Spline segments for a multi-segment curve. Of course, the curve is affected by the choice of order. With decreasing order the curve moves closer to the control polygon. When order equals 2, the curve is the control polygon: each piece of the curve is given by a simple parametric line equation.

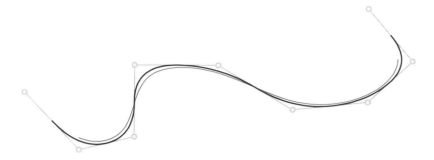

6.82: Order 2, 3 and 4 curves from the same control polygon. An order 2 curve is the control polygon. As the order increases from order 3 (black) to order 4 (red), the curve moves away from the control polygon and generally varies less.

B-Splines inherit all of the properties of Bézier curves and strengthen two. First, Figure 6.84 shows that the convex hull condition is much stronger. Whereas a Bézier curve lies within the convex hull of its control polygon, a B-Spline lies piecewise within the convex hull of its implied Bézier control polygons.

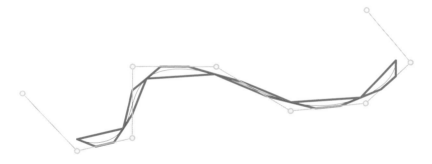

6.84: B-Spline curve segments lie within the convex hull of their implied Bézier control polygons. This allows for rapid approximate tests for likely intersections between the curve and other objects.

Second, B-Splines demonstrate true local control. Figure 6.85 demonstrates that moving a vertex of the control polygon for an order n curve affects at most the n curve segments whose control polygons use that vertex. When the vertex is close to the end of the control polygon even fewer segments are affected.

6.83: A B-Spline control polygon, implied Bézier control polygon and curve segment for each of the piecewise components of a B-Spline curve.

163

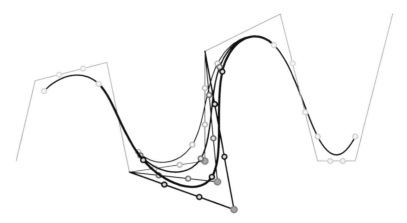

6.85: When a single control point (in eopdRed) of an order 4 B-Spline curve moves, only the four parts of the curve using that control point are affected. B-Splines implement true local control.

As described above, B-Splines introduce knots as a new control. Figure 6.86 shows that repeating knots internal to a B-Spline reduces the continuity at the affected vertex.

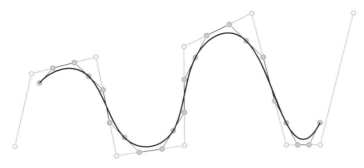

(a) Uniform knot vector $\langle 0, 1, 2, 3, 4, 5, 6, 7, 8, 9, 10, 11 \rangle$

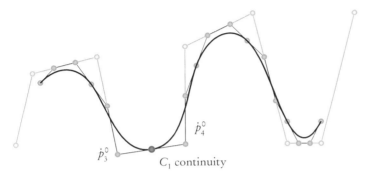

(b) Non-uniform knot vector, with two duplicate internal knots
$\langle 0, 1, 2, 3, 4, 4, 5, 6, 7, 8, 9, 10 \rangle$

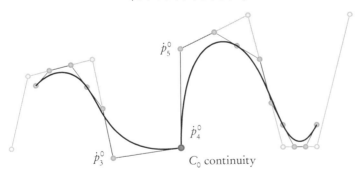

(c) Non-uniform knot vector with three duplicate internal knots
$\langle 0, 1, 2, 3, 4, 4, 4, 5, 6, 7, 8, 9 \rangle$

6.86: (a) In this order 4 B-Spline, non-duplicate knots guarantee C_2 continuity. (b) This non-uniform knot vector duplicates the fifth and sixth knots. This changes the blossom values at control polygon vertices $\dot{p}_3^0$ (blossom $\langle 3, 4, 4 \rangle$) and $\dot{p}_4^0$ (blossom $\langle 4, 4, 5 \rangle$) and reduces continuity between the Bézier curve segments 2 and 4. Bézier curve segment 3 has four identical control points, so essentially disappears. (c) A third duplicate knot spreads the change in blossom value to a third vertex: now $\dot{p}_3^0$, $\dot{p}_4^0$ and $\dot{p}_5^0$ have blossoms $\langle 3, 4, 4 \rangle$, $\langle 4, 4, 4 \rangle$ and $\langle 4, 4, 5 \rangle$ respectively. This reduces continuity to C_0 between Bézier curve segments 2 and 5; and makes curve segments 3 and 4 have all identical vertices.

6.9.13   Non-uniform rational B-Spline curves

Curves have one more control: *weights*, which are introduced in the step from B-Splines to *Non-Uniform Rational B-Splines* (NURBs). CAD system interfaces and marketing literature feature the word "NURB" as if it were some kind of magic. Some design literature goes even further, attributing high meaning to the term "non-rational". Reality is both more plebian and essentially below design. NURBs exist so that curves control polygons can be taken through a perspective projection and the curve computed afterwards. To do this, NURBs define *weights*. Mathematically NURBs are specified in a space one dimension higher than the geometric space in which they are embedded. The weights are the highest dimension coordinates of the control points in that space. In design terms, weights manifest as controls that draw a curve closer to a control point as the weight on that point is increased. Many CAD systems do not even provide access to either weights or knots. Such systems may claim NURB capability and be based on NURBs underneath the interface, but they essentially provide only B-Splines. NURBs do have one geometrically important feature. With the correct choice of weights, they can represent conic sections, a task B-Splines cannot do. For CAD systems this means that only the NURBs representation is needed. From a design perspective this matters much less.

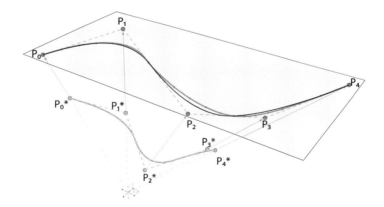

6.88: Increasing the z-coordinate of a B-Spline control point in three-dimensional space moves the two-dimensional NURB curve towards the two-dimensional projection of the control point. The z-coordinate of a control point of three-dimensional B-Spline is the weight of its corresponding point in the two-dimensional NURB. When weights are equal as, in the second from bottom curve, the two-dimensional projection of the B-Spline and the two-dimensional NURB are the same.

6.87: NURBs in two-dimensional space are B-Splines in three-dimensional space. The two-dimensional NURB (rendered in red), with control points P_0, P_1, P_2, P_3 and P_4, corresponds to a three-dimensional B-Spline (rendered in grey) with control points P_0^*, P_1^*, P_2^*, P_3^* and P_4^* when the z-coordinates of the B-Spline control points are equal. Otherwise, as is the case shown here, the NURB varies from the B-Spline.

Weights complete the lexicon of curve properties and controls. Béziers, B-Splines and NURBs form a sequence, each building on its predecessor. Here is how they compare.

Property	Bézier	B-Spline	NURB
convex hull	yes	yes	yes
symmetry	yes	yes	yes
endpoint interpolation	yes	optional	optional
affine invariance	yes	yes	yes
affine parameter invariance	yes	yes	yes
variation diminishing	yes	yes	yes
local control	pseudo	yes	yes
splining with continuity	hard to do	yes	yes
order control	no	yes	yes
knots	no	yes	yes
projective invariance	no	no	yes
conic sections	no	no	yes
weights	no	no	yes

From a design perspective, what is most striking with all of these properties is their relative irrelevance. Yes, we rely on each of these properties sometimes. For instance, affine invariance is important. As we move control points around as a group the generated curve does not change with respect to the control points. But the generic curve concepts are what count. That parametric and geometric distances differ, that the Frenet frame is (almost) always defined and that we want to control continuity are more important to design. Béziers, B-Splines and NURBs are the (not so simple) mathematical devices we need to get there.

6.9.14   The rule of four and five

How many control points are actually needed? What is a good choice for order? These are separate questions, but with linked answers. There are good reasons to keep each number small, and it turns out that just five control points and order 4 is sufficient for many, many modeling tasks. Five control points means that a curve can have a "dip" in it. Order 4 means that curves can join smoothly, without obvious joints, even under light re ection. Having a small number of control points makes it easier to predict how a model will change. The lower the order, the closer the curve is to the control polygon, and this also helps in understanding a model s behaviour.

 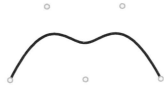

6.89: An order 4 curve with five points on its control polygon allows a single "dip". This simple and computationally light description is sufficient for many design situations.

6.10   Parametric surfaces

Parametric surfaces and curves share mathematical structure. Surfaces are more complex than curves so, naturally, their representation must be more involved. Rather than describe how surfaces work mathematically and parametrically, this section describes their behaviour from a modeling perspective.

Parametric surfaces comprise a point $\dot{p}(u,v)$ that moves along the surface as the parameters u and v change. (See Figure 6.90.) By convention curves have a parameter t, so surfaces get the next two letters of the alphabet.

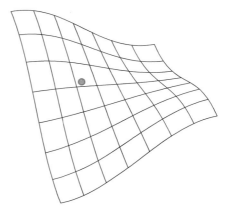

6.90: A uv point on a surface $\dot{p}(u,v)$.

Like curves, movement is not linear. (See Figure 6.90.) Unlike curves, there is no general way to make spacing uniform. This leads to many hard problems in subdividing surfaces.

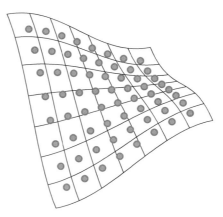

6.91: An array of parametrically equally spaced uv points on a surface. It is easy to see that the geometric spacing varies between pairs of points.

With exceptions similar (but more complex) to those for curves, Figure 6.92 shows that every point on a surface has a unique unit surface normal.

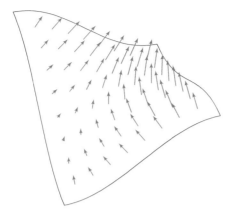

6.92: The unit surface normals at the *uv* points on the surface from Figure 6.90.

Lines in *u* and *v* parameter space map to curves on the surface. When either *u* or *v* is held constant, the line in parameter space is parallel to the parameter axes. The square *uv* parameter space is mapped to the surface, stretching like a rubber sheet in the process. The curve in geometry space stretches with the sheet, so lies on the surface in rough proportion to its position in parameter space. Such curves, where one of *u* or *v* is held constant, are called *isocurves*. Figure 6.93 shows four such curves.

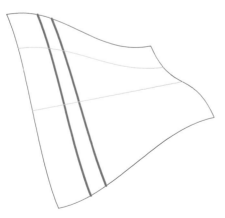

6.93: Isocurves with $u = 0.2$, $u = 0.3$, $v = 0.5$ and $v = 0.8$ on the surface from Figure 6.90.

At almost every point on a surface there is a coordinate system comprising the surface normal (z-axis), a vector in the local *u*-direction (x-axis) and a vector in the local *v*-direction (y-axis). Such a system is called a *uv*-coordinate system. Figure 6.94 renders an array of such systems at equal parametric intervals.

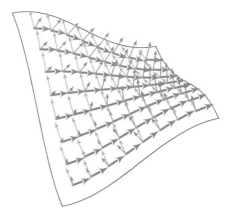

6.94: An array of *uv*-coordinate systems on a surface.

There is another coordinate system as well, shown in Figure 6.95. This points not along the *uv* isocurves but along the *lines of principal curvature*. At almost every point on a surface (excepting oddities like the sphere and the plane), there exist two planes at right angles to both the plane of the surface normal and to each other. Both planes intersect the surface. One holds the curve of maximum curvature; the other the curve of minimum curvature. The directions of these planes are called the *principal directions* of the surface at the point.

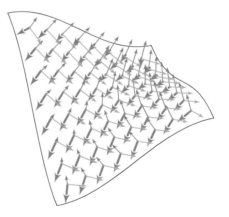

6.95: An array of principal direction coordinate systems on a surface.

Chapter 7

Geometric gestures

Architect: Kohn Pederson Fox Associates (KPF)

by Onur Yüce Gün

Parametric modeling enables designers to build complex designs with precise control. Through connecting discrete parts with hierarchical relationships, designs can be driven, updated and modified via the use of numerical, textual and logical values: parameters. The design model is no longer a fixed entity. It becomes malleable, granting us the opportunity to explore, test and evaluate design variations.

One of the greatest benefits of parametric modeling over conventional CAD modeling is the propagation graph, which enables simultaneous manipulation of parts across a design. This encourages the designer to think across a range of interconnected design ideas and enables discovering or establishing relational rules within design parts. One single action triggers a chain of reactions within the built system. When the logic of parametric modeling systems is combined with contemporary free-from modeling, form-finding and design exploration are vastly enhanced.

Unbounded and playful exploration in design is how we discover new ideas. More computational power and fewer geometric limitations simply mean a larger ground for innovation. However, the realities of design-construction practice eventually require more geometric and cost control. Once set into a parametric model, geometrical relationships, connections and limitations can be harnessed towards these practical ends.

When geometry is incorporated early into the design process, the well-known strategy of post-design rationalization becomes pre-rationalization: geometry and structure become form-making ideas in their own right. Through using such tools, designers gain insight and clarity.

7.1   Geometrical fluidity: White Magnolia Tower

Kohn Pedersen Fox Associates 68-storey White Magnolia Tower was designed in 2003 as the landmark building of the Luwan district of Shanghai. The digital model of the tower was built in Rhinoceros® 3.0, using non-uniform rational B-Spline (NURB) modeling techniques. The initial design was an exercise in sculpture using neither pre-rationalization nor parametric modeling techniques.

The original model of the tower comprised three identical surfaces that were extended in a slightly different fashion at the top of the building (Figure 7.1). A similar approach applied to the canopy development at the tower base.

7.1: 3D print of the tower.
Source: Robert Whitlock and KPF.

7.2: Surface curvature properties before (left) and after (right) geometrical rationalization.
Source: Onur Yüce Gün and KPF.

Driven mainly by form-making considerations, the designers made no attempt to control the surface curvature in the original digital model. The complex result had varying and irregular curvature values across the surface. Practical curtain wall design rewards regularities of almost any kind: curvature, planar faceting or common edge lengths (Figure 7.2). Smooth variation in curvature enables a more regular and cost-effective panelization. Flat panels still retain their historical advantages over warped panels, including production time and cost, durability and maintenance.

The design development studies of the White Magnolia Tower centred on the idea of generation and use of parametrically controlled torus patches. A torus, or a rectilinear torus patch, which is a cutout from the surface of a torus, can be subdivided into   at quadrilaterals. These quadrilaterals can be interpreted as   at panels for curtain-wall construction (Figure 7.1).

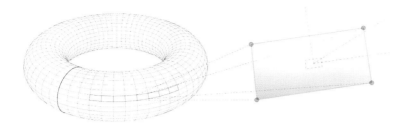

7.3: A torus surface can be panelized with at panels. The panels common to a horizontal row are the same size.
Source: ©2010 Onur Yüce Gün.

A parametrically controlled set-out generated the oor slab perimeters for each
 oor of the building. A set of circles with tangential dependencies defined a
series of co-tangential arcs forming in to a composed curve (Figure 7.4). At
each oor, the composite curve representing the slab perimeter lines was then
trimmed from both ends with trimming lines. These lines rotate a small amount
(0.44°) in successive oors, yielding 30° of twist overall across the 68 storeys
(Figure 7.5). Regardless of the twisted cut on the edges of the overall surface, the
shape of the surface remains the same.

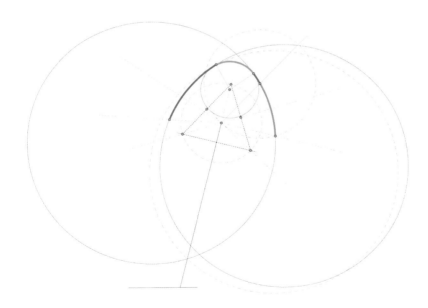

7.4: An underlying diagram of tangential circles create a continuous arc composite with
smooth transitions.
Source: Onur Yüce Gün and KPF.

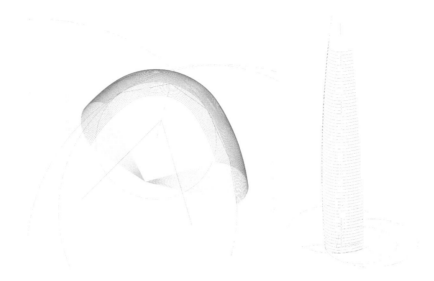

7.5: The composite base curve (in Figure 7.4) is trimmed by trimming lines (in orange) as
it is carried upward to generate all oor slab perimeters. Note the twisting effect created
by rotating the trimming lines.
Source: Onur Yüce Gün and KPF.

The composite slab perimeter curve scales as it moves along a vertical arc. The
manipulation of both the vertical arc and the composite slab perimeter curve
defines the overall form of the building, controlling the amount of tapering
and the maximum width in the middle of the building. When swept along one
of the base arcs, the vertical arc creates a torus patch. Since the base comprises
three co-tangential arcs, the resulting geometry is a compound surface of three
torus patches. However, the transitions between these patches are smooth since
the composite curve arcs have tangential continuity.

The parametric model of the White Magnolia Tower was developed in Bentley s
GenerativeComponents®. This model can be driven by both global variables,
and by editing associative dependencies between the underlying geometries,
which dynamically update in connection to any change in a geometric part.
Once running, designers used the parametric model to generate variations of the
tower for further evaluation (Figure 7.6).

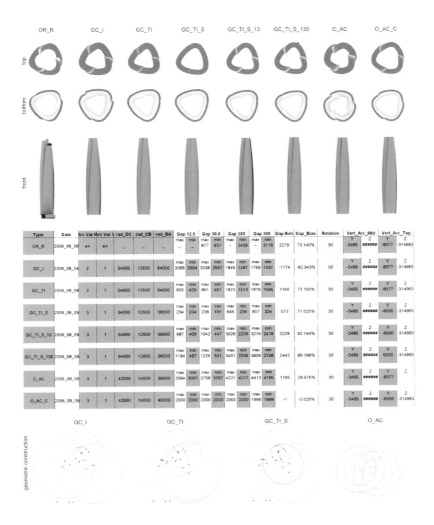

Type	Date	Arc Var H	Arc Var V	rad_DC	rad_CB	rad_BA	Gap 12.5		Gap 30.0		Gap 280		Gap 300		Gap Beh	Gap_Bias	Rotation	Vert_Arc_Mid		Vert_Arc_Top	
							max	min	max	min	max	min	max	min				Y	Z	Y	Z
OR_R	2006_06_06	e+	e+	–	–	–	~	~	877	837	~	3409	~	3116	2279	73.140%	30	-3495	######	-8377	-314963
GC_I	2006_08_04	2	1	54000	12600	54000	3089	2604	3038	2567	1845	1487	1759	1431	-1174	-82.043%	30	-3495	######	-8377	-314963
GC_TI	2006_08_08	2	1	54000	12600	54000	655	429	891	461	1623	1513	1878	1595	1166	73.100%	30	-3495	######	-8377	-314963
GC_TI_S	2006_08_09	3	1	54000	12600	36000	234	204	238	191	646	236	807	334	573	71.020%	30	-3495	######	-6000	-314963
GC_TI_S_13	2006_08_09	3	1	54000	12600	36000	987	409	1042	447	3026	2206	3215	2419	2228	82.144%	30	-3495	######	-6000	-314963
GC_TI_S_135	2006_08_09	3	1	54000	12600	36000	1164	487	1225	531	3401	2505	3606	2738	2442	89.186%	30	-3495	######	6000	-314963
O_AC	2006_08_09	3	1	42000	14000	36000	3694	3001	3758	3097	4221	4217	4413	4195	1195	28.476%	30	-3495	######	-8377	
O_AC_C	2006_08_09	3	1	42000	14000	40000	2000	2000	2000	2000	2000	2000	1999	1999	-1	-0.026%	30	-3495	######	-6000	-314963

7.6: Various towers as a product of the parametric model.
Source: Onur Yüce Gün and KPF.

During design studies the generated geometries were evaluated on both the ease and cost of construction and the proximity of the final form to the initial one. The visual shape of the tower also remained as one of the main considerations during the design studies (Figure 7.7).

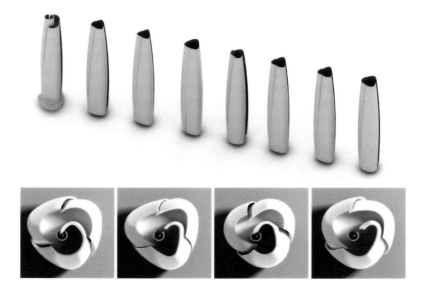

7.7: Preliminary renderings of tower variations. Note the differences regarding the gap between surfaces, and the varying visual sharpness created by different curvature values.
Source: Onur Yüce Gün and KPF.

Three-dimensional prints were used to compare and contrast the visual qualities of alternatives (Figure 7.8).

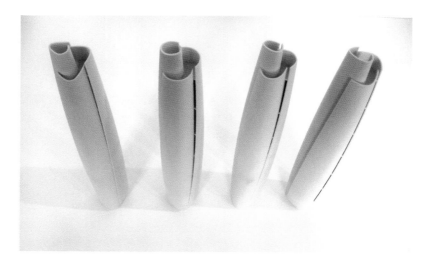

7.8: 3D prints help the designers understand the qualities of the tower form.
Source: Onur Yüce Gün and KPF.

In the next phase of the study, a script developed in McNeel s Rhinoceros[®] helped automate the tower panelization. The panel placement works as follows. The start point of the slab perimeter line is the centre of a circle, whose radius is equal to desired panel width. This circle intersects the slab perimeter line at a point, which determines the second base point for the panel. The next panel uses this second point of the first panel. The second point becomes the centre of the second intersecting circle, which determines the second point of the second panel. And the routine keeps creating the panels until it reaches the end of the slab oor perimeter line, and then the next oor is processed (Figure 7.9).

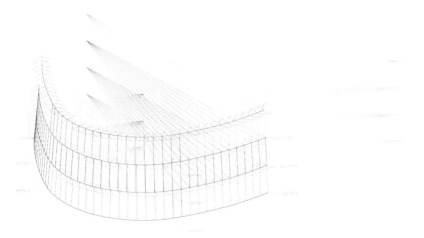

7.9: Each panel is created in reference to the previous one and to local geometrical guides. Source: Onur Yüce Gün and KPF.

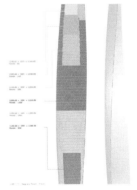

7.10: Panels grouped and colour coded with a 10mm tolerance in size.
Source: Onur Yüce Gün and KPF.

Once all the panels were created, they were grouped by their size and colour coded for a quick visualization of the number of panel types. A curtain wall construction tolerance of 10mm determined the boundaries between groups of like panels. With this technique, the tower can be panelized with six different panel types (Figure 7.10).

Computational design methodologies developed for the White Magnolia Tower in uenced KPF s ongoing studies for numerous towers, which, at the time of writing, were either under construction or confirmed for construction around the world. For example, geometrical models and construction documentation of the CSCEC Tower in Pudong, Shanghai and F3–F5 Towers in Songdo, South Korea, each extend the studies done for the White Magnolia Tower.

Design studies of the White Magnolia Tower kept the overall form appealing and interesting while achieving practical curtain wall construction. As the KPF (New York) Computational Geometry Group, we exhibited in several events and exhibitions, including the SIGGRAPH 2008 Design Computation Gallery in Los Angeles. During the preparation of this exhibit, we explored additional experimental structural façade patterns (Figure 7.11).

7.11: Fiber-façade: An interpretation by the KPF (NY) Computational Geometry Group as shown in the SIGGRAPH 2008 Design Computation Gallery.
Source: Onur Yüce Gün and KPF.

7.2   Designing with bits: Nanjing South Station

Kohn Pedersen Fox New York entered a competition for the Nanjing South Station, which was planned as part of China s high-speed and regular service railroad system. The station is sited in a shallow valley and is bisected through its centre by a "green corridor" connecting the area s major parks. Inside the station the green corridor takes the form of an intermodal hall, around which the arrival hall is located, and on top of which runs the station s platforms and departure lounges. Above the elevated departure lounges, a large sweeping roof protects passengers from rain, sun and wind (Figure 7.12).

The conceptual non-parametric CAD model, prepared as the first 3D model of the station, reveals the initial design intentions around massing and geometric organization (Figure 7.13). Large canopies cover 500m-long platforms lying between the 15 train-tracks aligned on an east–west axis. However, the tracks themselves are not covered in order to admit sunlight onto the platforms. The canopies transform into arced stripes to define the intermodal hall in the middle of the building. Additional canopies connected to the middle of the station on the north and on the south accentuate the entrances.

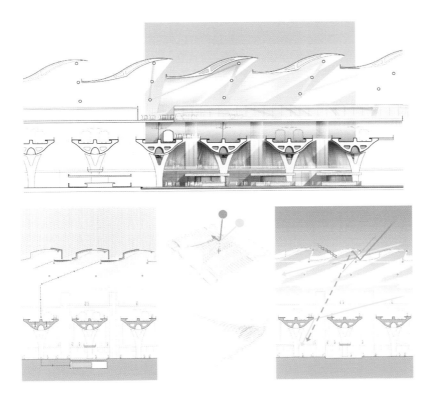

7.12: Section drawings prepared by the design team revealing the intentions about the performance of the sweeping roof. Note the scale of the roof surfaces in comparison to the trains and human figures.
Source: Nicholas J. Wallin and KPF.

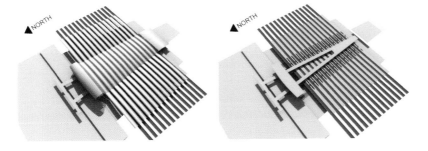

7.13: The first non-parametric digital model of Nanjing South Station prepared by the design team, showing the sweeping roof on the left and the train tracks on the right.
Source: David Malott and KPF.

The team intended an organic and uid form. Conventional non-parametric modeling requires that the very properties to be explored must be decided at the outset. Parametric modeling allows such decisions to be deferred to the end.

179

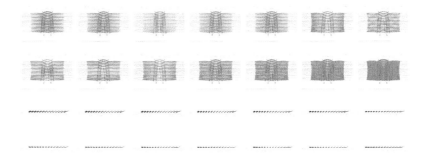

7.14: A parametric model enables the design team to generate and discuss various formal configurations.
Source: Onur Yüce Gün, Stelios Dritsas and KPF.

With references from the non-parametric CAD model, a basic parametric model was built in GenerativeComponents® to explore more formal organizations (Figure 7.14). In this model a global perimeter surface hosts all individual canopy surfaces as continuous forms. Simple parameters update the width and height of these surfaces enabling quick exploration. At this stage, the specific parametric relationships were less important than the overall form. Precise control came later.

In this more advanced modeling phase, a generative S-shaped section plays the main role in defining the characteristics of the surfaces. Although individually simple, under composition and parametric control the S-curve creates a range of different formal conditions (Figure 7.15). These include the steepness and depth of surface, and the amount of projection towards the side. A splitting function divides the S-curve at the higher portion of the roof, tearing an extra opening for more sun exposure where necessary (Figure 7.16). The split basically occurs right in the middle of the S-curve: while one half is elevated, the other remains in its place. The split ends are then tied with a vertical connector. The ends of the S-curves connect to the main structural elements below in a similar fashion. The connection angles are manipulated in reference to the underlying structural elements.

Various configurations, deformations and transformations of simple S-curves, driven by global rule sets and internal parameters for local adaptations, define the characteristics of the surfaces. While driving and determining the design form, these curves remain invisible. The resulting design form affects re ection from and penetration to the station of direct sunlight, as well as water drainage. Solar insolation in each season is affected in a similar manner (Figure 7.17). The final design configuration is a result of these rule-sets imposed on the S-curve system, rather than being a "hand-crafted" geometry.

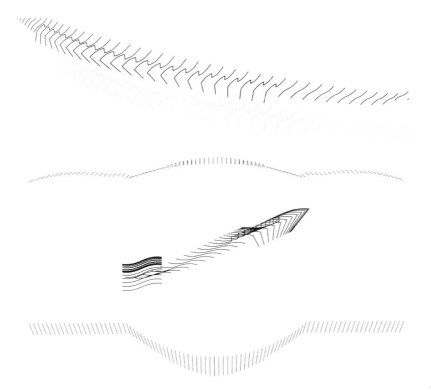

7.15: Simple S-curves and their power of generating variations.
Source: Onur Yüce Gün and KPF.

7.16: A split function creates a gap right in the middle of the S-curve, which is then connected with a linear member.
Source: Onur Yüce Gün and KPF.

While the exibility and freedom in the exploration phase helps discovery of different formal organizations (Figure 7.18), the limitations and constraints defined in the parametric system help develop precision and higher control over the geometry in later phases.

7.17: Solar insolation simulations done for spring, summer and fall give ideas about overall solar exposure of the roof surface.
Source: Onur Yüce Gün, Stelios Dritsas, Mirco Becker and KPF.

181

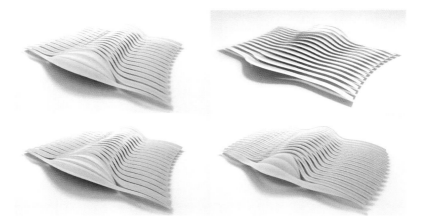

7.18: Variations derived from the source parametric model.
Source: Onur Yüce Gün and KPF.

The behaviours defined over the S-curves imposed constraints on geometric outcomes. This way, the model could be called pre-rationalized. With some anthropomorphic license, we can claim existence of a certain awareness in the model; it does not violate boundaries, either stopping or failing as it does. Most of the time it warns the user of impending failure. Thus there is some sort of intelligence, or at least part of the designers intelligence, embedded in it.

These efforts require custom tool-making, as the generic tools provided by CAD platforms are insufficient to resolve all the geometric requirements and intentions of even moderately complex building models (Figure 7.19). In this case, the GCScript language was used to construct arrays of nodes for references and generating geometric forms.

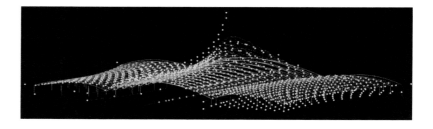

7.19: The Nanjing South Station model including data in various ranges, from the column layout to roof panelization.
Source: Onur Yüce Gün and KPF.

The parametric model helped generate the structural scheme via the creation of geometric placeholders – points, lines and curves. Files of these placeholders were passed to the structural consultant for analysis. The feedback from the consultants helped update the form towards greater structural efficiency.

The final form reveals the team s discovery of "gestural" form, especially when compared to the initial CAD model (Figure 7.20). Instead of a rapid uctuation in geometry, the canopies now rise and break apart in the middle to celebrate the intermodal hall. The entrances on the north and south are highlighted by projections. The train station represents a unified form, enabled by relating parts through common geometry and logic. Any manipulation on the global form dynamically updates the form of each canopy.

7.20: The Nanjing South Station entry became one of the two competition finalists. Source: KPF.

A 1/400 scale model, approximately two meters long, was built in China using the digital documentation. This was a rehearsal of actual construction since all the structural members and surface pieces were prototyped. The model, when complete, gave ideas about the configuration of the ribs supporting the canopies and the qualities of the double curved surfaces comprising the overall form.

7.3 Alternative design thinking

The two distinct projects shown here have much in common. The designs for the White Magnolia Tower and the Nanjing Train Station cover a wide range of concerns. Their studies are neither purely technical nor purely aesthetic. On the contrary, the tools developed for each design empower form-finding under technical constraint. Designs today require so many inputs that they no longer are, or can be, one "master s sketch". Likewise, they cannot be a technician s product. The competitive profession of design demands that a firm s whole knowledge be used. Successful design is a complex process done in teams.

Parametric models can carry the needed design complexity. They can embed multifaceted design concerns into a relational digital model. In contemporary practice, the design model is a exible entity that can be generated, manipulated and re-organized to produce elegant wholes comprising highly customizable and controllable interconnected parts.

Chapter 8

Patterns for parametric design

Abstraction is the hardest new skill for designers. Why? It involves thinking more like a computer scientist than a designer. But does it? Designers employ abstraction all the time as they organize projects and drawing sets. Removing unneeded detail helps keep focus on the issues to hand. Abstract representation enables progress on concrete issues such as circulation, light and structure.

Just as a designer would never specify a building (beyond a doghouse, of course) completely in a single drawing, a parametric modeler should never work in a single model. A complex model is made of (mostly reusable) parts.

Reusable, abstract parts are a keystone for professional practice. Over several years, my research group at Simon Fraser University has used design patterns to understand, explain and express the practice and craft of parametric design. In addition to the the patterns themselves, group members have written theses (Qian, 2004; Marques, 2007; Sheikholeslami, 2009; Qian, 2009) and publications (Qian and Woodbury, 2004; Woodbury et al., 2007; Qian et al., 2007, 2008). Ours is a shared enterprise; throughout this chapter, I use the first person plural to describe what we did together.

A pattern is a generic solution to a well-described problem. It includes both problem and solution, as well as other contextual information. Patterns have become a common device in explaining systems and design situations (Week, 2002; Tidwell, 2005; Evitts, 2000; van Duyne et al., 2002; Gamma et al., 1995). Authors express patterns in various ways. Here we adapt Tidwell s (2005) direct and self-explanatory style comprising *Title, What, Use When, Why, How* and *Examples*. The *Title* should be a brief and memorable name for the pattern. *What* uses an imperative voice describing how to put the pattern into action. *Use When* provides the context needed to recognize when the pattern might be applied. *Why* motivates the pattern and outlines the benefits that accrue to its use. *How* explains the pattern s mechanics. For us, a distinguishing feature of a pattern is that it explains its mechanism, that is, all instances of the pattern have similar symbolic structure. Examples, which we call *Samples,* provide concrete instances of the necessarily abstract pattern descriptions.

Patterns use the imperative voice. They are normative, describing what should or might be done. They have ancient precursors. Throughout Western history at least, authors have codified practice through text. Vitruvius s *The Ten Books on Architecture* (Pollio, 1914) is the sole architectural text surviving whole from Roman times. From the Renaissance comes Palladio s (1742) *The Four Books of Architecture*. In the 19th Century, Ruskin s (1844) *Seven Lamps of Architecture* looked largely to long past works as the basis for practice. In the 20th Century, Alexander (1979) gave the common "pattern" a specific meaning as a "Pattern" – a formal, rhetorical device expressing design intent. To a computer scientist or linguist, it seems obvious that Alexander was in uenced by the computational thinking of the time, particularly by Noam Chomsky s grammars. Alexander built a philosophy of architecture around his patterns. He used phrases such as a "Timeless Way of Building", "a process necessary for good" and "a quality without a name" to prescribe how people should use patterns in the world.

In the late 20th Century, software engineering discovered Alexander s work. In software, patterns became a tool to explain informal mid-level compositional ideas in computer programming (Gamma et al., 1995). The software engineers dropped all of the philosophy, leaving only the device itself. Their justification came from the world; they saw patterns as effective devices for achieving design goals. They grounded specific patterns in shared expertise within a group of authors and reviewers. Each design pattern systematically names, explains, and evaluates an important and recurring design in object-oriented systems. They intended patterns to help users choose design alternatives that make a system reusable and avoid alternatives that compromise reusability. The publication of Gamma et al. s (1995) book tipped the concept of design patterns to worldwide popularity in the domain of software engineering and other fields.

We now understand that patterns are useful because they foster communication. Rather than having to explain a complex idea from scratch, a group of designers can just mention a pattern by name. Everyone will know, at least roughly, what is meant. Through such sharing patterns have become a popular vehicle for the collection and dissemination of practices and semi-formal ideas.

Our patterns aim to help designers learn and use propagation-based parametric modeling systems. We have largely focused on the GenerativeComponents® system as this allows us to access a large group of designers who are currently learning both the system and the computational concepts underlying propagation-based systems. While we expect that our results could generalize to other systems, at the time of writing we have done limited trials in CATIA® and SolidWorks®. Tsung-Hsien Wang and Ramesh Krishnamurti (2010) have implemented all of our patterns in Rhinoceros®.

We intend that our patterns capture these acts of authorship, above nodes but below designs. Patterns can aid learning. We have taught parametric modeling to several hundred professionals and graduate students. Over time we noticed that our instruction has increasingly focused on this tactical level. We now use patterns as explicit elements in teaching and learning.

This chapter presents 13 patterns for parametric design, explaining each in the abstract and through several samples. Complexity increases throughout – the earlier patterns are simple, the later ones more involved. They group into five categories. The first pattern is in a class of its own; it calls for CLEAR NAMES throughout a model. CONTROLLER, JIG, INCREMENT and REACTOR outline basic model structuring techniques. Paired together, POINT COLLECTION and PLACE HOLDER convey a key method for specifying and locating compound objects. PROJECTION, REPORTER and SELECTOR present ways to abstract information from a model. The final three patterns, MAPPING, RECURSION and GOAL SEEKER, comprise the inevitable residual category of useful (and somewhat complex) ideas.

8.1   The structure of design patterns

Alexander (1979) defines a pattern as a three-part construct: context, problem and solution. His patterns have a common format: a picture (demonstrating a typical example), an introductory paragraph (to set context), a headline (essence of the problem), a long section (body of the problem), a paragraph explaining the solution, and a diagram of the solution. Gamma et al. (1995) use a graphical notation to describe design patterns and provide multiple concrete examples. Tidwell s user interface (UI) patterns (Tidwell, 2005) have a clear and strong structure: name, diagram (usually made by example screenshots), what, use when, why, how and examples. Patterns can be presented both in a formal structure and as a set of exible ideas. We build largely on software patterns (Gamma et al., 1995) and UI patterns (Tidwell, 2005) to develop a structure for parametric modeling design patterns as follows:

- **Name** is a noun phrase describing the pattern brie y and vividly.

- **Diagram** is a graphic representation of the pattern.

- **What** states a one-sentence description of the goal behind the pattern.

- **When** describes a scenario comprising a problem and a context.

- **Why** states the reasons to use this pattern.

- **How** explains how to adopt the pattern to solve the given problem.

- **Samples** illustrate the patterns with working code.

- **Related Patterns** show the connections among different patterns.

Of the eight pattern elements, samples are distinctive in our work in that they provide concrete, working code as pattern instances. We downplay the language aspects of patterns. Although many pattern authors aim for a complete pattern language that models a design s functional hierarchy, such comprehensiveness and authority proves itself elusive. In counterpoint, Week s (2002) short book of informally defined workplace patterns and Tidwell s (2005) extensive user interface pattern collection use simple categories of patterns and have achieved wide recognition with users and other experts.

8.2   Learning parametric modeling with patterns

Almost all computer manuals are example- and procedure-based. They take you through a series of worked examples, describing keystroke-by-keystroke what you must do to model the example. Some people learn well this way. If you do not, patterns may help. Through teaching parametric modeling to hundreds of people, we have developed a simple and effective three-step process. The first step is learning a minimal set of mechanical steps. You need to learn the basic interaction conventions of the modeler, a few modeling commands and succeed in making a very simple model. The second step is to make a model useful to you in your current work. Start with a sketch in any medium you wish; just make it quickly. Divide it into logical parts, so that each part can be modeled easily. We have found that good outside advice can really help you here. An experienced hand can clarify both the model and its division into parts. The third step is to model the parts and combine them into a whole. Here is where patterns shine. You will likely find that many of the parts resemble patterns (we derived the patterns largely from observing and interacting with designers as they worked). Copy and modify the pattern samples you think may be useful, combining each pattern sample into your model. The patterns will not make up the whole of your model, but the parts they do compose should be clear and clearly separate. This process helps you learn a powerful strategy you already know but in the new context of parametric modeling. Divide-and-conquer is a near-universal strategy in problem solving and design. It appears differently in each medium. In parametric modeling, patterns are one good manifestation.

8.3   Working with design patterns

We developed the design patterns in this book by working with and observing designers learning and using parametric modeling. Chapter 3 distills some of what we discovered into 14 classes of designer action. It would be no surprise if we argued that patterns may help in many of these, but such arguments are currently circular; we commit the *post hoc ergo propter hoc* fallacy when we use the same data to both form and verify theory. In the place of firm conclusions, I hypothesize that patterns can help design work and present several arguments supporting this hypothesis. In the rest of this section, I use the definite voice, presenting hypotheses as if they are established claims. The truth is that these are propositions to be tested by future research.

Four salient attributes of patterns is that they are explicit, partial (above nodes and below designs), problem-focused (shared problems) and abstract (generic).

Explicitness aids reflection. The acts of writing and reading patterns demands a mode of thought different from the flow of design. Like Schön s (1983) *reflection-in-action*, patterns provide a tool for advancing design skill. To write a pattern is to commit it to definite media for others to read in your absence. Patterns are a good tool for groups to build up a shared library of low-level modeling and design ideas. Though explicit, the samples in patterns are intended as throw-away code to be copied and modified at will. Since exact digital copies are freely available, samples cannot be ruined. Minimal work is lost in trying them out. Multiple samples for each pattern provide different roots from which to start. Pattern names are explicit handles for communication in design work.

That patterns are partial means they must be composed into designs. They provide parts with which to solve the "conquer" aspect of the divide-and-conquer strategy. By providing separate solutions to problem parts, they can help clarify the data flow through a model. Properly written, they are informal devices by which modules can be expressed in principle.

Patterns focus on solving problems. When well-written they state a problem and provide several clear solutions to it. They aid sketching by accelerating the creation of approximate models. They often combine geometric, mathematical and algorithmic insight. They demonstrate how to fuse these important and complementary skills.

Lastly patterns are abstract. To use them well evidences mastery of the "divide" part of divide-and-conquer. Using them at all helps develop the special form of divide-and-conquer demanded by parametric modeling.

8.4   Writing design patterns

Our research shows that writing your own design patterns may aid reflection on and reuse of design ideas. Patterns take time and effort to write, and return clarity and simplicity later. They can amplify your professional skill. To write a pattern is to listen to yourself and your colleagues. Are you doing the same thing again and again in variations? Can you describe it in a phrase? Do you have sample code that you reuse? If you answer "yes" to each of these questions, think about writing a pattern. Stick to the eight pattern descriptors. As you start, focus mostly on Name, What, When and How. Collect a set of Sample files. Look at these together to discover what they share. Refactor the code in each to be consistent. At this point, you may have the beginnings of a useful pattern. In the slow periods of your work, reflect on the pattern. Refine it for clarity and simplicity. Use it in your work. If it is useful, refine it again. Make it public within your group. Make it easy to find: online is best. Others may be interested in what you have done. Share it widely if you possibly can.

8.5   CLEAR NAMES
Related Pattern • ALL OTHER PATTERNS

Some likely good names

MainBeam3
RoofPanel
SouthFacade
DesignSurface
PlaceHolder
Truss8
Purlin8_3
Foundation
RoseWindow
Pane3_7
ColumnA_7
Hypotenuse

What. Use clear, meaningful, short and memorable names for objects.

When. Always, except for work you intend to throw away.

Why. Objects have names. You use these to remember how you have organized a model, to refer to parts as you create and edit links, and to communicate to others. Clear, meaningful, short and memorable names are a prerequisite for making a model useful beyond its immediate creation.

How. Good names are clear; they convey what you intend. They carry design meaning; usually they relate to form, function or location. They are as short as they need to be (and no shorter). A good and useful convention for concision is *CamelCasing,* putting words together with no spacing or linking punctuation and capitalizing each word (separate numbers with punctuation). Memorable names explain design concepts.

Some usually bad names

Point02
BSplineA
foobar
aardvark
here
there
angle6
parabola
thingamabob
IansPlane
abc
AfDrAp

Bad names are easier to invent than good ones. Perhaps the worst naming scheme is by object type. "Point01," "vector03" and "coordinateSystem06" provide no new information; the type of an object is one of its properties.

Naming is active. If you watch an experienced parametric designer, you witness a process of naming, re ection and renaming. As model complexity increases, this expensive refactoring returns a benefit. In its absence, modeling stalls in confusion and error. Be warned. Unless you are smarter than any parametric modeler I have ever seen, you need to attend carefully to the names of model parts. It takes time and effort, but returns capability and reliability.

Source for tag cloud:
www.wordle.net

8.6 CONTROLLER

Related Pattern ● JIG ● POINT COLLECTION ● REACTOR ● REPORTER ●
SELECTOR ● MAPPING

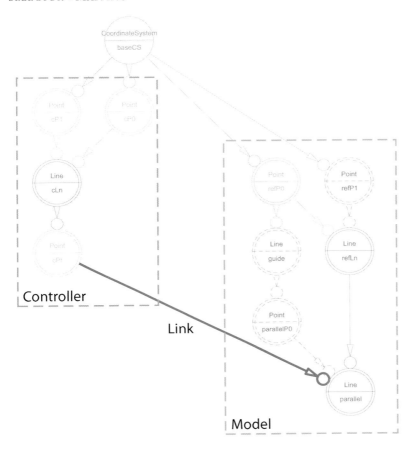

What. Control (a part of) a model through a simple separate model.

When. The essence of parametric modeling is the parameter – a variable that
in uences other parts of the design. Understanding how parameters affect a
design is a crucial part of the modeling process. Use this pattern when you want
to interact with your model in a clear and simple way, OR you want to convey
to others how you intend a model to be changed. *Remember, in the future you
may well be such another person if you have forgotten the model structure!*

Why. Isolating manipulations to a simple place away from the complex detail
of a model means that you can change the model more easily. Using a logic for
control that is different from the way the model is defined means that you can
use the most appropriate interaction metaphor. Changing a collection of objects
through a single interface simplifies the interaction task.

As models grow, so does the need for carefully considered CONTROLLERS. In particularly complex models, you may well design and implement a separate control panel that collects all of the CONTROLLERS into a single place in the interface.

How. A CONTROLLER can do either or both of the following: it can abstract an aspect of a model into a clear and simple device or it can transform an aspect of a model into a different form.

The key concept in a CONTROLLER is separation. You build a separate model whose outputs link to the inputs of your main model. The separate model is the CONTROLLER. It should express, simply and clearly, the way you intend to change the model.

CONTROLLERS can abstract or transform and they can do both at the same time. An abstracting CONTROLLER is a simple version of the main model that suppresses unneeded detail. Parameters on lines and curves are very simple cases of a CONTROLLER: they abstract a location on a curve into a single number. The layout of controls on a properly designed stovetop directly abstracts the layout of the burners. In contrast, the vast majority of stovetop controls fail to do this well.

A transforming CONTROLLER changes the way you interact with a model. For example, polar coordinates transform Cartesian coordinates into a different set of inputs. A rotating knob on a stovetop transforms the amount of energy delivered into an angle.

As one property changes in your model, one or more parts change; you can connect these changing properties to your model through a CONTROLLER. Then, you can simply change the CONTROLLER and see the result in your model. CONTROLLERS are thus independent – they have minimal connection to the model they control and are easily connected and disconnected as needed. This clear separation is the hallmark of a CONTROLLER: every well-designed CONTROLLER will have a symbolic model that shows only one or a scant few links between it and the model it controls.

CONTROLLER Samples

Vertical Line

When. Control the position of a vertical line on a curve with a CONTROLLER.

How. Curves and surfaces are complex objects. Their parametric structure is typically hidden from the interface – a point may move quickly in one part of a curve and slowly in another as its parameter changes. Further, curves and surfaces are usually part of a design. There may be many other objects around them that make it difficult to directly interact with their parametric points. Controlling a point on a curve through a parametric point on a line addresses both of these issues. You can see the relative parameterization of a curve point by examining its controlling point. Further, the controlling point can be in any position, near to or far from the model.

In this model, a single vertical line takes its position from a parametric point on the curve *pOnCrv*. The CONTROLLER is a line and a parametric point on it. Making the parameter of the point *pOnCrv* dependent on the point in the CONTROLLER transfers control from the curve to a straight line.

This is a very simple sample, but it demonstrates the essential idea of separation of control and model.

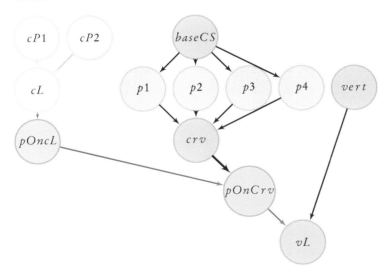

8.1: The CONTROLLER on the left joins to the main model on the right through only a single link. Such sparsity of connection is a hallmark of a CONTROLLER.

8.2: A simple CONTROLLER. The point on the line controls the point on the curve, which, in turn, is the base for a vertical line.

Line Length

When. Change the length of a vertical line with a slider.

How. This is a very simple sample of the CONTROLLER, but one that transforms a length in one direction to a length in another. Start with a vertical line and a horizontal CONTROLLER line. Connect the length of the vertical line to the parameter of the point on the CONTROLLER line. Moving the point in the CONTROLLER alters the length of the vertical line.

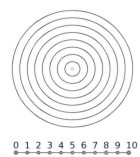

8.3: The previous sample maps the CONTROLLER S motion along a line to the controlled points motion along a curve. This CONTROLLER is less direct: it maps location along a line to the height of the controlled line.

Multiple Circles

When. Change the number of concentric circles with a slider.

How. The quantities controlled can be continuous (a real number) or discrete (an integer or member of a sequence or set). In this sample, a slider controls the numbers of concentric circles. The parametic point on the slider connects to the creation method of the circle. In this sample, the number of the circles is determined by the parameter of the point on the slider. As the parameter of the point changes from 0 to 1, the number of circles will change from m (in this case $m = 0$) to a predetermined number n. This CONTROLLER requires a mapping between $0 - 1$ and $1 - n$. The actual math is simple: the number of circles for a given parameter t is $\text{Floor}(t/(n-m))$. This idea of mapping though is so general that it has its own pattern: the MAPPING pattern.

Controlling a discrete result with a continuous slider creates visual dissonance: the slider seems smooth yet the result changes in steps. A typical solution is to mark the slider at the locations at which the number of discrete objects changes.

8.4: Control the number of circles in a model with a point on a line.

Cone Radii

When. Change the radii of a cone with a pair of concentric circles.

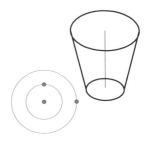

How. A single CONTROLLER can control multiple aspects of a design. Of course, this alone poses a design problem. The CONTROLLER must visually cohere with the object being controlled. In this sample, the aim is to control the top and bottom radii of a cone. The CONTROLLER maps from concentric, coplanar circles to the cone s top and bottom surfaces. Its circles are controlled by points on their boundary. Two links, one the radius property of each of the CONTROLLER S circles to the cone radii connect the CONTROLLER to the model. The CONTROLLER circles provide a visual reminder of the real objects being controlled: the top and bottom of the cone.

Most of the time, the relative size of the circles when compared with the cone suffices to distinguish the link between aspects of the CONTROLLER and model. Such geometric coincidence may fail to satisfy, for example, when viewing in perspective or when the two radii are very close. Other codes, such as colour (careful here!), text, line weight or graphic labels, might be useful.

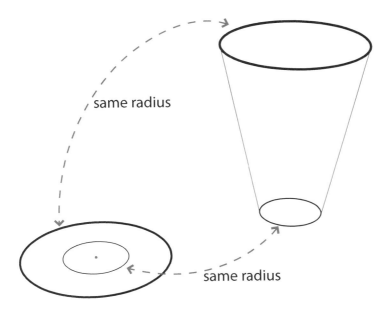

same radius

same radius

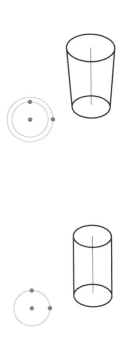

8.5: The CONTROLLER S circles visually map to the top and bottom of the cone.

195

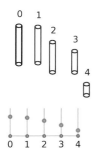

Equalizer

When. Adjust the height of multiple cylinders with an equalizer.

How. In this sample, the CONTROLLER takes advantage of a roughly linear arrangement of objects in the model by using the well-known design for a sound equalizer. The equalizer is a row of sliders, each interactively independent of the others. This design puts the controlled dimensions into visual proximity and thus reveals their relative sizes, which might well be obscured in the model due to location, size and perspective effects.

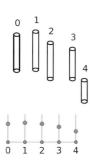

This CONTROLLER misses an important aspect of the design of a physical sound equalizer. With such a device an operator can use his or her entire hand to simultaneously control several dimensions and to achieve a smooth curve across dimensions. The computer mouse, with its relentless one-thing-at-a-time design impoverishes the potential interactivity of the CONTROLLER. Some of this could be recovered by using a REACTOR or SELECTOR pattern as part of the CONTROLLER itself.

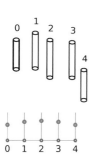

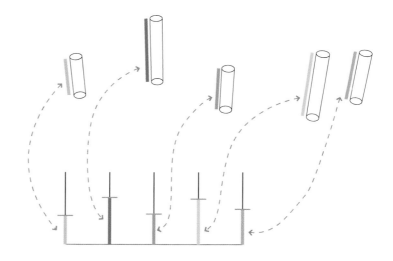

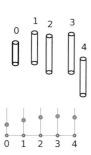

8.6: This CONTROLLER works like the familiar equalizer in sound systems.

Parallel Lines

When. Adjust the length and position of a line parallel to a reference line.

How. In this sample, a single CONTROLLER affects multiple parameters. It is the converse of the samples above, in which multiple independent controls form the CONTROLLER. A reference line establishes the direction and maximum length of the result line. The CONTROLLER comprises a single line carrying a parametric point. The line s direction and length determines the direction and length of a *guide* line that originates at one end of the reference line. A point on the guide line gets its parameter from the CONTROLLER and is the start point for the result. The result gets its direction from the reference and its length from the CONTROLLER.

If you move the CONTROLLER S parametric point, both the result s length and its distance from the reference change. If you move the CONTROLLER line, the guideline moves to remain parallel.

This CONTROLLER combines several of its properties (line length, direction and parametric distance) to control multiple aspects of its result (distance, length and radial position). It does this by combining controls, for example, both length and distance of the result line are a function of parametric distance along the CONTROLLER. Sometimes, such *interdependence* is both intentional and beneficial. More often though, it can confuse: the result of the CONTROLLER becomes opaque with increasing complexity in its relation to the model. Most usability experts, for example, Don Norman (1988), are highly critical of such linked controls.

Be warned: good CONTROLLERS can be hard to write.

8.7: The point on the control line controls both distance between the two lines and length of the controlled line.

Right Triangle

When. Create different right triangles with the same base.

How. The right triangle is a fascinating and useful geometric object. Some of its instances have Pythagorean triples as dimensions; its hypoteneuse is the diameter of its circumscribed circle; it combines to form rectangles; and the sum of its two non-right angles is 90°. Each of these could be the base for a CONTROLLER design.

This CONTROLLER uses the last of the above features, by using a half-circle to express the 180° triangle angle sum. The half-circle s base gives the direction and length of the resulting triangle base. Rays between the circle centre and two points on the circle represent the direction of the sides of the triangle. If these two points can move freely on the half-circle, they specify an arbitrary triangle. Presume that the half-circle has a $0 - 1$ parameter domain. If the parameter t of one of these points is constrained to the domain $0.0 - 0.5$ and the other to the domain $t + 0.5$, the generated triangle will always be right-angled. Further, all right-angled triangles can be reached.

This CONTROLLER reveals that right-angled triangles are but two-parameter objects: the hypoteneuse length and one angle suffice to uniquely determine the triangle up to a rigid body motion. It does visually invert both the angle and side when compared with the result. In reading across both CONTROLLER and model, you encounter the angles and lengths in reverse order. Some visual coherence has been traded for geometric insight.

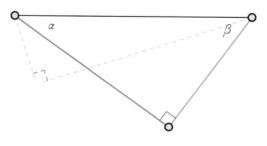

8.8: Controlling two angles fully determines a triangle if its base is known.

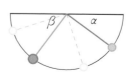

Hyperboloid of One Sheet

When. Abstract the geometry of a hyperboloid of one sheet to a plane.

How. A *hyperboloid of one sheet* is a ruled surface, that is, it can be formed from a sequence of straight lines. Further, it is doubly ruled: two such sequences can combine into a lattice, giving potential for structurally efficiency. Conceptually, a hyperboloid can be defined by twisting two parallel circles whose centres share a common line normal to the circles.

The hyperboloid s independent parameters are the radii of the two circles and the twist of one circle relative to the other. Starting with the CONTROLLER from the sample, add a twist control to one circle.

Of course, this CONTROLLER has limits. These range from −180° to 180° exclusive. A twist of 180° turns the hyperboloid into a cone. Two surfaces with twist parameter *a* and −*a* are geometrically the same but logically distinct. The difference is that the two sets of generating lines transpose. If one set carries information distinct from the other, the resulting design will differ as well.

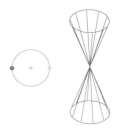

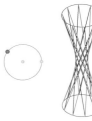

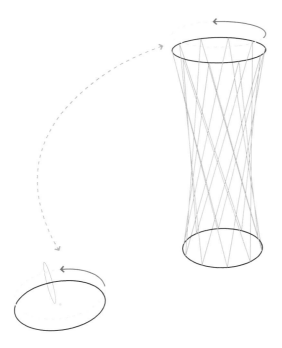

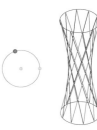

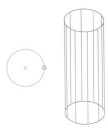

8.9: A single point on a circle maps directly to the degree of twist in a hyperboloid of one sheet.

Azimuth Altitude

When. Control a direction by its *azimuth* and *altitude*.

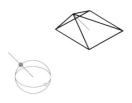

How. The *azimuth* of a point with respect to a reference is the horizontal angle from a reference direction. The *altitude* is the vertical angle from the horizontal plane. As controls, azimuth and altitude are independent: they specify clearly separate changes to a point. Of course, azimuth and altitude relate to two of the dimensions of a *spherical* coordinate system (*azimuth, zenith* and *radius*), with $zenith = 90 - altitude$.

An azimuth–altitude CONTROLLER comprises two concentric circles with equal radii: one horizontal and one vertical. A point on the horizontal circle determines both azimuth (where $azimuth = t * 360°$) and the vertical plane on which the altitude circle lies. A point on the altitude circle gives the altitude. The CONTROLLER is easily programmed to report the angles it produces.

In this sample, the model is simple: a pyramid with apex controlled by a line of fixed length and direction given by the CONTROLLER. Four points make the base of the pyramid. The start point of the controlling line is the intersection of the base diagonals. The direction is that of the azimuth–altitude CONTROLLER and the distance from start to end is a predetermined value, set outside of the CONTROLLER, in the model at large.

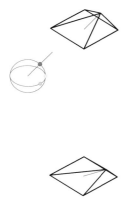

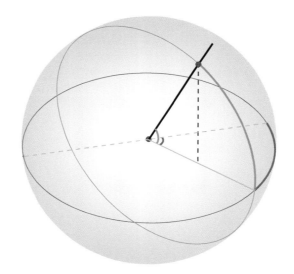

8.10: A complex CONTROLLER comprising separate controls for azimuth and altitude.

8.7   JIG

PATTERN ALIAS ● *Strut* ● *Reference*

Related Pattern ● CONTROLLER ● POINT COLLECTION ● PLACE HOLDER
● MAPPING

Source: Amy Taylor

What. Build simple abstract frameworks to isolate structure and location from geometric detail.

When. Designers sketch. Carpenters build jigs. Parametric modelers make JIGS. These acts share intent; they abstract away inessential detail, leaving only a simple framework that can be easily changed. Design sketches express structure and form. Carpenters jigs fix locations and tool paths in space. A parametric JIG mixes both of these traditions. Use this pattern when you want to quickly make and modify a simple version of your design and develop detail later.

Why. Most models contain many elements and a few controls. A JIG reduces the number of elements. It is an abstract model that reveals design structure and control behaviour without the distracting detail and slow interaction implied by a larger model. A JIG can be changed easily compared to a more complex model. Once developed, a JIG can be reused in other contexts, but only if it can be isolated from the rest of the model. JIGS are like abstracting controllers, but they are more specialized (they abstract a particular design). Further, JIGS typically describe the whole design and are embedded within the design rather than being separated from it. The design is built directly on top of the JIG.

201

How. A JIG should appear and behave as a simplified version of your intended design. A physical example is the strongback and stations used to build a small boat. The stations locate and support the hull when it is being constructed. Fairing, the process of making the hull smooth and continuous, can be done much more simply with a jig of stations than with a complete hull. JIGS are like construction lines in that they help locate elements. They are unlike such lines in that they are linked to the controls that enliven the parametric model.

JIGS typically connect to the model they control more richly than controllers, but still with a limited number of links. Most of these links should come from *sink* nodes. This is not a necessity – it is good programming style. Non-sink nodes capture the internal logic of the JIG. Connections from other than sink nodes run the risk of becoming invalidated when the JIG is refactored. In fact, if a sink node of a JIG is not used in the model it serves, it probably should not be there and can be deleted.

To make a JIG, you need to understand the parametric behaviour you want and how the JIG will be used to define the complete model. A good JIG typically has relatively few geometric inputs (for example, points, lines, planes, coordinate systems) and each of these is carefully named. The small number of geometric inputs allows you to easily locate the JIG. The names are the primary means by which you will understand the JIG when you (or someone else) reuse the JIG in the future.

Use the internal structure of the JIG to capture intended logical behaviour. For example, if the depth of a truss is proportional to its span, a JIG might comprise a line and a variable whose value is proportional to the length of the line.

Jig Samples

Controlled Surface Variation

When. Make variations starting from a surface with a parabolic cross-section. Use a Jig to model these variations in a controlled way.

How. Low-order curves and surfaces are easy to model and often display visual regularity that is difficult to achieve with higher orders. An order 3 curve can be represented by a higher-order curve by locating the control points of the higher-order curve in precise relation to those of the lower-order curve. In the curve literature this is called *degree elevation*.

A symmetric Jig comprising an upright and a crossbar provides a simple set of parameters that support controlled surface variations starting from a parabolic curve (see (a) below). To generate the control points of an identical order 4 curve from those of an order 3 curve (see (b)), divide the two sides of the order 3 control polygon in the ratio of 2 : 1 and 1 : 2 respectively. The order 5 control polygon divides the three sides of the 4 in the ratios 3 : 1, 2 : 2 and 1 : 3. Initially locate and size the crossbar to give these ratios. Varying the ratios (d) produces symmetric curves that are visually close to the parabola. Restoring the crossbar settings to the above defaults restores the initial parabolic surface section. This allows the designer to vary the surface cross-section in comparison to a known, simple and potentially fabricatable form.

(a)

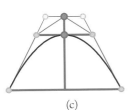

(c)

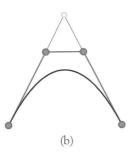

(b)

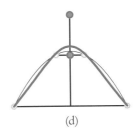

(d)

8.11: Two parameters give the overall height and width. Three more control variation away from the default parabola form: the proportional heights of the central points of the order 4 and 5 control polygons and the proportional width of the central points of the order 4 control polygon.

Tube

When. Use the local properties of a curve to determine the local radius and orientation of circular JIGS. Use the circles to define a tube. In turn use a curve as another JIG to apply a global form to the tube as a whole.

How. Start with a curve as the central path of the tube. See (a) below. It can be specified by four points with almost arbitrary x-, y- and z-coordinates. Along this curve, place a sequence of circles perpendicular to a global axis, here the y-axis. Evenly distribute the circles in parameter space, making the geometric spacing between circles vary along the curve. Each circle takes its radius from a property of its centrepoint, in this case the height above some external datum. In this sample, the radius is the absolute value of the centrepoint s z-value plus a small increment (to avoid the possibility of a zero or negative radius). Since these circles are the elements that construct the tube, they comprise a JIG.

Now (b) JIG the JIG. Make a simple curve using a low-order B-Spline. Substitute it for the existing curve used to define the JIG. The tube now re ects the simple, strong geometry of the curve.

Make (c) arcs comprising those parts of the circle JIGS above the xy-plane.

Lastly (d), change the planes on which the circle JIGS lie to be perpendicular to the defining curve, resulting in a subtle, but significant change to the tube s form.

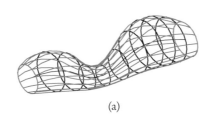

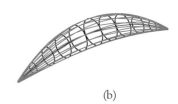

(a)

(b)

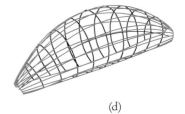

8.12: The control polygon for the JIG curve comprises three points only. In this sequence the middle point of the control polygon moves in all of the x-, y- and z-directions.

(c)

(d)

Sheet

When. Simplify controls for a surface by relating them to a quadrilateral.

How. Standard surface controls can provide too much freedom. This sample reduces the control available to model a surface by ensuring corner tangency conditions. It still provides a wide range of visually logical variation.

The JIG is hierarchical – it comprises JIGS built on JIGS, as shown below. The first JIG (a) is a quadrilateral, which may be planar or not. The second JIG (b) has two parts. The first comprises struts at each vertex, each perpendicular to the local plane of the quadrilateral (defined by the vertex and its predecessor and successor vertices). The second adds frames at the end of each strut, such that the *x*-axis of the frame aligns with the successor vertex and the *y*-axis with the predecessor vertex, but in the opposite direction (the quadrilateral has right-hand rule orientation, so the frame s *y*-axis has the same direction as the vector from the predecessor vertex to the vertex itself). The third JIG (c) comprises curves with end tangents defined by the *x*- and *y*-directions of the frames. The result (d) is the surface itself with the curves as its defining boundary.

The controls for this JIG comprise the quadrilateral itself and the four strut lengths. Each enters the system at a different level of the JIG.

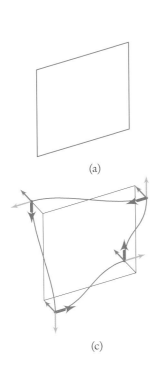

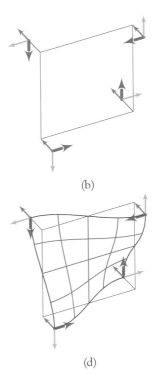

(a)

(b)

(c)

(d)

8.13: Four lengths, one for each of the corner struts, are sufficient to access a wide range of surface geometry.

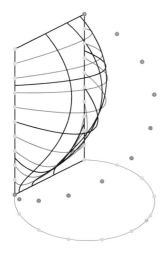

Scallop

When. Use the shape of a scallop as a point of departure in a search for form. The actual surface will be analogous to, but not a copy of, a scallop.

How. In plan, the geometry of a scallop is approximately that of a circular arc. The base of the scallop is a chord of the arc. Any point on the edge of the circle will subtend a constant angle with the base.

The idea is to "open" up the base of the scallop – to turn it from a line into a vertical rectangle. This JIG comprises a sequence of triangles on horizontal planes arrayed vertically from the base line. The apex of each triangle is the projection of a point on the circle onto the plane of the triangle. This JIG has three parameters: the angle subtended on the circle, the spacing of base points on the circle and the vertical spacing of the JIG elements. CONTROLLERS could be put on each of these to open a design space for the surface.

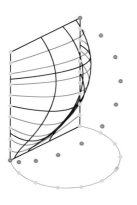

The generating triangles are actually modeled as order 2 B-Spline curves. This and the order of the surface itself give two additional controls. The resulting forms are far from the original scallop point of departure.

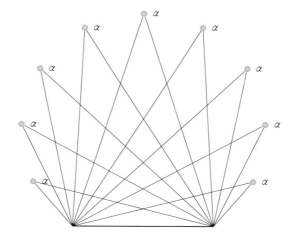

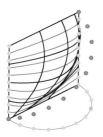

8.14: Developed initially from the constant angle subtended from a chord on a circle, the JIG for this design opens a space of related designs.

8.8   INCREMENT
Related Pattern • POINT COLLECTION • MAPPING

What. Drive change through a series of closely related values.

When. Parts may be similar in structure but vary in their inputs. Very often, input variations are gradual from part to part and parts in sequences or other arrangements are similar to their neighbours. Use this pattern when you are making collections of related parts.

Why. Being able to relate and edit parts through gradually changing inputs lends surety and control. As a form-making strategy, gradual change provides a background against which a strong figure can play.

How. Gradual change occurs in two forms. The first is the integers, stepping in units of one from low to high,

$$\ldots -1, 0, 1, 2, 3, \ldots$$

The second is the reals, varying continuously (infinitely divisible). Taken by themselves, the integers and reals can express only limited kinds of change. Functions transform sequences of integers and sampled reals into new sequences that may be dramatically different from the originals.

In turn, an INCREMENT uses the output of a function to drive change in any of a variety of ways, limited only by imagination. Length, size, angle, orientation, distance, colour, transparency and surface texture can all be changed in orderly (and disorderly) ways through incrementing along sequences of integers or reals.

The samples in this pattern develop increasingly complex curves traced by a single point moving through space. Each successive sample increases both the number of parameters on which an increment applies and the complexity of the incrementing functions. Throughout each sample, the structure of the model remains constant; only the values of the parameters change.

Even a single point can demonstrate the basic structure of an increment. Start with a point in space, located as it must be with respect to a coordinate system.

The point can be thought of having either Cartesian (x, y, z) coordinates or cylindrical (r, θ, z), where r is the radius, θ is the azimuth angle and z is the height of the point. Use cylindrical coordinates and increment the azimuth angle θ to make the point trace out an arc. If the azimuth angle increments from 0° to 360° the arc becomes a circle. Increment the radius to turn the arc into a spiral.

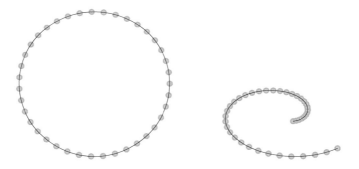

Incrementing the height of the point turns the arc into a helix and brings us to the first sample below.

INCREMENT Samples

Circular Helix

When. Move a point uniformly around a centre and upward in space.

How. As a point moves around the circle, increment its height by a uniform amount. The result is to trace out a simple circular helix.

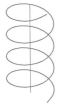 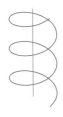  

Conic Helix

When. Add a reducing radius increment to change a circular to a conic helix.

How. In addition to the two increments (angle and height) for a circular helix, reducing the radius incrementally from an initial value to a minimum value produces a conic helix, that is, a helix whose points lie on a cone.

Tapered Radius Spiral

When. Taper the radius of a conic helix to produce a spiral.

How. As a point on a conic helix moves upward its radius shrinks. The point can be imagined to have a parameter that is 1 at the helix base and 0 at the top. Squaring this parameter will still result in a series that goes from 1 to 0, but the series will taper across this interval. Mathematically, the curve changes from a helix to a spiral.

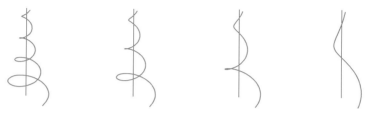

Tapered Height Spiral

When. Taper the height of a conic helix to produce a spiral.

How. Instead of tapering the radius, taper the height with the same device, by squaring the parameter. In this case, the parameter is 0 at the helix base and 1 at the top. The helix, now a spiral, appears to have been differentially stretched from its base to its top.

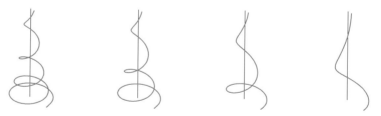

Tapered Radius and Height Spiral

When. Combining increments yields unpredictable forms.

How. Combining both radius and height tapers can be done independently in the model. They do not affect each other computationally, but combine in the geometric result. They produce a spiral that would be hard to conceive of itself, but naturally emerges from the parameterization.

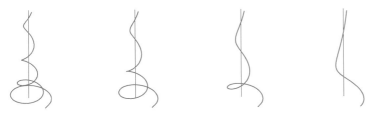

Elliptical Tapered Radius and Height Spiral

When. Change a circular spiral to an elliptical one.

How. In the prior samples, the radius, angle and height were independent in the model. In this sample, the radius becomes a function of the angle, by using a polar equation for the radius of an ellipse. If an ellipse has major axis of $r = 1$ and minor axis of $s = 0.5$, the radius as a function of θ is

$$\frac{rs}{\sqrt{r^2\cos^2\theta + s^2\sin^2\theta}} = \frac{0.5}{\sqrt{\cos^2\theta + 0.25\sin^2\theta}}$$

8.9   POINT COLLECTION

PATTERN ALIAS ● *Point Set* ● *Point Grid*

Related Pattern ● CONTROLLER ● JIG ● INCREMENT ● PLACE HOLDER ● PROJECTION ● RECURSION

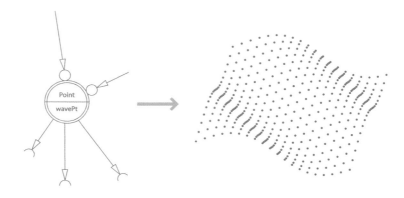

What. Organize collections of point-like objects to locate repeating elements.

When. Most designed artifacts have repeating elements. These may vary by both their absolute position and by their spatial relationships with nearby repeating elements. Use this pattern when you are able to think about the size and location of repeating elements in terms of a set of defining points.

Why. A collection of points organized to capture intended spatial relationships can greatly simplify the process of further model development. This saves time and effort in both modeling and reuse of a model in new contexts.

How. Point-like objects may be located in Euclidean space or parametric space, so a collection can be specified in either space. Euclidean space is the familiar space of everyday life. It can be represented through Cartesian, cylindrical or spherical coordinates. Most curves and surfaces (those defined internally by parametric equations) define a moving frame that gives locations on the curve or surface. Unlike those of Cartesian space, these parametric formulations may not preserve constant distance, either geometrically or along the defining object.

Use a collection of point-like objects as the input to define repeating elements. The logical structure of a collection is important – it provides the relationships through which points can be used to define objects. For instance, a collection structured as 2D array provides for each point P_{ij} easy access to the surrounding points, that is, $\dot{p}_{gh}$, where $g \in \{i-1, i, i+1\}$ and $h \in \{j-1, j, j+1\}$. In comparision, a collection structured as a tree provides for each point P, easy access to parent(P) and children(P).

The following samples specify POINT COLLECTIONS with functions. A given parametric system will provide its own particular commands for organizing collections, for example, replication in GenerativeComponents. The uniform and universal function notation here allows comparison among the samples.

POINT COLLECTION Samples

Spiral

When. Place a sequence of points along a spiral.

How. A spiral is a curve that turns around an axis at a continuously varying distance perpendicular to the axis. Spirals admit many parameterizations: this sample uses count, heightStep and radius. Count controls the number of points in the collection. HeightStep is the height increment between sequential points, not the entire height of the spiral. Radius decides the outer radius of the spiral: the distance from the first point of the spiral to the central axis. The function below generates a spiral.

The update method ByCylindricalCoords, which generates the actual spiral points, takes four arguments: a coordinate system, the point s distance from the origin, the point s angle of rotation from the x-axis, and the point s height above the xy-plane.

```
1  function spiral (CoordinateSystem cs,
2                   int count,
3                   double radius,
4                   double heightStep)
5  {
6    Point spiralP = {};
7    double radiusInt = 0.0;
8    for (int i = 0; i < count; ++i)
9      {
10       spiralP[i] = new Point();
11       radiusInternal=radius*(1—Pow(i/count,0.5));
12       spiralP[i].ByCylindricalCoordinates(cs,
13                                 radiusInternal,
14                                 30.0*i,
15                                 i*heightStep);
16     }
17   return spiralP;
18 };
```

8.15: Few can predict the form of the spiral from its parameters alone. In form-finding, designers typically iterate through cycles of coding and parameter play.

Parabola

When. Arrange a sequence of points along a parabola.

How. Simple mathematical functions pervade the modeling act. Functions must be described mathematically to work at all, and it pays to use evocative names for their variables. For example, the parabola $y = kx^2$ scales the most simple parabola $y = x^2$ in the y-direction by the factor k.

Placing count points along the parabola yields both the POINT COLLECTION and its organization as a linear sequence. Algorithmically, a *for-loop* steps through the points, adding each at the end of the sequence in turn. Sampling at count equal intervals along the domain of the parabola function yields an unequally spaced collection of count points. Thus the function below generates a POINT COLLECTION as a sequence along the parabola.

```
1  function parabola(CoordinateSystem cs,
2                    int count, double scale)
3  {
4    Point pointOnParabola = {};
5    for (int i=0; i < count+1; ++i){
6      pointOnParabola[i] = new Point();
7      pointOnParabola[i].ByCartesianCoords(cs,i,0.0,scale*i*i);
8    }
9    return pointOnParabola;
10 };
```

At the risk of repetition, this collection is a sequence – an array. Its members thus have indexes, that is, integers giving each member s position in the array. Members of pointOnParabola can thus be addressed as "pointOnParabola[i]", where i = 0...count−1.

Designers are often more interested in controlling the output range over which a function is used rather than its input domain. For example, to place a sequence of points along the part of a parabola below a given upper limit requires that the input to the function be scaled as in the following code.

```
1  function parabolaInRange(CoordinateSystem cs,
2                           int count,
3                           double scale, double range)
4  {
5    Point pointOnParabola = {};
6    double xStep = Sqrt(range/scale)/count;
7    double x = 0.0;
8    for (int i=0; i < count+1; ++i){
9      x = i*xStep;
10     pointOnParabola[i] = new Point();
11     pointOnParabola[i].ByCartesianCoords(cs,x,0.0,scale*x*x);
12   }
13   return pointOnParabola;
14 };
```

8.16: Several point collections, each along the positive arc of a parabola, each scaled by a real parameter. As this scale parameter increases, so does the slope of the parabola. The model limits the output range from zero to a set maximum value. The collections input parameters are spaced so that each has an equal number of points.

214

Waves

When. Simulate a waveform with a two-dimensional collection of points.

How. POINT COLLECTIONS in the previous two samples are one-dimensional. A two-dimensional collection can be organized as an *two-dimensional array*, an array of arrays. This sample demonstrates how to create such a two-dimensional collection. The generating function $f(x, y)$ is a sum of two sine functions, with two arguments taken respectively with domains along the x- and y-directions. The particular parameterization here comprises count the number of points in each direction (and the dimensions of the array), size the geometric extent of the collection in the x- and y-directions, amplitude the height of the wave function and startAngle the angle at which the sine curves starts.

A pair of nested *for-loops* makes the algorithm step through the points, row by row, defining each in turn. The structure of the algorithm maps directly to the structure of the collection!

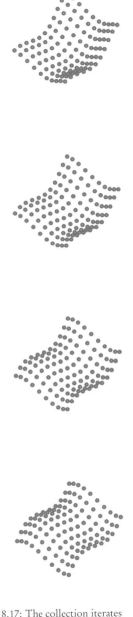

```
1  function wave (CoordinateSystem cs,
2                  int count,
3                  double size,
4                  double amplitude,
5                  double angleStart)
6  {
7    Point pt = {};
8    double anglei = 0.0;
9    double anglej = 0.0;
10   double ordinate = 0.0;
11   for (int i = 0; i<=count; ++i)
12     {
13     pt[i] = {};
14     anglei = (i/count)*360 + angleStart;
15     for (int j = 0; j <count; ++j)
16       {
17       pt[i][j] = new Point();
18       anglej = (j/count)*360 + angleStart;
19       ordinate = Sin(anglei) + Sin(anglej))*amplitude/2;
20       pt[i][j].ByCartesianCoordinates(cs,
21                               (j/count*size),
22                               (i/count*size),
23                               ordinate);
24     }
25   }
26   return pt;
27 };
```

8.17: The collection iterates through a complete sine curve in both parametric directions. The parameter angleStart has the greatest effect on the resulting form; it picks the place on the sine curve where the cycle begins.

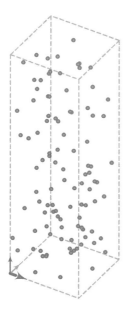

Point Cloud

When. Create a collection of random points to uniformly fill a volume.

How. The geometric and symbolic structures of collections need not be the same. Here, the symbolic structure is a sequence and there is no geometric structure, just randomness. This sample places uniformly-distributed random points within a rectangular bounding box. Its parameterization gives count, the number of points; lowerLeft, a frame defining the lower-left corner of the bounding box; and boundX, boundY and boundZ, reals that give the location of the upper-right corner of the bounding box. In this special case, the range of the function is a rigid body transformation of the domain. This means that the uniform distribution defined in the domain will persist into the range. Imagine using a random distribution in spherical coordinates. The points are random, but not uniformly distributed!

```
1   function cloud (CoordinateSystem lowerLeft,
2                   int count,
3                   double boundX,
4                   double boundY,
5                   double boundZ)
6   {
7     Point randomP = {};
8     for (int i = 0; i < count; ++i)
9     {
10      randomP[i] = new Point();
11      randomP[i].ByCartesianCoords(lowerLeft,
12                                   Random(0.0,boundX),
13                                   Random(0.0,boundY),
14                                   Random(0.0,boundZ));
15    }
16    return randomP;
17  };
```

8.18: A random sequence likely has little utility in design (but designers always surprise us). This sample shows that symbolic and geometric structures may have any kind of relation, including the null relation of randomness.

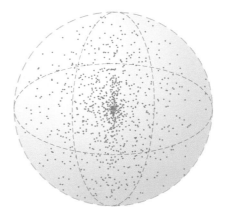

Points on a Parametric Curve

When. Position a sequence of points along a parametric curve.

How. A parametric curve provides both a curve and a way to place points along it. A sequence of points along the curve at intervals of its parameter t yields a collection of points in which the symbolic successor of a collection point is the geometric successor of the corresponding curve point. The sequence can be made either by replication or an explicit function (shown here). Section 4.10 introduces replication as a convention of specifying a collection of values for a node property. The collection causes the system to generate an object for each item of the collection in nodes using the replicated property.

```
1  function pointOnCurve (Curve curve, int count)
2  {
3    Point p = {};
4    double tStep = 1/(count−1);
5    for (int i = 0; i < count; i++)
6    {
7      p[i]=new Point();
8      p[i].ByTParameter(curve, i*tStep);
9    }
10   return p;
11 };
```

8.19: A collection organized by its members parametric position on a curve.

Points on a Parametric Surface

When. Array points on a parametric surface.

How. Analogous to a parametric curve, a parametric surface provides both a surface and locations on it through the parameters u and v. This gives a natural organization for the collection as an array of points, with neighbours in the array corresponding to neighbours on the surface. As with a curve, a surface can be generated by replication or by an explicit function.

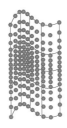

```
1  function pointOnSurface (Surface surface, int uCount, int vCount)
2  {
3    Point p = {};
4    double uStep = 1/(uCount−1);
5    double vStep = 1/(vCount−1);
6    for (int i = 0; i < uCount; i++)
7    {
8      p[i]={};
9      for (int j = 0; j < vCount; j++)
10     {
11       p[i][j]=new Point();
12       p[i][j].ByUVParameters(surface, i*uStep, j*vStep);
13     }
14   }
15   return p;
16 };
```

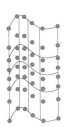

8.20: A collection organized by its members parametric positions on a surface.

8.10   PLACE HOLDER
Related Pattern • JIG • POINT COLLECTION

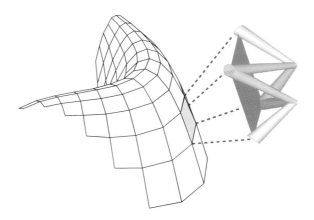

What. Use proxy objects to organize complex inputs for collections.

When. Designs have parts. A single model may represent many variations of a part, for example different window designs. An effective modeling strategy copies the model, one copy for each part, and adjusts the model inputs to each copy. Typically a part has multiple inputs – customizing each one is a lot of work. Use this pattern when you are able to describe the multiple inputs to a model through a smaller number (preferably one) of abstract proxy objects.

Why. A very common scenario arrays a module across a target surface or along a set of curves. If this module requires point-like inputs themselves defined on the target, organizing these inputs is sure to be complex and error prone. If you can define the inputs to the complex module through a simple construct such as a polygon, it is often much easier to place the module. An arrangement of polygons on the goal surface creates proxies on which the module can be later (and easily) placed.

How. PLACE HOLDERS have two parts. First is the proxy: a simple object that carries the module inputs. For example, a rectangular module requires four input points, one for each corner. A four-sided polygon can act as a proxy for these points: each of the vertices of the polygon provides one of the points. The proxy simplifies the arguments provided to the module: instead of four points, use only one polygon. The second part relates the proxy object to the model. For example, a polygon proxy can be placed using a rectangular array of points: the ij^{th} polygon s vertices are the points $\dot{p}_{i,j}$, $\dot{p}_{i+1,j}$, $\dot{p}_{i+1,j+1}$ and $\dot{p}_{i,j+1}$. The code placing a generic object such as a polygon is more simple and reusable than the code for a specific module.

PLACE HOLDER Samples

Hedgehog

When. Use a POINT COLLECTION as a PLACE HOLDER to locate and orient components (spines) that are perpendicular to a surface.

How. Every point on a surface defines a single frame comprising the surface normal and the vectors of principal curvature. This is sufficient information to place and size spine-like objects on the surface. The point provides location; the surface normal provides the direction for the spine; and the vectors of principal curvature provide information for further adapting the spine to context. Make a POINT COLLECTION structured by its u and v point-on-surface parameters. Instead of points, use frames – remember they have points inside them! Each of the frame points will serve as the base of a spine. Define two graph variables *count* and *height*. The POINT COLLECTION produces *count* frames in each parametric direction. At each of the frames, use the frame s z-direction and the parameter *height* to define a cone.

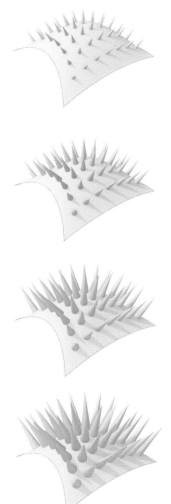

Kunsthaus Graz, Austria, by Peter Cook and Colin Fournier

Source: Anita Martinz

8.21: This simple PLACE HOLDER uses frame located on a surface to hold geometric information for placing cones.

219

Truss

When. Use lines as PLACE HOLDERS to locate the members of a truss.

How. Each member of a truss might carry information such as the member section, material, moment of inertia and modulus of elasticity. In addition, the parametric model for truss members may be able to shape its ends depending on the context in which it is placed. Placing a truss member though requires only the baseline along which the member lies. First, develop a feature representing a truss member and requiring only a line as a geometric input. Second (and in a new model!), create an abstract truss comprising line segments to represent the truss members. Applying the truss member feature to these baseline PLACE HOLDERS, places the detailed truss members. Of course, this simplifies a real truss member PLACE HOLDER in which the truss member parametric model would need sufficient information to shape its sectional properties and details. Taking this next step would require that the PLACE HOLDERS become spatially more sophisticated and that the truss member feature use that new information to specify its details.

Firth of Forth bridge, Scotland
Source: Kenneth Barker

8.22: A simple representation for the *Firth of Forth bridge* comprises three long and two short lines. These act as PLACE HOLDERS for more complex representations of the bridge segments.

Paper Folding

When. Use quadrilaterals as PLACE HOLDERS to simulate origami.

Source: Ray Schamp

How. Parametrically modeling folded paper is hard. The problem is physics – paper has actual dimensions and folds in it constrain the spatial configurations it can achieve. These real-world constraints inevitably imply that any model will require the solution of simultaneous equations, which propagation-based systems cannot do. (The GOAL SEEKER pattern gives a partial solution to this problem.) That said, design sketching is approximation and this sample shows a way to simulate a folded paper system, ceding from reality some dimensional variation in the individual panels.

In a folded structure, the pattern of folds can be thought of as separate from the size and location of the folded panels. Further, the folding pattern will belong to one of the 17 possible symmetry groups on the plane (each group represents one of the fundamentally different ways of arranging a collection of like motifs on the plane (Grünbaum and Shephard (1987, pp. 37-45); Weisstein (2009))). In each such group, there is a repeating module that imposes geometric conditions on where the paper edge must be to connect to the next module. The modeling task splits into three parts: the paper folds, ensuring geometric connection at the joints and arranging the resulting module across a surface.

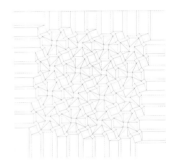

The choice of module is key to clarity and simplicity. This sample comprises a collection of identical parallelograms (for symmetry *a cianados*, arranged in symmetry group *pmg* in crystallographic notation). It is much simpler though to combine parts of six parallelograms to form a module needing only simple

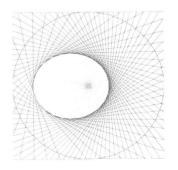

8.23: Some origami folding patterns.
Source: Ray Schamp

translational symmetry (symmetry group *p1*). Using two whole and four half parallelograms defines a module in which it is easy (or at least, easier) to relate the geometric boundary conditions to the proxy PLACE HOLDER.

To connect adjacent modules requires coincidence along each edge and at each vertex at which modules join. Four edge points connect two modules each and four vertex points connect four modules each. The edge points are easy: they lie at edge midpoints on the PLACE HOLDER, so are guaranteed to coincide. Vertex point coincidence requires that, at each vertex, adjacent modules share a common vector from the vertex to the module point. Here, this vector is a global property of the surface. With slightly more work, the PLACE HOLDER object could hold individual direction vectors at each of its vertices.

A POINT COLLECTION – a rectangular point array by *u* and *v* parameters on a parametric surface – locates a collection of quadrilateral polygons. Using these quadrilaterals as PLACE HOLDERS, the modules cover the surface to look like origami. They aren t of course: on a general surface, edge lengths will differ from the initial paper and polygons will be non-planar. Adding constraints can allow true folded paper models. For instance, the GOAL SEEKER pattern can be used to find feasible configurations for folding models of Persian Rasmi domes from single sheets of paper (Maleki and Woodbury, 2008).

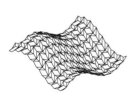

8.25: An approximation of folded paper geometrically attached to a surface.

8.24: A dome structure folded from a planar assembly of triangles. Source: Maryam Maleki

8.11   PROJECTION

Related Pattern • POINT COLLECTION • REPORTER • MAPPING

Source: Alexandre Duret-Lutz. Creative Commons Attribution Share-alike.

What. Produce a transformation of an object in another geometric context.

When. "Here" and "there" pervade design. Eyes, ears, the sun, lights, ducts, pipes, columns and beams all relate a "here" to some distant "there". Often a geometric line or curve provides the needed link. Use this pattern to construct coherent, reproducible relationships between "here" and "there".

Why. Projection is a simple, yet open-ended tool for producing new objects from old. Its origins lie in the Renaissance and before. For designers, it is most associated with the field of *descriptive geometry*, an 18th-Century invention (Gaspard Monge, 1827) and one which, until recently, was a mandatory part of design curricula worldwide. Descriptive geometry codified procedures for deriving two-dimensional drawings of three-dimensional objects by projecting the three-dimensional objects onto surfaces. Parametric modeling supports a much richer collection of projective ideas than was practical with older, manual techniques. With tongue somewhat in cheek, one could argue that parametric modeling is the 21st-Century replacement for descriptive geometry. The idea of projection has three parts: (1) a *source object* to be projected, (2) a *projector* or *projection method*, and (3) a *receiver*, the object on which the source object s projection appears. Its most simple form is orthogonal projection: points are projected onto a receiving plane such that the projection lines are perpendicular to the plane. The projection and intersection tools common in most parametric modeling systems enable a wide range of projective form-making ideas. The two main effects of projection are indirection and separation. With it, a model can be the indirect cause of a sculptural effect. With it, different object aspects can be separated into distinct views that may enable special views and inferences on the object. A very common example is a light (essentially a point source) that *projects* through a patterned screen onto a surface.

How. Every PROJECTION has the three above parts: (1) the projected object, (2) the projection method and (3) the receiving object. The projected object is a point or any composite of points: a line, ray, line segment, curve, polygon, surface, or 3D object. The three most common projection methods are *parallel projection* in which all projecting rays are parallel; *normal projection* in which the projecting rays are normal to the receiving object; and *perspective projection* in which all projecting rays pass through a single point. There are a wide range of other methods. For instance, cartographic projections can be explained as the mapping of parametric coordinates from one surface to another.

The common receiving objects are planes, polygons, surfaces, lines and curves, as well as composites of these. While possible, PROJECTIONS to points and 3D objects seem to be less common in practice.

A wide variety of projections exist (Anderson, 2009). Computing projections typically involves either mathematical projection or geometric intersection. Mathematical projection provides direct solutions to relatively simple cases such as projecting one vector $\vec{u}$ onto another vector $\vec{v}$ with result $\vec{w} = \frac{\vec{u} \cdot \vec{v}}{|\vec{v}|} \vec{v}$. More complex situations involve intersecting objects. For example, projecting a point onto a surface amounts to computing the intersection between the surface and projecting ray.

For simple cases, a parametric modeler will provide direct tools for computing projections, for instance, projecting a line onto a plane. It is a fact of life though that designers will push these bounds. In these more complex situations, using the PROJECTION pattern involves three steps: (1) sampling key object points, (2) projecting these points onto the receiver, and (3) reconstructing the object as projected on the receiver.

PROJECTION Samples

Surface Sampler

When. Project a collection of points onto a surface.

How. The mathematics of parametric surfaces ties both the surface shape and its uv-parameterization to the control polygon. Often, only part of a surface is actually needed in a design. Projecting a POINT COLLECTION onto the surface makes a subset of the surface with its own independent parameterization.

The source object is a point collection. In this sample, the collection lies on a plane and is a simple array, but other geometric and data arrangements can be used. The projector is parallel projection, with projecting rays being parallel to a line from the centroid of the collection to a controlling point in space. As an alternative, the projector could be a perpendicular line from the source plane and a control could allow the source to be moved within its plane. The receiver is the surface.

Shadows

When. Simulate a row of posts casting shadows on the ground.

How. Start from a line (abstracting a post) standing vertically on the xy-plane. Define a free point as the moving light. The *shadow point* is the projection of the free point onto the xy-plane. The shadow is a line between the base of the post and its shadow point. Replicating the startpoint of the posts gives a row of posts, each with its own shadow. In this case, the source is the free point, the projection is a perspective projection through the source and the receiver is the xy-plane.

8.26: The planar array of points projects to the surface. The geometry is that of the surface, the data organization that of the array.

8.27: This very simple sample illustrates the basic idea of projecting a source to a receiver using a method. In this case the method is simple perspective projection (all rays pass through a point).

Skylight

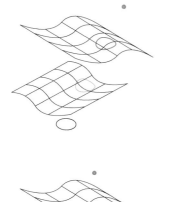

Source: Pieter Morlion

When. Create a daylight "lens" that focuses on a circle.

How. Two free-form surfaces represent a roof and a ceiling. The xy-plane is the floor. A circle on the floor can be daylit by projecting it through the ceiling and roof surfaces. The direction of daylight is nearly uniform, but the two separated holes will act as a very fuzzy lens to focus daylight on the circle. Similar to the *Surface Sampler* sample, the projection direction is controlled by a free point. If the direction is constrained to be within the sun's annual range, for a specific model instance the sun will shine directly on the circle exactly twice a year. If the direction is chosen to lie on either of the two solstice paths, this reduces to exactly once per year. Fixed architecture can have difficulty in responding to moving phenomena.

The projection of a circle onto a surface, or even an angled plane, is no longer a circle. While some parametric modelers provide curve-onto-surface projection tools, a good approximation can be had by projecting sampled circle points and reconstructing the curve from the projected points. The resulting curve will not exactly coincide with the surface in which it should lie. Alternatively, if the modeler has surface trimming tools, trimming the surface with a sweep of the circle along the projection line will yield a new surface with a hole.

When rotating the model, you can see that three circles perfectly coincide at a specific viewing angle (in a parallel viewing projection).

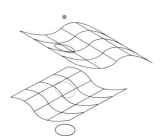

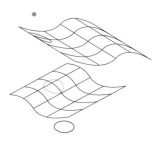

8.28: The point in space controls the location of a parallel projection of a circle through the two surfaces.

A famous example of projection used in form-making is Le Corbusier's 1953 *Monastery of Sainte-Marie de La Tourette* in France (shown in the image above).

Spotlight

When. Model a metaphorical spotlight projecting a circle onto several surfaces.

How. This sample is very similar to the previous one. The main difference is that all the projecting rays intersect at the light point. Each projecting ray starts from the light point and goes through the sampled points of the base circle. While rotating the model in a parallel projection view, you can see the projected circles do not coincide at any angle. If you use a perspective view the projected circles coincide when the camera and light source coincide.

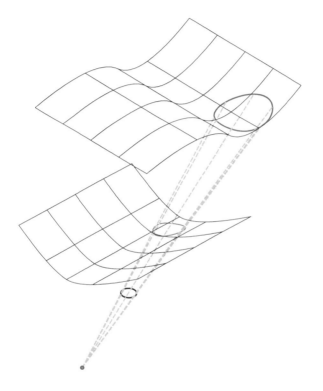

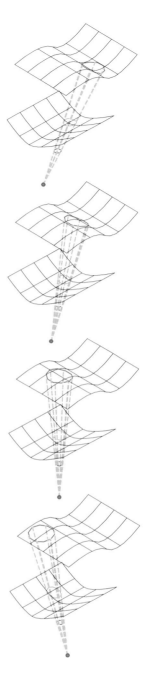

8.29: Projection through a point creates a cone of intersection through the surfaces. Two objects: (1) a projection point and (2) a circular "lens", control the projecting cone. In this case, the circle is parallel to the xy-plane – giving an ellipse as the result.

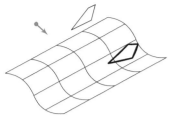

Solar Polygon Shadow

When. The shadow of a polygon cast by the sun on a curved surface.

How. The source is a polygon, the receiver a free-form surface. The projector is the sun, therefore the projecting rays are parallel.

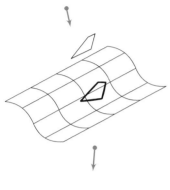

Straight lines project as curves onto a surface. For specific surface types, such as conic sections, closed-form equations for these curves exist. For free-form surfaces, approximations must suffice. Even though your favourite parametric modeler may have a curve projection tool, approximation techniques remain important tools in a modeler s kit. The key is sampling. Sample each source line with a sequence of points. The choice of how many points depends on the complexity of the receiving surface: high curvature and rapidly changing surface normals require more samples. Project the sampled points onto the surface and reconstruct a curve "on" the surface from the sampled points. The word "on" is advisory – the curve will not lie exactly on the surface. Much representation is approximation. If the curve and surface must exactly coincide, either sample very densely or find a modeler that supports exact curve-to-surface projection.

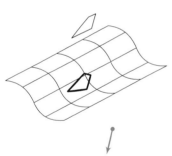

It is clear that the shadow is no longer bounded by four straight lines, but by four curves. Note too a further simplifying assumption. Non-planar polygons can be thought of as defining a minimal surface. If the source polygon is non-planar then its orientation must be such that no part of this minimal surface projects outside of the projection of the polygon s edges. Else, the shadow will not model reality. This may be good enough – again, much representation in design is approximate.

8.30: The boundary of the polygon projects onto the surface. The red vector controls the direction of projection. Even when the polygon has straight sides, the projection will be curved on the surface.

Pinhole Camera

When. Model a pinhole camera.

How. A pinhole camera replaces a conventional glass lens with a tiny hole. Such a hole in very thin material can focus light by confining all rays from a scene through a what is effectively a single point. To produce a reasonably clear image, the aperture diameter has to be less than about 1/100 of the distance between the pinhole and the screen.

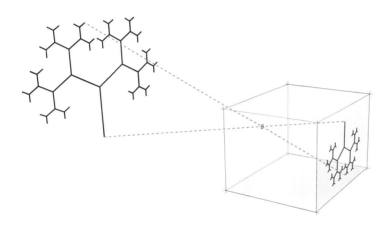

The principle of a pinhole camera is that light rays from an object pass through a small hole to form an image on the screen (shown in image above). To model this effect, simply place a point (modeling the pinhole) between the source and receiver and project from the source through the pinhole to the receiver. Use either direct model reconstruction or the sampling technique from the *Solar Polygon Shadow* sample above to reconstruct the source on the receiver.

Note that the image is re ected both top-to-bottom and left-to-right. This is equivalent to a 180° rotation about the axis normal to the receiving plane and through the pinhole (providing the receiver is a plane).

8.31: Putting the projection point between the source and destination objects produces a pinhole camera.

8.12   REACTOR

Related Pattern • CONTROLLER • GOAL SEEKER

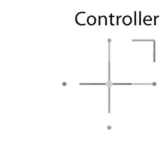

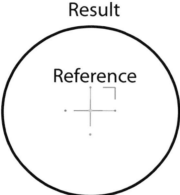

What. Make an object respond to the proximity of another object.

When. The essence of parametric modeling is expressing object properties in terms of the properties of upstream objects. A problem arises when the relation between the object and its upstream precedents is based on proximity. The new location for the object becomes based on the old location for the object, making the object definition become circular! Propagation graphs cannot have cycles.

Use this pattern when you want to make an object respond to the presence of another object.

Why. Designers often use the metaphor of *response* in which one part of a design depends upon the state of another. Reversing the perspective, is as if part of a design becomes a tool for shaping the other. This situation is very much like that encountered in the CONTROLLER pattern, but with a key difference – the controlling property is proximity.

How. The essential idea: connect an *interactor* to a *result* through a *reference*.

The trick is to join the *interactor* and the *result* through a mediating and usually fixed object, which we call a *reference*. The *interactor* and the *reference* interact to produce the *result*.

For example (see sample *Circle Radii and Point Interactor* below), you have a point and a circle, and you want the circle to get bigger (or smaller or elliptical) as you move the point closer. This can be done by using the REACTOR pattern. As you might have guessed, the point is an interactor and the circle is a result (which can be replicated to give us an array of circles). The circles have to be somewhere. This somewhere is the reference. The reference is usually hidden in a REACTOR.

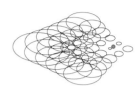

Position is a complex property that can manifest in many ways. Position is any combination of location and direction, for instance, the length or direction of lines, parameter or number or position of points, direction of planes, radius of circles and even additional properties such as colour if they are made to depend on position.

REACTOR Samples

Circle Radii and Point Interactor

When. Control the size of a set of circles by proximity to a point.

How. Perhaps the simplest definition of a circle requires just its *centre* and *radius*. The *centre* (a point) is the reference and the *radius* is the result. The free point is the interactor. Making the *radius* a function of the distance between the *centre* and the controlling point completes this instance of the REACTOR pattern. In this case, the function is a direct relationship – its value shrinks as distance shrinks. As the interactor moves closer to the circle, the circle gets smaller.

Replicating the reference causes all of the circles to react to the movement of the interactor. Hiding the reference creates an illusion of direct control from interactor to result.

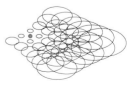

8.32: The collection of circles reacts to the prescence of an interactor point.

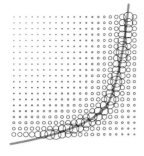

Circle Radii and Curve Interactor

When. Control the size of a set of circles by proximity to a curve.

How. In modeling terms, this sample hardly differs from the previous one. In both, the radii of circles in an array change with proximity to an interactor. The only differences are that the interactor here is a curve and the radii grow with proximity rather than shrink. The distance from a reference point to the curve is the distance between the point and its projection onto the curve – this is the shortest distance between the point and curve.

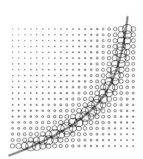

Hiding the reference removes each circle s visual fixed point. The eye focuses only on the changing displayed part.

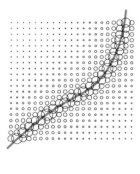

Source: NASA Earth Observatory image created by Jesse Allen, using Landsat data provided by the University of Maryland s Global Land Cover Facility.

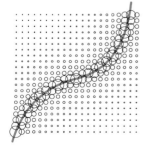

8.33: In this sample the *interactor* is an entire curve, itself controlled by a set of points.

Lift

When. Make a line s length increase as you move a point closer to its start point.

How. Define two points; call one the reference and one the interactor. On the reference define a vertical line: the result.

The length l of the result must increase as the distance between the reference and the interactor shrinks. Choosing a "good" function for l takes work. In this sample $l = 1/(\text{distance}(interactor, reference) + 0.1)$. The small amount of 0.1 that is added within the function prevents the line from becoming infinitely long as the distance between the points approaches zero. The MAPPING pattern gives a process for reliably using other functions.

Replicate the start point and hide it. Now you have a set of lines that react to the movement of the interactor. In turn, use the line endpoints to define the shape of another object using the lines, such as a roof surface.

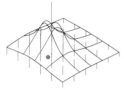  

8.34: With a reactor a single point can replace the 16 points needed for general control of a surface. Of course, generality is lost; some surfaces cannot be modeled.

Repeller

When. Make a point move away from a controlling point.

How. Define two points; call one the reference and one the interactor. The result will lie on the infinite line defined by the reference and the interactor.

The result is the sum of the reference and a vector. The vector s direction is the same as the vector between the interactor and the reference. Its length results from a function of the distance between the interactor and the reference: as the interactor moves towards the reference, the length increases.

The function in this sample is $SD/(\text{distance}(interactor, reference) + SD * 0.01)$, where SD stands for *Standard Distance*. As SD grows, so does the distance over which the pattern has an effect. The small quantity of $SD * 0.01$ added to the distance prevents the result from moving infinitely as the interactor approaches the reference.

8.35: The only effective difference between this and the previous sample is that the line on which the result lies is directly defined by the interactor and reference.

Replicate and hide the reference. The result points now appear to respond to the interactor. In turn, use the result to define other objects, such as a surface.

Vector Field

When. Rotate a bound vector as a controlling point moves, so that it always has the same angle to the point. Replicate to define a vector field.

How. Define two points: an interactor and a reference. The goal is to define a vector bound to the reference such that it is right-handedly perpendicular to the imaginary line that connects the two points. Create a frame on the reference point by using the interactor point to locate its *x*-axis. Making the result vector on the *y*-axis of this frame ensures that it will always be perpendicular to the *x*-axis and consequently to the connecting line.

Note that the reference can be more than one object. In this case both the start point of the vector and the frame comprise the reference. The frame and start point could combine, simplifying back to a single reference. Such reduction is not always possible.

Replicate the reference point in one, two or three dimensions and hide it. All of the result vectors will react to the position of the interactor and portray a continuous vector field.

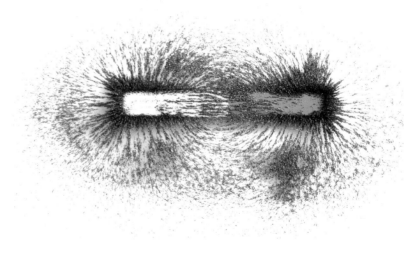

Source: Dayna Mason

8.36: The point appears to directly control the vector field. Hidden, as with most REACTORS, is the reference, in this case, a point and a frame located at the point.

234

Dimple

When. Make the local shape of a closed curve react to a nearby point.

How. Define a circle and two points on the circle. Call one of these points the reference and the other the interactor. Draw a line from the reference point to the circle s centre. Place the result, a parametric point on this line, that moves toward the center if the interactor gets *too close* to it. The trick is to assign the parameter of the result point a higher value (here 0.4) if the distance between the interactor and the reference (measured by the modular distance between their parameters) becomes less than a value d (explained later), otherwise set it to another value (here 0.2). This distance condition can be defined as follows:

```
1  function modular01Distance (double t0, double t1)
2  {
3    object result = t0—t1;
4    return
5      result > 0.5 ?
6        1 — result :
7      result >= 0 ?
8        result :
9      result > —0.5 ?
10       Abs(result) :
11       result + 1.0;
12 }
```

The parameter d here can be a number less than or equal to 0.5 and greater than or equal to half of the distance between each two references. The lower limit is needed so that the test is always true for at least one point. With *count* equally distributed references, a minimal value is $d = 1/(2*count)$.

After replicating the reference, create a closed curve interpolating the result points. This curve will look like a circle deformed by the interactor.

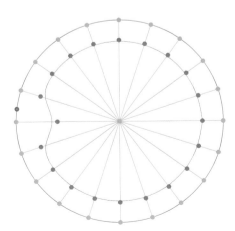

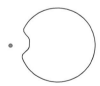

8.37: A simple interaction hides a complex mediating reference structure. The point appears to directly control a dimple on the circle.

8.13   REPORTER

Related Pattern • CONTROLLER • PROJECTION • SELECTOR

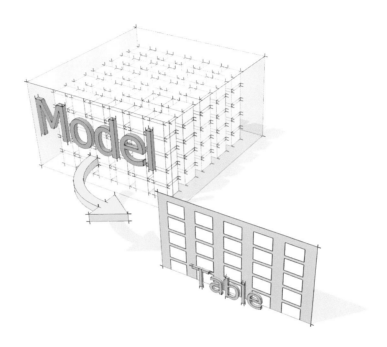

What. Re-present (abstract or transform) information from a model.

When. Models can be complex. Finding and using the relevant parts of a model can be tedious and error-prone. Further, some "parts" of a model may only be implied – computation may be needed to construct them from primary model data. Use this pattern when you need to use some aspect of a model in another process or another part of the model.

Why. Models can be complex and hard to understand. They can express far more information than they directly contain. Such implicit information must be uncovered through functions applied to the model. Using a REPORTER allows you to present only the information you need to another part of the model. This makes your model structure more clear and helps you work with other people who may use your model.

REPORTERS may abstract (simplify) or transform (re-present). They report a design or its parts from a different point of view. In analogy to a relational database, the REPORTER pattern is akin to a view table extracted from a database.

How. Data from a REPORTER must be conceived, extracted and envisioned. Deciding what to report requires judgment, for example, when reporting façade element planarity, the most effective report may, or may not, be the minimal vertex movement that restores planarity. Extracting the data may demand a complex algorithm, for example, a convex hull of a set of points. Envisioning that data so that it makes sense to the person receiving it has been the subject of entire books (Tufte) (1986; 1990; 1997) – it is likely that a simple, textual list will not be best. Of course, if the purpose of the REPORTER is to provide data to another program, a textual or numeric list might be exactly right.

You can use the REPORTER pattern in many different ways.

- Displaying properties of an object. For example, a collection of point coordinates might be displayed numerically in a table, or their minima and maxima might be instanced as two points.

- Defining an element in a different way. For example, a point defined in one frame can be reported in another.

- Conditionally selecting parts from your model. In this use, a REPORTER is very similar to a SELECTOR. For example, a roof surface comprising polygons might be reported by the degree of non-planarity in each.

- Creating new objects from reported objects. In this case of indirection, a property of an object is used to define another object. For example, a REPORTER on line segments might comprise new segments coincident with the originals central third. Another REPORTER example produces a *dual* polygon mesh (the mesh generated by replacing centroids with vertices, and edges between vertices with edges between centroids).

- Sampling a model and then reporting this simplified version somewhere else and with different conditions to create a more complex model.

- Copying. Generally, copying is reporting the model as many times as needed in different places, therefore features such as copy, mirror, clone and rotate are all kinds of reporting.

The REPORTER pattern typically combines with other patterns. This pattern feeds information to downstream objects or directly to the designer. In many ways, it is a normal part of parametric modeling in that models are defined in terms of other models. The difference is that a REPORTER is often not a part of the design, but rather a view on the design or an intermediary in the model construction process.

In some sense, the REPORTER pattern is an anti-CONTROLLER pattern. In a CONTROLLER, information flows from the control to the target – typically from a simple model to a complex one. In a REPORTER information flows the other way – it typically is an abstraction of a larger model.

$\alpha = 39.01$
$\beta = 39.01$

$\alpha = 39.01$
$\beta = 39.01$

$\alpha = 39.01$
$\beta = 39.01$

$\alpha = 39.01$
$\beta = 39.01$

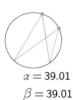

$\alpha = 39.01$
$\beta = 39.01$

Reporter Samples

Subtended Angle

When. Envision information from the model as text.

How. In a circle, any inscribed angle subtended by a chord of a given length is constant. A good demonstration juxtaposes as text a suite of angles subtended by a common chord. This model comprises a circle and two pairs of lines that represent two angles and share a common subtending chord. Showing both of those angles together demonstrates this simple geometric theorem. Text is the simplest REPORTER. Sometimes it is actually effective.

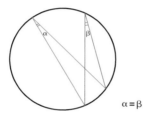

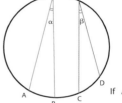

8.38: Angles subtended by a common chord are the same. Conversely two points subtending the same angle from a line segment lie on a common circle for which the line segment is a chord.

Array Depth

When. Extract properties of a collection of points organized as an array.

How. Collections of point-like objects define many properties, some pertaining the points themselves and some to their organization in a collection. Examples include the extremal coordinates of the points, the longest path in the collection (the array depth) and the number of elements in the collection. In this case, the REPORTER pattern extracts such data from the model. A function iterates over each element in a collection, accumulating the desired measures as it proceeds.

Rank = 3

Dimensions = { 5 ,6 ,2}

$BBox_{ll} = \{0.0, 0.0, 0.0\}$

$BBox_{ur} = \{4.0, 5.0, 1.0\}$

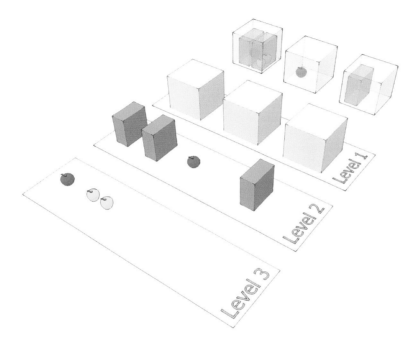

Level 1

Level 2

Level 3

Rank = 3

Dimensions = { 4 ,5 ,3}

$BBox_{ll} = \{0.0, 0.0, 0.0\}$

$BBox_{ur} = \{3.0, 4.0, 2.0\}$

Rank = 3

Dimensions = { 3 ,4 ,4}

$BBox_{ll} = \{0.0, 0.0, 0.0\}$

$BBox_{ur} = \{2.0, 3.0, 3.0\}$

8.39: Arrays are complex objects. Understanding their structure can be hard. This REPORTER puts a display of array structure directly in the three-dimensional model.

Fabrication

When. Transform design data for fabrication.

How. Planes slice a solid into a set of closed curves. A common fabrication technique is to use such curves to cut *stations* out of a sheet material and use the stations as internal formwork that is covered with other sheet or strip material. The curves forming the stations can be reported in a variety of ways, in both 2D and 3D and through mediating transformations. In this sample, one report is a scaled 3D version and the other is a 2D layout suitable as a draft cutting plan for sheet material.

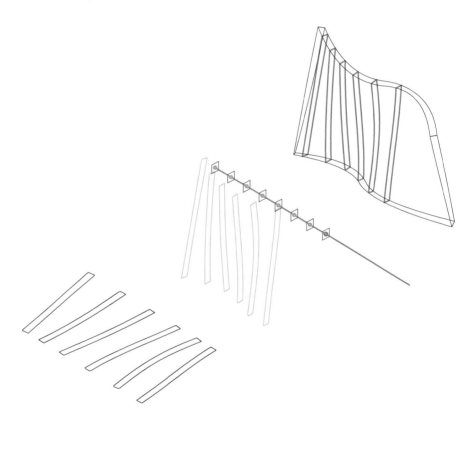

8.40: The model reports data for fabrication. Parametric systems typically provide such outputs. The principle though is simple: transform parts of the model into a separate view or location.

Mirror

When. Mirror a curve through an axis.

How. Define a curve based on a point collection, and a line to use as a mirror axis. In 3D the line would be a plane. Now re ect the curve poles through the axis to create poles for a new curve. Finally create the new curve from the new poles; this curve is a mirror of the first curve. In general, mirrored objects are *enantiomorphs*, that is, identical except for handedness.

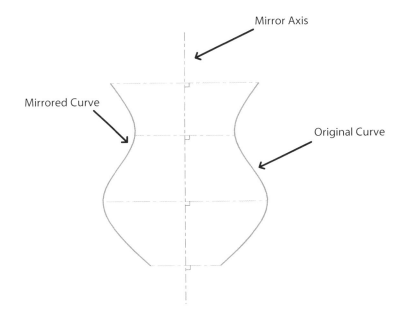

Mirror Axis

Mirrored Curve

Original Curve

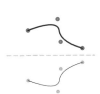

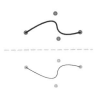

8.41: A mirror can be seen as either a REPORTER or a PROJECTOR.

Out of Plane

When. Report the out-of-plane polygons of a surface both by colour and text.

How. Create a curved surface and subdivide it with polygons. Some polygons may be non-planar. The amount of non-planarity depends on the local surface. Iterate over the collection, extracting the polygons that exceed a threshold out-of-plane measure. Visualize the resulting polygons both *in situ* with colour and in a tabular report.

The out-of-plane polygons are:

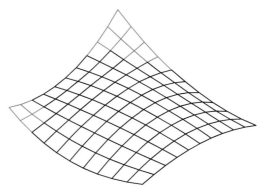

1 . polygon01[0][0]

2 . polygon01[0][1]

3 . polygon01[0][2]

4 . polygon01[0][8]

5 . polygon01[0][9]

6 . polygon01[1][0]

7 . polygon01[1][1]

8 . polygon01[1][8]

9 . polygon01[1][9]

10 . polygon01[2][0]

11 . polygon01[2][1]

12 . polygon01[3][0]

8.42: Understanding and controlling anomalies is both enabled and produced by parametric modeling. REPORTING directly in the model can provide much more effective feedback than a table of text.

Snapper

When. Report a triangle snapped onto a grid.

How. Parametric "sketches" (yes, a parametric model can be sketch-like!) are continuous. They may be abstracted into a discrete system, such as a grid. This REPORTER maintains the original model and ability to smoothly interact with it and reports the model as it would appear were it snapped onto a specified grid. The reporting takes two steps. First, report the original triangle s vertices in a new frame. Second, select and report the nearest point on the grid to each triangle vertex. Construct the reported triangle on these abstracted points.

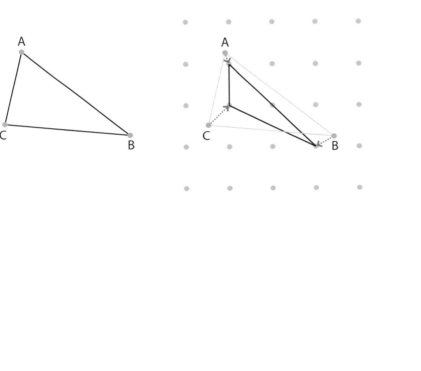

8.43: This REPORTER builds the usual system-level snapping interaction directly into a model.

Triangle

When. Rotate and scale a triangle.

How. This sample separates the shape of an object from the space in which it is embedded, giving independent control of each. It reports a triangle developed in one frame (the baseCS) in another system (the reporterCS) and also provides rotation and scaling controls for that new frame.

Ironically, this REPORTER uses a REPORTER internally. In order to compute the rotation of the reporterCS system, a point is defined in the baseCS system at the origin of the reporterCS system, but one unit along the *x*-axis of the baseCS system. Reporting this point in the reporterCS system provides the arguments needed for the function Atan2 to fully compute the rotation angle.

Scale: 1.63
Rotation: 15.35°

Scale: 1.3
Rotation: 10.33°

Scale: 0.98
Rotation: 1.91°

Scale: 0.7
Rotation: 13.89°

Scale: 0.53
Rotation: 44.29°

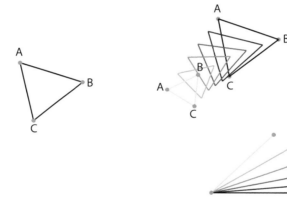

8.44: This REPORTER separates local editing (of the triangle) from its actual location in space.

8.14   SELECTOR

Related Pattern ● CONTROLLER ● REPORTER

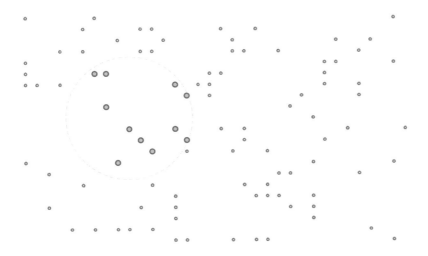

What. Select members of a collection that have specified properties.

When. Selection is a universal in interactive systems. In parametric systems, it can be part of the model itself. At each update of the propagation graph, objects can select the arguments to their update methods. Use this pattern when you want to locally and dynamically restructure a model depending its state.

Why. Creating objects and using objects are different acts. You may specify, say, a set of points by giving their Cartesian coordinates. When using these points, you might be interested only in those that are close to a line. The SELECTOR pattern allows you to separate object creation and later use, and express these two common operations in the terms most suitable for each.

How. In the SELECTOR pattern, there is always a collection of given objects and a collection that is the outcome of the SELECTOR s action. We call the first list the *target* and the second list the *result*. The SELECTOR mediates between these by determining which elements of the target to include in the result. The properties that objects must have or conditions they must meet in order to be selected we call the SELECTOR s *behaviour*.

For example (see the sample *Distance between Points* below), the target may be a list of points and the SELECTOR a compound of a point, circle and function. The point specifies the location of the SELECTOR; the circle the distance within which selection will occur; and the function how points will be selected and how selected points will be constructed, that is, the SELECTOR s behaviour. The function must select those points whose distance to the SELECTOR point is less than (or perhaps greater than or approximately equal to or within some range of...) the parameter d of the SELECTOR s behaviour.

The simplest representation of a SELECTOR s behaviour is a function treating each of the target points individually. For each target, it computes the behaviour and returns a copy of any objects that conform. For instance, with selection by distance, it compares the distance between the target and the SELECTOR against the threshold d. If the target object satisfies the condition, the function creates a coincident point and returns this point (acting in a sense as a REPORTER). As a result, the function s (and SELECTOR s) output will be a new list of points.

The result is not a subset of the target. Rather, it is a new set of points, identical to the selected points in the target.

```
1  function selectByDistance(Point selector,
2                            Point target,
3                            double distance)
4  {
5    for (value i = 0; i < target.Count; ++i)
6    {
7      if (Distance(selector,target[i]) < distance)
8      {
9        Point result= new Point(this);
10       result.ByCartesianCoordinates(baseCS,
11                                     target[i].X,
12                                     target[i].Y,
13                                     target[i].Z);
14     }
15   }
16 };
```

An actual call to the SELECTOR s behaviour function would take the following form:

```
selectByDistance(selector,target,distance);
```

where selector and target are points (or point collections) in the model and distance is a value held in a model variable or object property.

SELECTOR Samples

Distance between Points

When. Select points based on their distance from a SELECTOR point.

How. First write a function giving a condition for selecting target points. In this sample example, the distance between the target and the SELECTOR point must be less than variable d.

Write a behaviour function that iterates over the target points and compares the distance between each point and the SELECTOR point using the threshold d. For each member of the list, if the condition is met, the behaviour function creates a copy of the target point.

The behaviour function returns a new list of result points within distance d of the SELECTOR point. Note that the structure of the target and result may differ. For instance, the target may be a 2D array and the result a 1D array. You have to make and remember such choices.

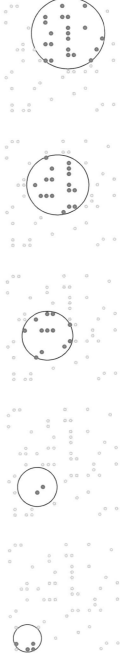

8.45: Selecting from a collection based on distance from a target point is identical to selecting points within a circle centred on the target and with radius of the chosen distance.

Part of Curve

When. Select part of a curve depending on its distance to a point.

How. Place a collection of parametric points on a curve. Use the SELECTOR mechanism from the sample *Distance between Points,* that is, a function that checks each of the points and reports them if they satisfy the distance condition.

Placing a curve through the selected points yields an approximate copy of part of the original curve. Moving the SELECTOR point controls the part of the curve to be copied. The more points on the original curve, the more accurate the curve selected.

The original points sample the curve and so will seldom capture the exact point on the curve that is at the specified distance. Solve this problem by searching between the last selected point and the first non-selected point for the point at which the distance to the SELECTOR is exactly the threshold. However, if the original points are widely spaced, very small sections of the curve that are within the threshold might fail to be detected. Resolve this issue by projecting the SELECTOR point onto the curve. If the distance to the SELECTOR point is less than the threshold, search on either side of the projected point for the exact end points of the curve.

8.46: It is often easier to conceive an overall model from which the intended design component is extracted by selection. In this case, the SELECTOR returns a part of the curve near the target point.

Lines inside Curve

When. Select all lines that are completely inside a closed curve.

How. This SELECTOR has two parts.

First, if a line segment is entirely inside or outside a curve it does not intersect the curve. In order to check the position of a line against a curve, first compute the intersection. If the result is null, the line may be either inside or outside.

Lines intersect the curve.

Lines do not intersect the curve.

Second, if an endpoint of a non-intersecting line is inside the curve, so is the line. The Jordan Curve Theorem states that a point is inside a closed curve if a line segment between the point and a point external to the curve intersects the curve an odd number of times. Use the Jordan Curve Theorem to determine the position of either end of the line segment against the closed curve. Don t count tangencies as crossings! If the number of intersections is odd, the line is inside the curve.

Odd number of intersections.
Point is inside the curve.

Even number of intersections.
Point is outside the curve.

Write a function that performs both of the above tests in turn. If both succeed (non-intersection of the segment and odd intersections of a ray from an end point) copy and return the line.

8.47: The Jordan Curve Theorem, applied twice, gives a simple and correct test for lines inside closed curves.

Points inside Sector

When. Select the points inside a 2D sector (two vectors bound to a point).

How. The sector comprises a base point and two vectors $\vec{u}$ and $\vec{v}$ bound to it. Taken in order, these define an angle between 0° and 360°. Imagine a target vector $\vec{a}$ for each target point connecting from the base point to the target point. Take the two cross products $\vec{u} \otimes \vec{a}$ and $\vec{a} \otimes \vec{v}$. Remember from Section 6.5.1 that the right-hand rule gives the cross product s orientation. If the angle between the vectors $\vec{u}$ and $\vec{v}$ is less than 180°, a target point is between two SELECTOR vectors if the z-components of both the cross products of its vector with the SELECTOR vectors are positive. If the angle is greater than 180°, the target point is in the sector if one or both of the cross products are positive.

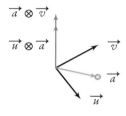

$\angle \vec{u} \vec{v} <= 180°$
$\vec{a}$ is inside the sector.
Both cross products positive.

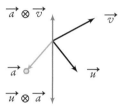

$\angle \vec{u} \vec{v} <= 180°$
$\vec{a}$ is outside the sector.
One or both cross products negative.

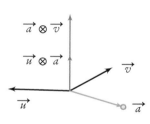

$\angle \vec{u} \vec{v} > 180°$
$\vec{a}$ is inside the sector.
One or both cross products positive.

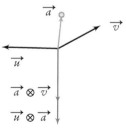

$\angle \vec{u} \vec{v} > 180°$
$\vec{a}$ is outside the sector.
Both cross products negative.

The cross product determines if the sector is greater than 180°. If the sector is between 0° and 180°, the z-component of $\vec{u} \otimes \vec{v}$ is positive. If the sector is between 180° and 360°, $\vec{u} \otimes \vec{v}$ is negative. When $\vec{u}$ and $\vec{v}$ are colinear, the sector is either 0° ($\vec{u} \bullet \vec{v} \geq 0$) or 180° ($\vec{u} \bullet \vec{v} \leq 0$).

The SELECTOR function iterates over the target points one by one. For each point, it computes the two cross products $\vec{u} \otimes \vec{a}$ and $\vec{a} \otimes \vec{v}$. Using the rules above it returns each point that lies within the sector.

8.48: The cross and dot products combine in a robust point-in-sector test.

Points inside Box

When. Select points that lie inside a box.

How. Write a behaviour function that checks the position of the target points against the box. The function reports their position in the coordinate system of the SELECTOR box one by one and compares their new coordinates to two opposite corners of the box. The function then reports them in the result list if they are inside the box.

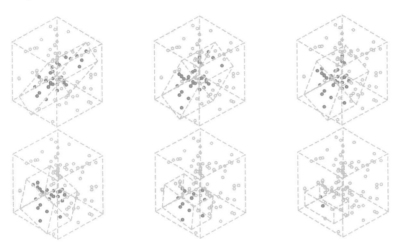

8.49: By defining a SELECTOR box in its own frame and reporting the target points in that frame, the box can have any orientation in space.

Length of Line

When. Select lines based on their length.

How. Given a list of lines, select those whose lengths are between the lengths of two SELECTOR lines.

Use a function that iterates through the target lines. For each target line, if it has the desired length, the function reports it and puts it in a new list of result lines.

8.50: This SELECTOR contains a CONTROLLER. The actual SELECTOR object comprises the upper and lower threshold given by the CONTROLLER s points.

251

8.15   MAPPING

Related Pattern • CONTROLLER • JIG • INCREMENT • PROJECTION

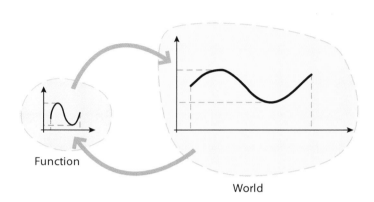

Function

World

What. Use a function in a new domain and range.

When. A function accepts inputs and produces a value. Geometric functions such as f(x) = sin(x), f(x) = cos(x), f(x) = x^2 and f(x) = $1/x$ are extremely common in parametric modeling. In fact, they form an indispensable base for much modeling work. These functions are all naturally defined over their own domains and ranges. Use this pattern when you want to use a function in the domain and range specific to a model.

The terms *domain* and *range* need to be explained. The domain of a function is the set of input values over which it is defined or used. The range of a function is the set of output values it generates. For example, we might choose to use a domain of 0° to 360° for the sin(x) function. This corresponds to its natural repetitive cycle. The range generated by sin(x) over this domain is −1 to 1.

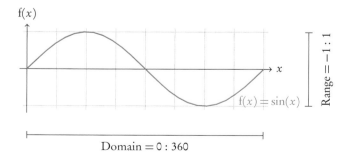

f(x)

x

f(x) = sin(x)

Range = −1 : 1

Domain = 0 : 360

Why. Much form-making comes directly from relatively simple functions, for many reasons. The repetitive use of simple functions can unify a design across its parts and across design scales. If the ease and cost of fabrication is a concern, simple functions can help control complexity and cost (but do not necessarily do so). In contrast, the so-called *free-form* curves and surfaces provide interfaces to more complex functions, but cede some control of the form-making process to the underyling algorithms.

Simple functions come with natural domains and ranges. It is much easier to think about a function in its natural domain and range than in a transformed version.

To use a function in a model requires reframing it so that it makes sense in the model. Reframing turns out to be surprisingly difficult and error-prone for many designers. Yet, there is a universal method of precisely seven parameters that works for almost all reframing tasks. Further, this method is based on one simple equation – essentially the same equation that defines a one-dimensional *af ne map* or, equivalently, an *af ne function*.

The term "affine map" is extremely common in linear algebra and its dependent fields (computer graphics and geometric modeling). It has a crisp mathematical meaning, and we use this meaning here – precision of language is important! An affine map is a *linear transformation* followed by a translation. In turn, a linear transformation preserves vector addition and scalar multiplication – you can add or multiply before or after the transformation and the result is the same. In one dimension (the real number line), the only linear transformation is scaling. A 1D affine map changes a function s scale and moves it along the real number line. The function $f(x)$ becomes $g(x)$ under the affine map.

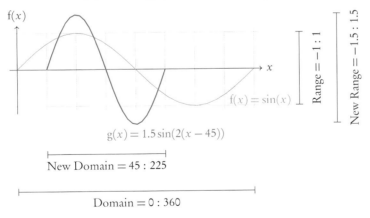

The problem for modeling is that determining the new function $g(x)$ is not easy. If you watch a modeler trying to get such a mapping to "work" you will see much trial and error. Looking at the function in the figure above, that is, $g(x) = 1.5\sin(2(x-45))$ gives some indication why the task is so hard. Which number does what? Why?

This pattern replaces all of the function-specific changes with a uniform structure and set of parameters. You never have to work with a function in any but its simplest form. MAPPING separates where the *model* uses a function from where the function is defined.

How. Consider two rectangles, called the *function* and the *model* respectively. The function rectangle is given by the domain and range of the function within it. The model rectangle can be any size and location you choose. The goal is to place the original function into the model. The basic idea is to always use the function rectangle when computing the function. To find a point on the model function, map from the model domain to the function domain (blue arrow 1 below), compute the function (red and green arrows in the function box) and then map from the result back to the model range (blue arrow 2 below).

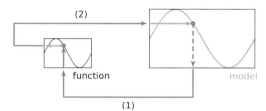

What follows precisely defines the diagram. Variables relating to a domain start with or have within a d; those over the range start with or have within an r. In one dimension, an affine map has a single equation, which we introduce first over the domain interval 0 to 1. Imagine a parametric function $f(d)$ over this interval. An affine map $r(d)$ from the interval 0 to 1 to the interval $[r_l, r_u]$ with parameter d has the equation

$$r(d) = r_l + d(r_u - r_l),\ 0 \le d \le 1$$

Reversing the map to go from the range (r) to the domain (d) gives

$$d(r) = \frac{r - r_l}{r_u - r_l},\ r_l \le r \le r_u$$

The map has domain d with bounds 0 to 1 and range r with bounds r_l and r_u.

Generalizing, to any domain produces the maps between d and r as follows:

$$d(r) = \frac{(r - r_l)(d_u - d_l)}{r_u - r_l} + d_l,\ r_l \le r \le r_u$$

$$r(d) = \frac{(d - d_l)(r_u - r_l)}{d_u - d_l} + r_l,\ d_l \le d \le d_u$$

Mathematically, these are simple equations, but require attention every time they are used. The purpose of this pattern is to abstract these equations so that designers can freely use generic and simple functions in their models.

WARNING. When using affine maps to apply a function, there are actually two
maps to consider. One goes between the domain of the model and its domain in
the function. The other goes between the range of the function and its range in
the model.

Since the range of the function is determined by the function itself, this means
that mapping between function and model had exactly seven parameters: the
lower and upper bounds of the function s domain (fd_l and fd_u); the lower and
upper bounds of the model s domain (md_l and md_u); the lower and upper bounds
of the model s range (mr_l and mr_u); and the function parameter d itself.

These seven parameters describe every possible situation in which you want to
use a function in a model. *Every possible situation!* Applying them though takes
some insight. The archetypal problem is this: you have a value in the model and
need to find the corresponding value of the function in the model. Giving more
detail to the diagram above, the solution has three parts: (1) an affine map from
the model to the function; (2) an application of the function; and (3) an affine
map from the result of the function to the result in the model. The diagram
below illustrates this   ow, showing how the various parameters and bounds
relate.

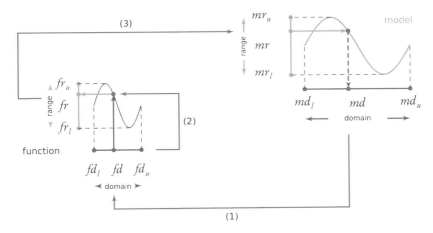

For example, imagine a roof whose profile is a sine curve. The roof spans from
a point $\dot{p}$ in the model to another point $\dot{q}$. A point $\dot{m}(t)$ with parameter t gives
the location of the roof point along the line between these two points. The
maximum roof height is given by a parameter *height*. Between $\dot{p}$ and $\dot{q}$ the roof
goes through two complete cycles of the sine function. Then the following are
the six mapping parameter settings. The seventh parameter is t, which gives the
parametric location of a varying point on the roof.

$$
\begin{aligned}
\mathrm{f}(x) &= \sin(x) \\
fd_l &= 0.0 \\
fd_u &= 720.0 \\
fr_l &= -1.0 \quad \text{(defined by the function – computed automatically)} \\
fr_u &= 1.0 \quad \text{(defined by the function – computed automatically)} \\
md_l &= 0.0 \quad (\dot{m}(t) \text{ is parameterized by } t \text{ over the domain 0 to 1)} \\
md_u &= 1.0 \\
mr_l &= 0.0 \quad \text{(the height is added to the } z\text{-value of } \dot{m}(t)) \\
mr_u &= height \quad \text{(the height is chosen in the model)}
\end{aligned}
$$

In summary, the whole process comprises these three steps:

- Given a model domain value, find the equivalent domain value in the function.

- Apply the function to get a value in the function s range.

- Find the equivalent model range value.

MAPPING Samples

Reciprocal

When. Feather a curve. Make a curve taper gently.

How. The multiplicative reciprocal is the function $f(x) = 1/x$. It is seductive as it provides a simple function that tapers to a non-zero value (is asymptotic to the x-axis), making it possible to feather effects on a curve or surface. It traps the unwary – it increases exponentially as its argument approaches zero and is undefined at zero. Thus it is important to set the function domain so that zero and values close to it are not included. In general, using this function produces poor results. It is included here to demonstrate that sometimes the function domain choice is crucial.

Here are the parameter settings for a useful mapping. The model point $\dot{m}(t)$ is parametric over the domain 0 to 1.

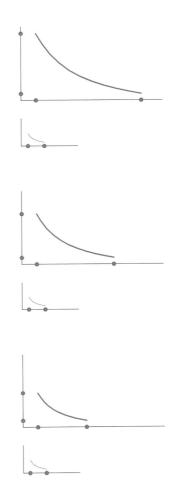

$f(x)$	$=$	$1/x$	
fd_l	$=$	0.25	
fd_u	$=$	100.0	
fr_l	$=$	0.01	(defined by the function – computed automatically)
fr_u	$=$	4.0	(defined by the function – computed automatically)
md_l	$=$	0.0	($\dot{m}(t)$ is parameterized by t over the domain 0 to 1)
md_u	$=$	1.0	
mr_l	$=$	0.0	(the height is added to the z-value of $\dot{m}(t)$)
mr_u	$=$	*height*	(height is chosen in the model)

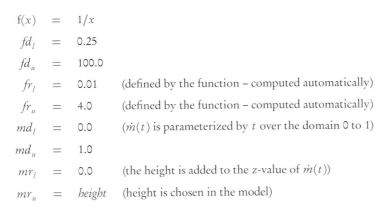

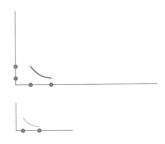

8.51: Beware the reciprocal.

$$f(x) = 1/x$$

It seems to taper nicely along the x-axis but goes to infinity along the y-axis. Using it usually leads to anomalies in the model.

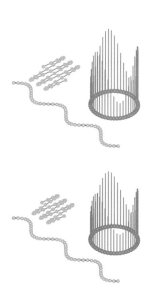

Sine and Cosine

When. Use sine and cosine functions in complete periodic cycles.

How. The basic trigonometric functions $\sin(x)$ and $\cos(x)$ repeat in periods of 360° and span 180° between function minima and maxima. Both functions have domains from $-\infty$ to ∞ and ranges from -1 to 1. Choosing a finite part of the domain such that the function starts and ends at a minimum, maximum or zero-crossing yields clean control over the end-conditions in the model.

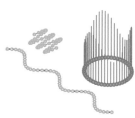

Here are sample parameter settings. The model point $\dot{m}(t)$ is parametric over the range 0 to 1. In this case, $\dot{m}(t)$ is bound to a circle, and vertical lines from each instance of $\dot{m}(t)$ have length given by the function result.

$$
\begin{aligned}
f(x) &= \cos(x) \\
fd_l &= 0.0 \\
fd_u &= 1080.0 \quad \text{(yields three complete cycles)} \\
fr_l &= -1.0 \quad \text{(defined by the function – computed automatically)} \\
fr_u &= 1.0 \quad \text{(defined by the function – computed automatically)} \\
md_l &= 0.0 \quad \text{($\dot{m}(t)$ is parameterized by t over the domain 0 to 1)} \\
md_u &= 1.0 \\
mr_l &= height_{min} \quad \text{(the minimum length of the lines on $\dot{m}(t)$)} \\
mr_u &= height_{max} \quad \text{(the maximum length of the lines on $\dot{m}(t)$)}
\end{aligned}
$$

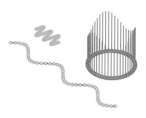

When sampling periodic functions and those with minima or maxima within the chosen domain, the choice of sampling interval is crucial if the sampled points will be used to regenerate the mapped function in the model. Samples must be chosen to coincide with function minima and maxima. Poor sampling can dramatically affect the shape of the reconstructed curve.

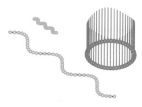

8.52: Three cycles of the cosine function mapped into space at different scales. Vertical lines from points on a circle use the y-coordinates of the mapped points as their length.

Function Parts

When. Choosing a small part of a function can yield an intended form.

How. Simple functions can yield surprisingly rich forms. A classic example in three dimensions is Foster + Partner s extensive use of parts of the torus as a generator of form (see Chapter 5).

The function is the sine function: $f(x) = \sin(x)$. The trick is that an appropriate choice of function domain can yield local segments of the sine curve that do not display the archetypal repetition of the entire curve.

Here are sample parameter settings. The model point $\dot{m}(t)$ is assumed to be parametric over the range 0 to 1. In this case, the model range minimum and maximum would be chosen by the modeler to suit the application to hand. The figures on the side bar vary only by $FDu = 180.0$ the upper function domain bound.

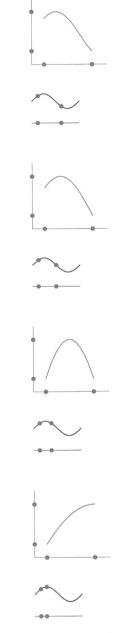

$$
\begin{array}{rcll}
f(x) & = & \sin(x) & \\
fd_l & = & 45.0° & \text{(increases in steps of 22.5°)} \\
fd_u & = & 180.0° & \\
fr_l & = & -1.0 & \text{(defined by the function – computed automatically)} \\
fr_u & = & 1.0 & \text{(defined by the function – computed automatically)} \\
md_l & = & 0.0 & (\dot{m}(t) \text{ is parameterized by } t \text{ over the domain 0 to 1)} \\
md_u & = & 1.0 & \\
mr_l & = & height_{min} & \text{(minimum height is chosen in the model)} \\
mr_u & = & height_{max} & \text{(maximum height is chosen in the model)}
\end{array}
$$

8.53: Choosing part of a function can lead to surprising and useful results. If the underlying function has known "nice" properties, such as maxima or minima at known inputs, so will the selected function.

8.16   RECURSION

Related Pattern • POINT COLLECTION

What. Create a pattern by recursively replicating a motif.

When. Hierarchy in design con ates wholes and parts. The parts copy and transform the whole. This naturally leads to a hierarchial information structure of *layers*, where the properties of a layer derive from the layer immediately superior to it. Recursive algorithms are natural traversers of such hierarchical structures. Use this pattern when you are working with hierarchy in design.

Why. Some complex models such as spirals, trees or space-filling curves can be elegantly represented with a recursive function. In fact, it can be so difficult to represent such structures non-recursively that designers give up and try easier forms. A recursive function typically takes a motif and a replication rule and calls itself on the copies of the motif that the rule generates. A word of warning – recursive algorithms are often hard to understand in the abstract. We humans struggle to envision a pattern from a motif and a replication rule (Carlson and Woodbury, 1994). Another word of warning. Recursive algorithms as update methods can be slow. Typically, limiting the depth of the recursion is the only way to maintain an adequate interactive update rate.

How. RECURSION requires a motif (a geometric object) and a replication rule. The simplest rule is merely a coordinate system with some combination of translation, rotation, scale and shear. Other more complex rules are possible, including ones that change or abstract the motif itself.

The recursive function uses the replication rule to generate a collection of clones of the motif. It then calls itself on each clone, typically (but not necessarily) with the same replication rule. So, in each step, the recursive function takes an existing motif, replicates it and calls itself. Every recursive function requires a termination condition to specify when to stop this process.

RECURSION Samples

Square

When. Nest a sequence of squares inside an initial square.

How. Start with a square (actually, any polygon will do). This is the initial motif – the input to the recursion.

The recursive function must transform the motif as a copy and call itself on the copy. In this sample, the transformation is specified as a parameter t. The new motif's vertices are parametric points on the original motif's edges with parameter t.

In a computer recursions must stop (though this is not true in mathematics!). They either stop by design or by overflow of some data structure, typically the recursion stack in the programming language. In this sample, the variable *depth* controls the recursion and is thus an argument to the function. Each subsequent call to the function reduces the depth argument by one. Inside the function, a test for depth returns the motif unchanged if *depth* is equal to one, else proceeds with the recursion.

Assigning each of the squares an elevation results in a 3D "stack" of polygons. Using this stack as the arguments for a surface gives a twisted vertical pyramid.

This sample defines one copy of the motif at each recursive call. The result is a linear list of motifs – the structure of the list mirrors the geometric structure of the result. Defining more than one motif within the function results in a *tree*.

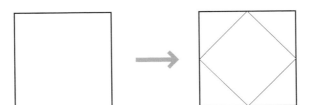

8.54: A simple one-dimensional recursion.

Tree

When. Define a tree – both graphically and as a data structure.

How. In this sample, the motif is a single line. The focus here is more on the geometric layout and data structure and less on the resulting pattern.

The motif transformation places two copies of the motif, each starting at the endpoint of the original motif. The copies are rotated by the parameter *rot* and scaled by the parameter *scale*.

As for any recursive function, you need to make sure that the recursion will stop. As in the prior sample, the stopping condition is set by the depth of the recursion.

With the hindsight gained by seeing the recursion in operation, we can form a good idea of what this particular function will produce as the *rot* and *scale* parameters change. With compound motifs and more complex transformations, such intuitions completely dissolve (Carlson and Woodbury, 1994).

A tree is a data structure that has branches. Each branch is either null or itself a tree. The recursive function determines the data structure. The preferred structure provides a *path* to each of the motifs that mirrors the geometric structure. For example, a sensible path might be one that starts with the root of the tree and that records which branch of the tree is followed to reach the motif. Thus, for a tree with depth 4 (with the base motif at depth 0), one path to a node would be tree[1][2][2][1]. Interpret this as taking the right branch on a 1 and the left branch on a 2. The data structure is thus a list where the first item in the list is the right branch of the tree and the second item in the list is the left branch of the tree. The motif itself must be stored somewhere and is assigned to the 0th branch of the data structure. So a path to a motif needs an index of 0 at its end, for example, tree[1][2][2][1][0].

```
1  treeFn function (CoordinateSystem cs,
2                   Line startLine,
3                   int depth, double rotation, double scale)
4  {
5    Line resultLine = {};
6    if (depth < 1){
7      resultLine[0] = null;
8      resultLine[1] = null;
9    }
10   else{
11     CoordinateSystem rightCS = new CoordinateSystem();
12     rightCS.ByOriginRotationAboutCoordinateSystem
13           (startLine.EndPoint,
14            cs,
15            rotation,
16            AxisOption.Y);
17     CoordinateSystem leftCS = new CoordinateSystem();
18     leftCS.ByOriginRotationAboutCoordinateSystem
19           (startLine.EndPoint,
20            cs,
21            -rotation,
22            AxisOption.Y);
23     Line rightLine = new Line();
24     rightLine.ByStartPointDirectionLength
25            (rightCS,
26             rightCS.ZDirection,
27             startLine.Length*scale);
28     Line leftLine = new Line();
29     leftLine.ByStartPointDirectionLength
30            (leftCS,
31             leftCS.ZDirection,
32             startLine.Length*scale);
33     resultLine[0]=treeFn(rightCS,
34                    rightLine,
35                    depth-1, rotation, scale);
36     resultLine[1]=treeFn(leftCS,
37                    leftLine,
38                    depth-1, rotation, scale);
39   }
40   resultLine[2]=startLine;
41   return resultLine;
42 };
```

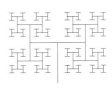

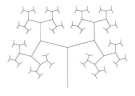

Note the internal calls to the treeFn function. The two separate calls ensure that the right and left branches of the tree are themselves trees. The base case of the recursion occurs when the depth is less than one and results in a tree with null branches being returned. At the end of the function, the motif is stored in the second member of resultLine, completing the data structure, which now stores both the tree structure and all the motifs.

A word to the wise. Writing recursive functions so that they return useful data structures is careful, error-prone work. Doing it well is key to making sense of the results.

8.55: The tree recursive function should produce a data structure that maps to the tree geometry. Each of the figures above shares a common data structure – the geometric variation is due to parameter settings alone.

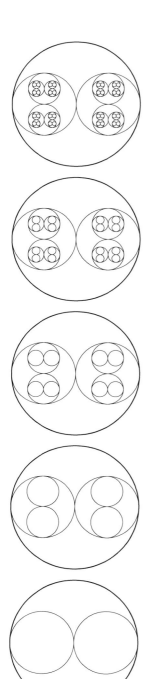

Circles

When. Nest circles within a circle, changing the nesting direction at each level.

How. The motif is a circle. It replicates twice inside itself, with the two new circles of half the radius and tangent to both themselves and the original circle. The line joining their centres is initially horizontal. At each recursive level, the line needs to alternate between horizontal and vertical. This requires a check on the parity of recursion depth within the function. As with the prior samples, the recursion is depth-limited.

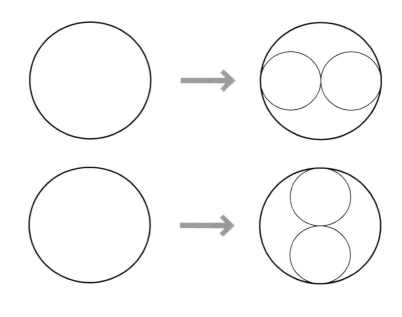

8.56: In this recursion much of the coding effort is devoted to changing the orientation of the circle pair at successive recursive levels.

Golden Rectangle

When. Subdivide a golden rectangle into a square and another golden rectangle.

How. A *golden rectangle* is a rectangle whose side lengths are in the golden ratio $1 : \phi$, that is, approximately 1 : 1.618. A distinctive feature of this shape is that when a square section is removed, the remainder is another golden rectangle, that is, having the same proportions as the original.

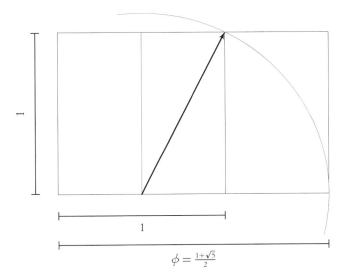

$$\phi = \frac{1 + \sqrt{5}}{2}$$

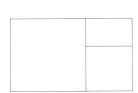

This sample represents a golden rectangle of length l as a sequence of rectangles. If there is only one member of the sequence, it is a golden rectangle with the short side of length l and long side of length $(1 + \sqrt{5})/2$. If there is more than one member, each member but the last is a square, starting with side length l and reducing by $1/\phi$ at every member. The final member is a golden rectangle. Each successive square is located $l * \phi$ away and rotated 90° from the last.

In this sample, the recursion condition is area. When the area of the next square would be less than a threshold $minArea$, the function produces a single golden rectangle and returns. Such a constraint is more realistic than recursion depth – in design there may be a minimum feature size for fabrication.

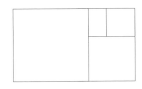

The data structure produced is simple: a linked list of rectangles, all but the last being a square.

You can also create golden rectangles from the "inside out" by adding squares to a seed rectangle.

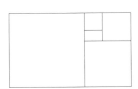

8.57: The golden rectangle is an archetypal recursive form. At each level, the rectangle comprises a square and another, smaller golden rectangle.

Sierpinski Carpet

When. Define a Sierpinski carpet.

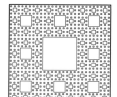

The Sierpinski carpet is a plane fractal, that is a recursive, self-similar form. Wac aw Sierpiński discovered it in 1916. Its construction begins with a square. Conceptually, the square is cut into nine congruent subsquares in a 3×3 grid, and the central subsquare is removed. The same procedure applies recursively to the remaining eight subsquares.

How. At each recursive level, the carpet comprises a motif: a square of $1/3$ the size of the carpet at that level and placed as the centre of the carpet. At all but the base levels, it has eight additional carpets arranged around the motif. Both the recursive function and the data structure should re ect this arrangement.

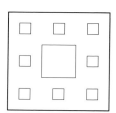

The number of times a recursive function calls itself at a single level is called its *branching factor*. A level 0 carpet has a single motif. A level 2 carpet has nine motifs. The number grows very quickly. A level 6 carpet has

$$1 + 8 + 64 + 512 + 4096 + 32768 + 262144 = 299593 \text{ motifs.}$$

Clearly, you have to be careful to limit recursion depth when faced with high branching factors.

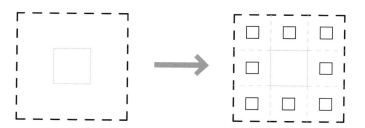

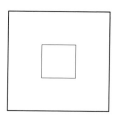

8.58: At each recursive level the Sierpinski carpet "cuts away" 1/9 of the remaining square and applies itself to the rest.

3D Planes

When. Recursively divide space with three perpendicular polygons.

How. The motif comprises a 3D cruciform of square polygons. The cruciform divides the space it occupies into eight cubes and, at each level, the recursive function places a scaled copy of the cruciform into three of these.

This sample displays more architectural reality than the prior samples. In fact, it resembles a recurrent motif in the work of Arthur Erickson, for example, the image below shows the Simon Fraser University academic quadrangle.

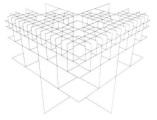

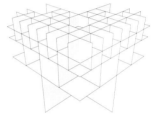

Academic Quadrangle, Simon Fraser University, by Arthur Erickson
Source: Greg Ehlers / Media Design, Simon Fraser University

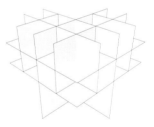

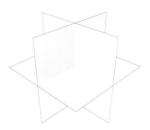

8.59: Recursion is the computational implementation of the design strategy of hierarchy. Of course, actual designs require recursive functions more specific than this simple sample.

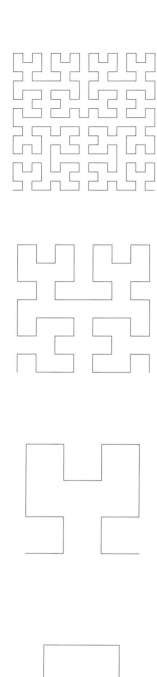

Hilbert Curve

When. Progressively fill space with a single curve.

How. The Hilbert curve fills space. At the nth recursive level it visits every point in a $(2^{n+1}) \times (2^{n+1})$ integer dimensioned space. For example, at the 0th level it visits all points in a 2×2 space.

At the 0th level, shown in (a) below, the curve comprises three lines, joining centres of the four quarters of the 2×2 space. At the second level, shown in (b), a new 2×2 space replaces each of the four points. The points of this space define four new curves. Joining the endpoints of each curve segment (c) with the start point of the next produces a continuous curve. At each subsequent level (d), a further 2×2 space replaces each point at the previous level. Successive levels of the Hilbert curve thus form a progressively elaborating sequence (d).

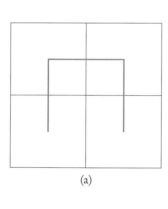

(a)

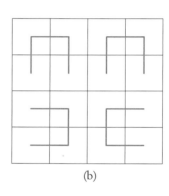

(b)

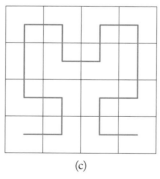

(c)

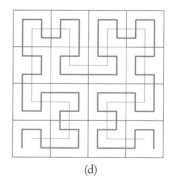

(d)

8.60: As the recursion level increases, the Hilbert curve progressively fills the space it occupies.

8.17   GOAL SEEKER

Related Pattern • REACTOR

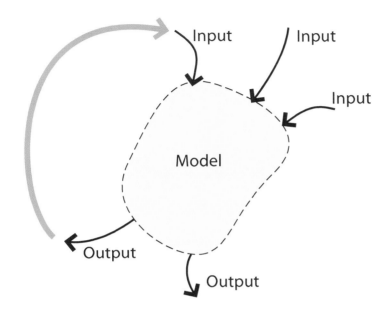

What. Change an input until a chosen output meets a threshold.

When. Parametric models are acyclic – data   ows downstream. In other words, you need to know parameter values to produce a result. Sometimes though, knowledge works the other way. You know a goal for a particular variable and want to discover a set of input values that will achieve it. Use this pattern when you want to adjust inputs until you reach a goal.

Why. Without values for its independent variables, a model is *undetermined*, that is, it does not contain sufficient information to give values to its dependent variables. Typically, a model can exist in an indenumerable infinity of states, depending on the choice of its input values. Sometimes, you know a property of such a state. You may even be able to adjust input values until the property is achieved. But accuracy and reproducibility are important. A GOAL SEEKER can compute the needed input values.

How. A model has inputs and some outputs. A GOAL SEEKER requires a choice of both: an output that will be evaluated and an input that will be adjusted. The output is called the *result* and input the *driver*. The threshold that the result should meet is called the *target*. The process of calculating the result from the inputs is the *update method*.

The GOAL SEEKER script runs the update method then checks the result. If it meets the target, the job is done and it returns. If not, it goes back, slightly changes the driver, runs the update method and checks the result again. This loop continues to run until the desired result is achieved.

A simple way of being systematic is to use a binary search, in which an estimate of the distance to the target determines changes to the driver. While searching, the incremental step change of the driver may cause the result to pass the target. If this happens, the script reverses and reduces the step size. Then it continues changing the driver until it passes the target again. It repeats the search process until the result meets the target (with adequate precision).

The simple GOAL SEEKERS presented in this pattern require that the model (or at least the result) changes smoothly with changes in the driver. If the result varied in sharp jumps, the strategy of slowly changing the driver to approach a result would not work. Such situations present complex problems of *discrete search* or *constraint satisfaction* that are beyond the scope of simple elements of parametric design.

GOAL SEEKER Samples

Local Maximum

When. Locate the point on a curve at which the curve is at a maximum.

How. Elementary calculus (or just looking at a curve) tells us that, at maximum (or minimum) points, the tangent to a curve is horizontal. The angle between the tangent and a horizontal line is zero. Searching for a fixed value simplifies the GOAL SEEKER script in comparison to looking for an unknown maximum. The tangent changes predictably as a point moves across a maximum. Its slope is greater than zero on one side of the maximum and less than zero on the other side. This gives a very simple rule for changing the driver: always move towards zero.

The essential idea is simple. Start at a known point on the curve. Always step upwards. At each step measure the slope. If it is zero, stop. If it changes sign, turn around, takes smaller steps and keep going. Not surprisingly, this is called a hill-climbing strategy. It has some problems. If there is a local hilltop in the direction you start walking, you will reach it and be trapped, even if you can see a taller hill nearby. If the hilltop is really small, that is, small in relation to the steps you are taking, you might miss it altogether.

Key to writing a working GOAL SEEKER is understanding how to build the desired measure into the system. Understand how the result will change with changes to the driver. In this case, the tangent measure makes the choice easy. In other cases code may be needed to check the effect of change of the driver on the result and to choose the appropriate direction of change.

The code for this GOAL SEEKER is relatively simple. Unfortunately, other GOAL SEEKERS require significantly more complex code. There are two nested while loops. The outer loop implements the binary search, the inner one the "walk" towards the target. The inner loop has a test

```
driver > driver.RangeMinimum && driver < driver.RangeMaximum
```

that ensures that the point remains on the parametric curve. If a curve end is a local maximum, the GOAL SEEKER will approach the end, but never overshoot, and will finally arrive at it.

Tangent angle = 0

T value = 0.468

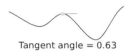

Tangent angle = 0.63

T value = 0.467

Tangent angle = 13.41

T value = 0.45

Tangent angle = 27.66

T value = 0.425

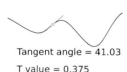

Tangent angle = 41.03

T value = 0.375

8.61: To seek a local maximum move a point "uphill" along the curve. When the point passes the maximum, change direction and divide the size of the move by two.

Code for the LOCAL MAXIMUM sample.

```
1   function generalNumericTest (object booleanTest,
2                                double a, double b)
3   { //provides conditional test of two numeric variables
4       //based on an input string.
5       switch (booleanTest){
6       case ">=": return a >= b;
7       case "<=": return a <= b;
8       case ">" : return a > b;
9       case "<" : return a < b;
10      case "==": return a == b;
11      default: return true;
12      }
13  }
14
15  double currentDriver = driver.Value;
16      //driver is a named variable in the model.
17  double target = 0.0;
18  double closeEnough = 0.000000001;
19  int giveUpWhen = 200;
20  int incrementAdded = 0;
21  int incrementSubdivided = 0;
22  double increment = 0.2;
23  object startingSide = "gt";
24  int incrementSign = 1;
25
26  if (result>target){
27      startingSide = ">";
28      incrementSign = 1;
29  }
30  else{
31      startingSide = "<=";
32      incrementSign = −1;
33  }
34  while (increment > closeEnough &&
35          incrementSubdivided < giveUpWhen)
36  {
37      ++incrementSubdivided;
38      increment = increment/2.0;
39      while (generalNumericTest(startingSide,result,target) &&
40              incrementAdded < giveUpWhen &&
41              driver > driver.RangeMinimum &&
42              driver < driver.RangeMaximum)
43      {
44          ++incrementAdded;
45          currentDriver = driver.Value;
46          driver = currentDriver+(incrementSign*increment);
47          UpdateGraph();
48      }
49      driver = currentDriver;
50      UpdateGraph();
51  }
```

Curve and Point Distance

When. Adjust a curve until it is exactly a given distance to a point at its closest approach.

How. In this sample the goal is a minimal distance. Every point on a curve is some distance from a given point. One (or more) of the curve points lie at the least distance. Such points are *projections* of a point onto a curve.

Clearly, any of the control points on a curve can be changed. For each of these points, any direction of change could be used. Using a GOAL SEEKER requires choice of both point and direction of movement. Other choices of point and direction can yield vastly different curves, but they will be at the goal distance (if the GOAL SEEKER works).

Once a control point and direction of movement are chosen, a GOAL SEEKER works as described above: walk towards the target until you overshoot; back up and take smaller steps; and keep doing this until you are as close as you can discern.

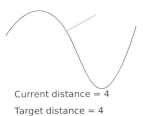

Current distance = 4
Target distance = 4

Current distance = 3.928
Target distance = 4

Current distance = 2.984
Target distance = 4

Current distance = 2.107
Target distance = 4

8.62: A curve can be moved in an infinity of ways. In this sample one of the control points moves along a chosen line.

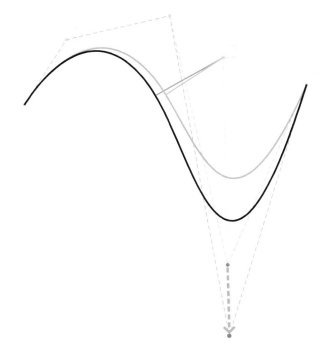

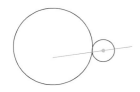

Area

When. Adjust a control point of a curve until the curve encloses a given area.

How. The goal here is the area of a closed curve. As in the previous sample, any of the control points of the curve can be moved in any direction. The modeler must choose. This particular sample moves the chosen control point away from the centroid of all other control points. This is a useful approximation, but, with some work, any other direction could be chosen.

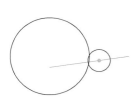

The GOAL SEEKER is almost identical to previous GOAL SEEKERS. The details of the curve, the chosen point and its direction are all factored into the single variable called *driver*.

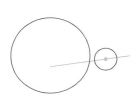

Area = 234   Area = 254   Area = 274   Area = 300

8.63: This GOAL SEEKER moves a control point of a curve along a line until the area of the curve reaches a threshold (in this case 300).

Two Circles

When. Given a circle constrained to move along a line, find the position of its centre such that it is tangent to another circle.

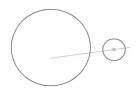

How. Computing tangency is easy if the circles are free. The two circle centres form a line. Move one circle along the line until its centre is plus or minus its radius from the intersection of the line and the other circle. This situation is different – the centre of one circle is constrained to lie on an arbitrary line. The circle centre is governed by the parameter t, which the GOAL SEEKER adjusts until the tangency conditions are met. The GOAL SEEKER must operate twice: once for each tangency condition.

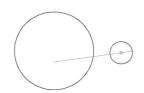

8.64: The small circle s centre moves in increments along a line until the two circles intersect. The direction of movement reverses and the increment size halves. These two steps repeat until the two circles touch.

Chapter 9

Design space exploration

by Mehdi (Roham) Sheikholeslami

9.1   Introduction

Clearly, exploring multiple alternatives can lead to better designs. Despite this well-known fact, current computer-aided design systems provide only the most rudimentary tools for generating, storing and visualizing alternatives. *Hysterical space* is a novel approach to discover alternatives in the solution space by using the interaction history with a parametric model.

Implicit in any parametric model are the states a designer might have reached by combining variable settings in new ways. Such a model exhibits hysteresis, that is, path dependence – thus the name hysterical space. Based on my Master s thesis (Sheikholeslami, 2009), I present a simple definition of hysterical space as the Cartesian product of variable settings. It provides orderings of the space that yield feasible interactive search strategies. In turn, the orderings suggest interface designs, which I report as working prototypes. Limited user evaluation supports a claim that hysterical space may be a useful approach to design space exploration.

Given our limits, we rely utterly on our external memory to achieve complex tasks (Norman and Dunaeff, 1994). Computation holds out the promise of making this medium active, that is, being able to perform some of the cognition externally.

A key limitation, explained largely by short-term memory capacity and latency, is our ability to create, compare and consider alternatives. Hysterical space is a new concept and computational device for wresting many alternatives from a small number of designer interactions with a parametric modeling system.

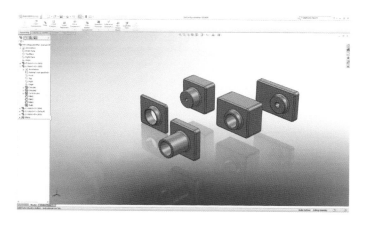

9.1: SolidWorks® Configuration Manager is a way to explore multiple variations of a single model.
Source: SolidWorks® screenshots reprinted with the permission of SolidWorks.

Current CAD systems focus mainly on *single states,* with notable exceptions such as the SolidWorks® Configuration Manager (Figure 9.1) and the Autodesk Showcase® (Figure 9.2). Predictably, designers find workarounds – they invent techniques (mostly manual) for design alternatives, such as copying entire files or copying parts of the model within the same file, often using layer structures.

9.2: Autodesk Showcase® has a feature for storing alternatives. Different materials and design are stored as alternatives of a sports car.
Source: Autodesk screen shots reprinted with the permission of Autodesk.

9.1.1   Design space

Despite the differences in design theories, we can claim that all of them admit the existence of a space that contains the solutions to a design problem.

This work mainly uses Woodbury and Burrow s (2006) definition of design space,which, on one hand, describes a general conception of design space and, on the other, entails specific mathematical concepts describing a limited, but sound and tractable design space representation. In short, they argue that design activity is well-modeled by a network structure and the extent of this network is determined by the strategies and the structure of the designer s exploration. They define several terms such as *implicit, explicit* and *hysteresis*, which we explain as follows.

Implicit Design Space: This all-encompassing object comprises every possible design solution reachable by a symbol system. It is a network depicting those paths that contain all design solutions, feasible or not, complete or not, that may or may not be visited by the designer.

Explicit Design Space: Woodbury and Burrow (2006) argue that an explicit design space comprises those states that have been visited, in the current or an available past exploration episode. They state "design space paths are embedded in both implicit and explicit design spaces". The latter is a smaller portion of design space. Explicit design space is developed through the design process. It gains its structure through the exploration behaviour of designers; especially through choices of strategies re ecting the limits of either computation, designer knowledge; or both.

Design Hysteresis: Woodbury et al. (2000) coin the term *design hysteresis* in the *Erasure in Design Space Exploration*. In essence, the idea is to use data from the explicit space states to construct (discover) implicit nodes by erasing and recombining known data. In this definition, design hysteresis is a part of implicit space of solutions that may not be explicitly visited by the designer during the design process. In fact, design hysteresis discovers explicit states in the implicit space without direct designer action.

We coin the terms *hysterical state* to describe states in design space that are reached by such recombination, and *hysterical space* to describe the set of states so reached. This work poses the research question, "How can a parametric modeling system support the recombination of prior decisions into new states that are meaningful to designers?"

9.3: The explicit space (in orange) expresses the path(s) taken by a designer to reach a solution. It is a subgraph of the implicit space (in grey).

9.1.2   Alternatives and variations

We narrow our research to parametric modeling, specifically, to architecture and building engineering. The reasons for this choice are that (a) recently more architects and engineers are using parametric modeling tools in their design; and (b) parameters admit model variations, which enables design space exploration.

A parametric model is an adaptive structure based on a set of parameters. The values of the parameters at any given time define a (usually infinite) space of

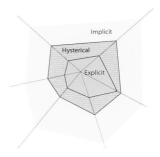

9.4: Graphical representation of implicit, explicit and hysterical space.

model instances. Therefore, parametric models intrinsicly enable exploring great numbers of alternatives and variations.

As a heuristic, we define alternatives as structurally different solutions to a design. In contrast, variations are the design solutions with identical model structure but having different values assigned to the parameters. Typically in a parametric modeling system, variations are considered informally, by moving input points and altering values on an ad hoc basis. Hysterical space expands the set of instances visited to a larger space of variations. We hypothesize that this hysterical space could be a novel approach to enhancing the design process by recombination of prior decisions into new states that are meaningful in design.

9.2   Hysterical space

Defining a hysterical space requires a representation scheme and an interaction history. The representation scheme describes the symbol structures with which we compute a design and its consequent hysterical space. The designer interacts with the representation to create the explicit space – the set of designs actually visited. The interaction history describes what a designer has done and how (s)he has done it – hysterical space amplifies these actions into a collection of representations.

There are many ways to characterize a hysterical space from a parametric model. This work illustrates only the most obvious – the Cartesian product of visited parameter values. The interaction history of the independent variables of a fixed parametric model gives the explicit space, that is, a collection of variations of a parametric model.

To illustrate hysterical space, we developed two design patterns – RECORDER and HYSTERICAL STATE in addition to those in Chapter 8. A RECORDER stores a designer s interaction history with the model, and a HYSTERICAL STATE generates new variations based on the data the RECORDER captures.

9.2.1   Recorder pattern

Currently there is no clear support in the parametric systems for recording the user interactions. Changes to parameter values and other interactions with the system simply ow with minimal recording processes. We introduce the RECORDER pattern that expresses the idea of storing variations of a model based on explicit user choices. Since the current configuration of a parametric model is defined entirely by its parameters, restoring a model to an earlier state requires only reassigning the original values to the parameters (Figure 9.5).

Like the other design patterns in Chapter 8 we define the RECORDER pattern in the following structure:

What. Store user-defined choices selectively.

When. Record some of the explicitly visited variations of a model in order to revisit them in the future.

Why. Design is an iterative process in which several variations of one alternative will be visited in the design process. At each phase the designer, the design team or the clients may choose some of these variations for further development. Therefore, having a system that provides the possibility of storing the desired variations seems essential. By using the RECORDER pattern one can restore the design model to a previously visited state.

How. First, identify the variables that define the desired part of the model. Second, create an array storing the recorded values of those variables. Third, restore the model to a desired state by reassigning the corresponding recorded values in the array.

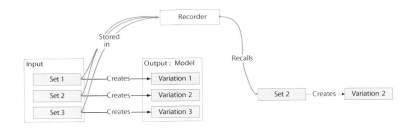

9.5: A schematic view of the RECORDER pattern. Three assignment sets of variables create three different variations of the model, and by recording the second set the designer can restore the model to the second variation.

Our primary tool to assess these ideas is GenerativeComponents®. Figure 9.6 illustrates the symbolic representation of the RECORDER pattern for a simple point. The *object of interest* is the part of the model that the designer desires to record. The parameter *varsToRecord* is the variable or variables from the object of interest that the designer chooses to record in the system. The designer may choose to focus on only a subset of the interaction history. The *recoArray* stores all these recorded values. The nodes of Figure 9.6 inside the dashed rectangle show the mechanism of the recording process in GenerativeComponents®. The *recoOnOff* is a Boolean variable specifying whether to record the values or not. If *true*, the RECORDER will record the values, otherwise not. The function *recoFunc* is the core of the recording process that records values whenever it is triggered. The *recoFuncTrigger* triggers the recorder function. Which object should trigger the function is the decision of the designer. It could be anything in the file that updates the model. Based on the structure of the software we may not need this variable, however; we use this variable to cleanly distinguish the recording process from the model.

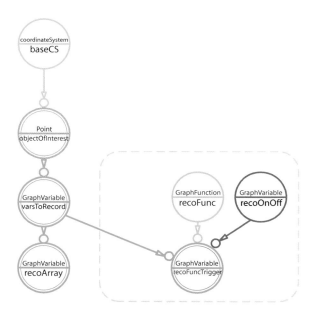

9.6: The structure of the RECORDER pattern in GenerativeComponents®.

For example, a point in a frame is defined by its x-, y- and z-coordinates (see Figure 9.7). Therefore, by recording these variables, the system can restore the position of the point to a desired state (Figure 9.8).

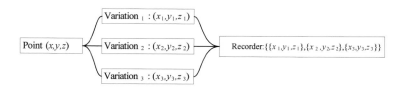

9.8: The recording array for storing the variations of the point contains x, y, and z.

9.2.2   Hysterical State pattern

We limit our examples to the simplest version of the hysterical space, that is, the Cartesian product of the recorded values. The HYSTERICAL STATE pattern illustrates the implementation of the Cartesian product hysterical space.

A parametric model can be restored to an earlier state entirely or partially, based on the parameters that are recorded in the system. If we record all the parameters of the model, we will be able to fully restore it to the recorded state.

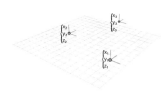

9.7: A point in frame is defined by x, y and z coordinates.

On the other hand, recording just some of the parameters gives us the option to restore only parts of the model related to those parameters (Figure 9.9).

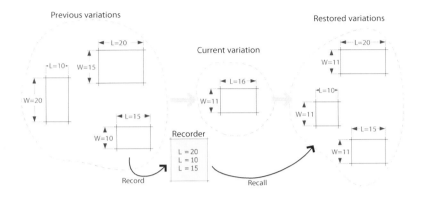

9.9: Recording parts of the model results in partial restoration. By recording only the length of the rectangle, the restored version retains the current width with the stored lengths.

What. Create new variations of a parametric model by recombining prior decisions stored as recorded parameters. In our case, this recombination is the Cartesian product of the recorded values.

When. Explore more variations of a model based on what has been explicitly visited in the previous stages.

Why. The HYSTERICAL STATE pattern uncovers new nodes in the implicit design space by combining previously recorded parameter values. Visiting the resulting new model variations may lead a designer to explore novel and maybe meaningful directions.

How. The first step is to record the user interactions with the model with the RECORDER pattern. The next step is to generate the Cartesian product of the recorded values. The simplest function iterates through all the recorded values making all combinations. Recreating a model for each of these combinations results in all possible variations in the hysterical space (Figure 9.10).

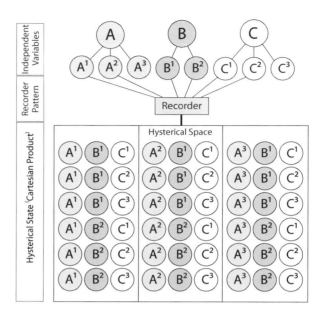

9.10: By generating the Cartesian product of the recorded values, the system can provide several variations of the model.

9.3 Case study

The *Aviation Museum* was the capstone project for my Master of Architecture degree (Sheikholeslami, 2006) (Figure 9.11). One part of the museum is used in this case study of hysterical space. This comprises a single roof corresponding to the size of the objects underneath it. For example, larger aircraft result in a larger roof span. Each primary exhibit object in the museum is represented by a circle, such that the circle encompasses that object (Figure 9.13). To cover these circles with a single roof, I used the Metaballs implicit surface representation. Metaballs are visually organic objects in *n*-dimensional space (Blinn, 1982). I used a two-dimensional Metaballs algorithm for the museum roof plan.

Since all of the recorded parameters in this example affect the 2D plan of the roof, in Figure 9.13 we brie y describe the logic relating the plan and roof.

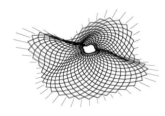

9.11: A roof variation for the Aviation Museum modeled in GenerativeComponents®.

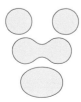

9.12: Two Metaballs distort and combine based on proximity.

- Create a point grid for the museum base and the Metaballs algorithm. Parameters control both size and density of the grid. The parameter *gridDensity* specifies the density of the point grid and, consequently, the smoothness of the museum s roof.

- Position circles on the point grid to represent the main exhibits in the museum. The radius of each circle (parameter *radii*) re ects the size of an aircraft. (Figure 9.14). We refer to each circle by its centrepoint.

- Apply the Metaballs algorithm to generate the boundary of the roof. The parameter *threshold* defines how much a MetaObject s surface, in our case a circle, in uences other MetaObjects. As the threshold increases, so does in uence that each MetaObject has on others (Figure 9.14).

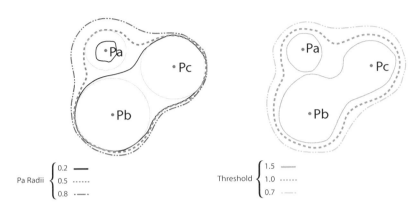

9.14: (a) The effect of *radii* of the points on the museum s boundary, in this figure radius of (Pa) changes. (b) The effect of the *threshold* on the museum s boundary.

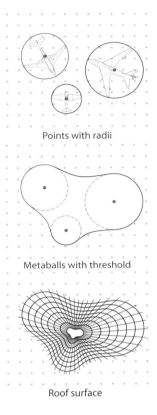

Points with radii

Metaballs with threshold

Roof surface

9.13: The steps to create a 2D plan of the aviation museum.

We record four parameters, three of which are the radii of the circles $\{r_a, r_b, r_c\}$ and one is the *threshold* t (Equation 9.1).

$$V = \{V_1, V_2, V_3, V_4\}$$
$$= \{r_a, r_b, r_c, t\} \tag{9.1}$$

We record two variations of the roof with the following values for the recorded parameters:

$$S_*^0 = \{r_a^0, r_b^0, r_c^0, t^0\} \qquad \text{(first variation)}$$
$$= \{0.5, 1.0, 0.6, 1.0\}$$
$$S_*^1 = \{r_a^1, r_b^1, r_c^1, t^1\} \qquad \text{(second variation)} \tag{9.2}$$
$$= \{0.7, 0.5, 0.8, 0.6\}$$

So now we have recorded two values for each of the variables. The Cartesian product of these values generates 16 different combinations and thus 16 roof variations (Equation 9.3).

$$|\mathcal{H}| = |T_0^*| \times |T_1^*| \times |T_2^*| \times |T_3^*| = 2 \times 2 \times 2 \times 2 = 16 \tag{9.3}$$

Figure 9.15 shows the two recorded variations of the roof in comparison with all possible combinations of the recorded values. As you can see, some of those variations are entirely different from what has been explicitly visited.

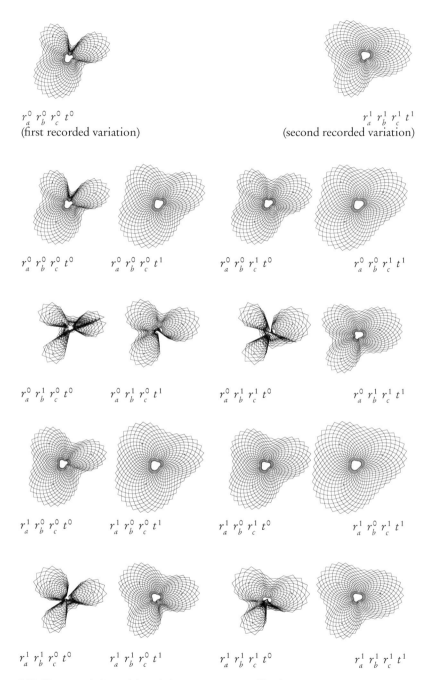

$r_a^0 \; r_b^0 \; r_c^0 \; t^0$
(first recorded variation)

$r_a^1 \; r_b^1 \; r_c^1 \; t^1$
(second recorded variation)

$r_a^0 \; r_b^0 \; r_c^0 \; t^0$ $r_a^0 \; r_b^0 \; r_c^0 \; t^1$ $r_a^0 \; r_b^0 \; r_c^1 \; t^0$ $r_a^0 \; r_b^0 \; r_c^1 \; t^1$

$r_a^0 \; r_b^1 \; r_c^0 \; t^0$ $r_a^0 \; r_b^1 \; r_c^0 \; t^1$ $r_a^0 \; r_b^1 \; r_c^1 \; t^0$ $r_a^0 \; r_b^1 \; r_c^1 \; t^1$

$r_a^1 \; r_b^0 \; r_c^0 \; t^0$ $r_a^1 \; r_b^0 \; r_c^0 \; t^1$ $r_a^1 \; r_b^0 \; r_c^1 \; t^0$ $r_a^1 \; r_b^0 \; r_c^1 \; t^1$

$r_a^1 \; r_b^1 \; r_c^0 \; t^0$ $r_a^1 \; r_b^1 \; r_c^0 \; t^1$ $r_a^1 \; r_b^1 \; r_c^1 \; t^0$ $r_a^1 \; r_b^1 \; r_c^1 \; t^1$

9.15: Sixteen variations of the aviation museum, created by the combining the variables of the two recorded variations.

9.4   Representing the hysterical space

The number of states in a Cartesian product hysterical space (we contract to *hysterical space* when not ambiguous) grows exponentially with the number of variables.

The simplest hysterical space representation comprises lists of its assignment sets, that is, the *n* sets that from which the Cartesian product is defined. Such a representation is *unevaluated*, which means it must be further processed to produce explicit representation of its states. A naïve evaluated representation is thus an *n*-dimensional array with each dimension capturing an assignment set. In all but the most simple of hysterical spaces, such a representation would be defeated by sheer size—it would grow exponentially with the number and size of the assignment sets. We therefore seek representations that compute only those parts of the hysterical space actually visited in an interaction, reserving the array representation for those subsets of hysterical space that are rendered in their entirety. A representation can be conceived as a choice of *ordering* a subset of states that are somehow *picked, computed* or *ltered* from the hysterical space. Our strategy will be to use such orderings to pick out subsets of the hysterical space that are then generated and displayed in their entirety as an array.

What, then, is the effective maximum size for a subset of hysterical space that can be represented directly using an array representation? We propose several methods for representing the hysterical space, for example, order of generation, range of inputs (Figure 9.16) and interpolation. See Sheikholeslami (2009).

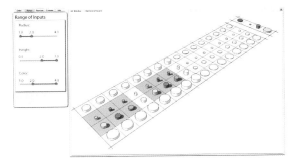

9.16: Representing the hysterical space by a range of inputs. One can filter the hysterical space by specifying the range of the input variables. In this figure the coloured cylinders are the ones that are filtered by the user s choice.

9.5   Visualizing the hysterical space

Since hysterical space is multi-dimensional, visualizing it presents challenges. Although we implemented several prototypes, in this section we describe the main one, called the *Dialer,*. It is implemented in GenerativeComponents®.

The Dialer comprises concentric rings. Each ring represents one parameter and the divisions of a ring correspond to its parameter s recorded values. The outmost ring illustrates the members of the hysterical space. Figure 9.17 shows three variables with three values for each (three division for each of the inner rings). As a result, the $3 \times 3 \times 3 = 27$ divisions on the outmost ring correspond to the items of the hysterical space.

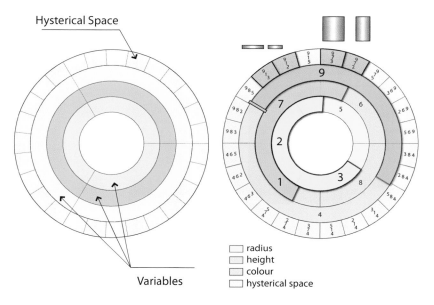

9.17: The Dialer: each ring represents one variable and the outmost ring shows the hysterical space.

9.18: The Dialer for the parametric cylinder, three rings represent three variables and the outmost ring shows the 24 variations of the cylinder.

Each ring has a slider with adjustable size that selects the values on the ring. The Cartesian product of the selected values highlights the corresponding items in the hysterical space (Figure 9.18).

The Dialer in Figure 9.18 shows three parameters – *radius, height* and *colour* – with $3, 4$, and 2 values for parameters respectively. By moving and resizing the sliders on each ring, a designer can select the desired values, and as a result, the corresponding items will be highlighted in the outmost ring, which represents the hysterical space. For example, in Figure 9.18, by selecting $\{2, 3\}$ for radius, $\{7, 1\}$ for height and $\{9\}$ for colour, four items in the hysterical space become highlit.

The circular arrangement of the values in the Dialer makes a relatively more compact visualization than a linear arrangement. However, as the number of values for a parameter increases, the growing number of the divisions in the corresponding ring may defeat this interaction scheme.

9.6   Conclusion

In the domain of parametric modeling, in which models are explicitly defined in terms of a set of parameters, the idea of exploring the designs engendered by the parameter space is already well-established. For all but trivial designs, the space is vast indeed. Hysterical space defines a potentially interesting subspace in which all designs are parametrically close to what has already been found. The Cartesian product model of hysterical space presents a novel way to access these implied states. Its structure is both simple and clear. Its near triviality masks a surprising richness. We were able to quickly envision a variety of ways to order (and thus search and visualize) states in the hysterical space. We are confident that there is much more to discover, in both representation and interaction.

It seems difficult to design visualizations that adequately capture the structure of variations, yet these are important in conveying the mechanism of a model (and thus its implied design space). Furthermore, parametric proximity does not imply geometric similarity of designs. Two models may be very similar in geometry but considerably different in parameters. Conversely, two very close values of the parameters may result in quite a distinct model. Further work would search for algorithms covering a wide range of hysterical space without overwhelming designers by representing very similar variations.

We simply do not understand the cognitive importance of the explicit states, which form the basis for hysterical space. Our interfaces provide no place for these. With the gift of hindsight, we are astonished at our lack of foresight.

We do not know if hysterical space can cause early commitment to a premature design or idea. The Cartesian product hysterical space generates variations of the same alternative, which may not be the best solution to the design problem. The mastermind of the design is still the designer and it is her decisions that lead in particular hysterical space.

This work provides a basis from which to search for new ideas for structuring hysterical space and the promise that there may be some fertile ground to cover in such a search. There may be new discoveries in the generated items that lead to completely new designs. By looking at the variations of hysterical space in the case studies, we discover distinct forms and models from the explicit space that may be worth considering in the design process.

The Cartesian product model *may* be useful in design. This claim gains support from the reactions of designers to the model and interface prototypes, and from our initial (and admittedly idiosyncratic) demonstrations of chosen designs. We informally discussed the idea with a number of designers and applied the hysterical space to their work. From the feedback that we received, it seems that it can be beneficial in their design process. However, more studies with users in real design situations need to be done to determine both positive and negative effects of the hysterical space on the design process.

Contributor biographies

Onur Yüce Gün, BArch (Middle East Technical), MSc (MIT), initiated and led the Computational Geometry Group of Kohn Pedersen Fox Associates New York. Through his work on more than 40 projects from 2006-2009, he focused on developing methods and tools for complex geometric building design. He is currently a faculty member at İstanbul Bilgi University and continues his research and professional practice in his design laboratory: O-CDC.

Brady Peters, BSc (Victoria), BEDS, MArch (Dalhousie), specializes in complex geometry in architectural design and, more recently, in architectural acoustics. First at Buro Happold and then Foster + Partners (where he was promoted to Associate Partner) he worked on projects including the Smithsonian Courtyard Enclosure, the Copenhagen Elephant House, the Khan Shatyr Entertainment Centre, Thomas Deacon Academy, the West Kowloon Great Canopy, and the SECC Arena. Currently, he is a PhD fellow at the Royal Danish Academy of Fine Arts.

Mehdi (Roham) Sheikholeslami, MSc (Shahid Beheshti), MSc (SFU), combines research, teaching and practice in parametric modelling systems. His research is in computational design, parametric modeling and design space exploration.

Bibliography

Aish, R. and Woodbury, R. (2005). Multi-level interaction in parametric design. In Butz, A., Fisher, B., Krüger, A., and Oliver, P., editors, *SmartGraphics, 5th Intl. Symp., SG2005*, LNCS 3638, pages 151–162, Frauenwörth Cloister, Germany. Springer.

Alberti, L. B. and Grayson, C. (1972). *On Painting and On Sculpture. The Latin Texts of De Pictura and De Statua [by] Leon Battista Alberti.* Phaidon. Edited by Cecil Grayson.

Alexander, C. (1979). *The Timeless Way of Building.* Center for Environment Structure Series. Oxford University Press.

Anderson, P. B. (2009). Map projections. Accessed at http://www.csiss.org/map-projections/ on 13 October 2009.

Beck, K., Beedle, M., van Bennekum, A., Cockburn, A., Cunningham, W., Fowler, M., Grenning, J., Highsmith, J., Hunt, A., Jeffries, R., Kern, J., Marick, B., Martin, R. C., Mellor, S., Schwaber, K., Sutherland, J., and Thomas, D. (2009). Manifesto for agile software development. Accessed at http://agilemanifesto.org on 29 May 2009.

Berlinski, D. (1999). *The Advent of the Algorithm: The Idea that Rules the World.* Harcourt.

Blinn, J. F. (1982). A generalization of algebraic surface drawing. *ACM Transactions on Graphics*, 1:235–256.

Borning, A. (1981). The programming language aspects of ThingLab, a constraint-oriented simulation laboratory. *ACM Transactions on Programming Languages and Systems*, 3:353–387.

Bowyer, A. and Woodwark, J. (1983). *A Programmer's Geometry.* Butterworths.

Bringhurst, R. (2004). *The Elements of Typographic Style.* Hartley & Marks Publishers, 3rd edition.

Buxton, B. (2007). *Sketching User Experiences: Getting the Design Right and the Right Design.* Morgan & Kaufmann.

Carlson, C. (1993). An algebraic approach to the description of design spaces. PhD thesis, Department of Architecture, Carnegie Mellon University.

Carlson, C. and Woodbury, R. (1994). Hands-on exploration of recursive patterns. *Languages of Design*, 2:121–142.

Davies, C. (1859). *Elements of Descriptive Geometry; with Application to Spherical, Perspective, and Isometric Projections, and to Shades and Shadows.* A. S. Barnes and Co.

Dertouzos M. et al., (1992). ISAT Summer Study: Gentle Slope Systems; making computers easier to use. Presented at Woods Hole, MA.

Euclid (1956). *The Thirteen Books of Euclid s Elements, Translated from the Text of Heiberg, with Introd. and Commentary by Sir Thomas L. Heath.* Dover Publications.

Evitts, P. (2000). *A UML Pattern Language.* Macmillan Technical Publishing.

Farin, G. (2002). *Curves and Surfaces for CAGD: A Practical Guide.* Series in Computer Graphics and Geometric Modeling. Morgan Kaufmann.

Flaherty, F. (2009). *The Elements of Story: Field Notes on Non ction Writing.* Harper, 1st edition.

Flemming, U. (1986). On the representation and generation of loosely-packed arrangements of rectangles. *Environment and Planning B: Planning and Design*, 13:189–205.

Flemming, U. (1989). More on the representation and generation of loosely packed arrangements of rectangles. *Environment and Planning B: Planning and Design*, 16:327–359.

Gamma, E., Helm, R., Johnson, R., and Vlissides, J. (1995). *Design Patterns: Elements of Reusable Object-Oriented Software.* Addison-Wesley Professional.

Gantt, M. and Nardi, B. A. (1992). Gardeners and gurus: patterns of cooperation among CAD users. In *CHI 92: Proceedings of the SIGCHI Conference on Human Factors in Computing Systems*, pages 107–117, New York. ACM.

Garrett, J. J. (2002). *The Elements of User Experience: User-Centered Design for the Web.* Peachpit Press.

Gaspard Monge, B. B. (1827). *Géométrie descriptive.* V. Courcier, imprimeur.

Grünbaum, B. and Shephard, G. (1987). *Tilings and Patterns.* W. H. Freeman.

Harada, M. (1997). Discrete/continuous design exploration by direct manipulation. PhD thesis, Carnegie Mellon University.

Henderson, D. W. (1996). *Experiencing Geometry: On Plane and Sphere.* Prentice-Hall Inc.

Highsmith, J. (2002). *Agile Software Development Ecosystems.* Addison-Wesley.

Hoffmann, C. M. and Joan-Arinyo, R. (2005). A brief on constraint solving. *Computer-Aided Design and Application*, 2:655–663.

Itten, J. (1970). *The Elements of Color*. Wiley.

Johnson, W. B. and Ridley, C. R. (2008). *The Elements of Mentoring*. Palgrave Macmillan, revised and updated edition.

Kundu, S. (1988). The equivalence of the subregion representation and the wall representation for a certain class of rectangular dissections. *Communications of the ACM*, 31:752–763.

Lakatos, I. (1991). *Proofs and Refutations: The Logic of Mathematical Discovery*. Cambridge University Press.

Maleki, M. and Woodbury, R. (2008). Reinterpreting Rasmi domes with geometric constraints: a case of goal-seeking in parametric systems. *International Journal of Architectural Computing*, 6:375–395.

Marques, D. M. (2007). Federation modeler: a tool for engaging change and complexity in design. Master s thesis, School of Interactive Arts and Technology, Simon Fraser University.

Maxwell, R. and Dickman, R. (2007). *The Elements of Persuasion: Use Storytelling to Pitch Better, Sell Faster & Win More Business*. HarperBusiness.

McCullough, M. (1998). *Abstracting Craft: The Practiced Digital Hand*. MIT Press.

Miller, H. W. (1911). *Descriptive Geometry*. The Manual Arts Press.

Mitchell, W. J., Liggett, R. S., and Kvan, T. (1987). *The Art of Computer Graphics Programming: A Structured Introduction for Architects and Designers*. Van Nostrand Reinhold.

Monahan, G. (2000). *Management Decision Making: Spreadsheet Modeling, Analysis, and Application*. Cambridge University Press.

Myers, B., Hudson, S. E., and Pausch, R. (2000). Past, present, and future of user interface software tools. *ACM Transactions on Computer–Human Interaction*, 7:3–28.

Norman, D. and Dunaeff, T. (1994). *Things That Make Us Smart: Defending Human Attributes in the Age of the Machine*. Basic Books.

Norman, D. A. (1988). *The Psychology of Everyday Things*. Basic Books.

Palladio, A. (1742). *The Architecture of A. Palladio; in four books*. Printed for A. Ward, S. Birt, D. Browne, C. Davis, T. Osborne and A. Millar.

Palladio, A. (1965). *The Four Books of Architecture*. Dover Publications, Inc.

Peters, B. (2007). The Smithsonian courtyard enclosure: a case-study of digital design processes. In *Expanding Bodies: Art • Cities • Environment: Proceedings of the 27th Annual Conference of the Association for Computer Aided Design in Architecture*, pages 74–83, Halifax (Nova Scotia). Riverside Architectural Press and Tuns Press.

Piegl, L. and Tiller, W. (1997). *The NURBS Book*. Springer-Verlag, 2nd edition.

Piela, P., McKelvey, R., and Westerberg, A. (1993). An introduction to the ASCEND modeling system: its language and interactive environment. *Journal of Management Information System*, 9(3):91–121.

Pollio, M. V. (1914). *The Ten Books on Architecture*. Harvard University Press. Translated by Morris Hicky Morgan.

Pollio, V. (2006). *The Ten Books on Architecture*. Project Gutenberg. Accessed at http://www.gutenberg.org/etext/20239 on 11 June 2009.

Pottmann, H., Asperl, A., Hofer, M., and Kilian, A. (2007). *Architectural Geometry*. Bentley Institute Press. Edited by D. Bentley.

Qian, Z., Chen, Y., and Woodbury, R. (2007). Participant observation can discover design patterns in parametric modeling. In *Expanding Bodies: Art • Cities • Environment: Proceedings of the 27th Annual Conference of the Association for Computer Aided Design in Architecture*, pages 230–241, Halifax (Nova Scotia). Riverside Architectural Press and Tuns Press.

Qian, Z. and Woodbury, R. F. (2004). Between reading and authoring: patterns of digital interpretation. *International Journal of Design Computing*, 7. Accessed at http://wwwfaculty.arch.usyd.edu.au/kcdc/ijdc/vol07/articles/-woodbury/index.html on 28 February 2010.

Qian, Z. C. (2004). A pattern approach to support digital interpretation. Master s thesis, School of Interactive Arts and Technology, Simon Fraser University.

Qian, Z. C. (2009). Design patterns: augmenting design practice in parametric CAD systems. PhD thesis, Simon Fraser University.

Qian, Z. C., Chen, Y. V., and Woodbury, R. F. (2008). Developing a simple repository to support authoring learning objects. *International Journal of Advanced Media and Communication*, 2:154–173.

Ramsay, C. and Sleeper, H., editors (2007a). *Architectural Graphics Standards*. American Institute of Architects, 11th edition.

Ramsay, C. and Sleeper, H., editors (2007b). *Architectural Graphics Standards*. American Institute of Architects, 4.0 CD-ROM edition.

Rockwood, A. and Chambers, P. (1996). *Interactive Curves and Surfaces: A Multimedia Tutorial on CAGD*. Series in Computer Graphics and Geometric Modeling. Morgan Kaufmann Publishers.

Rogers, D. (2000). *An Introduction to NURBS: With Historical Perspective*. Morgan Kaufmann Publishers.

Rogers, D. F. and Adams, J. A. (1976). *Mathematical Elements for Computer Graphics*. McGraw Hill Book Company.

Rottenberg, A. T. and Winchell, D. H. (2008). *Elements of Argument: A Text and Reader*. Bedford/St. Martin s Press, 9th edition.

Ruhlman, M. (2007). *The Elements of Cooking: Translating the Chef s Craft for Every Kitchen*. Scribner s.

Ruskin, J. (1844). *The Seven Lamps of Architecture:lectures on architecture and painting ; the study of architecture*. A.L.Burt, New York.

Ruskin, J. (1857). *The Elements of Drawing in Three Letters to Beginners*. Smith, Elder, London, 2nd ed. edition.

Sannella, M., Maloney, J., Freeman-Benson, B. N., and Borning, A. (1993). Multi-way versus one-way constraints in user interfaces: experience with the Delta Blue algorithm. *Software – Practice and Experience*, 23:529–566.

Schneider, P. L. and Eberly, D. H. (2003). *Geometric Tools for Computer Graphics*. Morgan Kaufman Publishers.

Schön, D. (1983). *The Re ective Practitioner: How Professionals Think in Action*. Basic Books.

Sheikholeslami, M. (2006). The aviation museum. Master of Architecture Thesis, Shahid Beheshti University.

Sheikholeslami, M. (2009). You can get more than you make. Master s thesis, School of Interactive Arts and Technology, Simon Fraser University.

Smith, T. M. and Smith, R. L. (2008). *Elements of Ecology*. Benjamin Cummings, 7th edition.

Steele, G. L. (1980). The definition and implementation of a computer programming language based on constraints. PhD thesis, MIT.

Strunk, W. and White, E. B. (1959). *The Elements of Style / by William Strunk; with revisions, an introduction and a new chapter on writing by E.B. White*. Macmillan.

Sussman, G. and Steele, G. (1980). CONSTRAINTS - a language for expressing almost hierarchical descriptions. *Arti cial Intelligence*, 14(1):1–39.

Sutherland, I. (1963). Sketchpad: a Man–Machine Graphical Communication System. Technical Report 296, MIT Lincoln Lab.

Tidwell, J. (2005). *Designing Interfaces: Patterns for Effective Interaction Design*. O Reilly Media, Inc.

Tufte, E. R. (1986). *The Visual Display of Quantitative Information*. Graphics Press.

Tufte, E. R. (1990). *Envisioning Information*. Graphics Press.

Tufte, E. R. (1997). *Visual Explanations: Images and Quantities, Evidence and Narrative*. Graphics Press. 4th printing with revisions.

van Duyne, D. K., Landay, J. A., and Hong, J. I. (2002). *The Design of Sites: Patterns, Principles, and Processes for Crafting a Customer-Centered Web Experience*. Addison-Wesley Professional.

Vince, J. (2005). *Geometry for Computer Graphics: Formulae, Examples & Proofs*. Springer-Verlag.

Wang, T.-H. and Krishnamurti, R. (2010). Design patterns for parametric modeling in Grasshopper. Accessed at http://www.andrew.cmu.edu/org/tsunghsw-design on 6 March 2010.

Week, D. (2002). *The Culture Driven Workplace*. Assai Pty Ltd.

Weisstein, E. (2009). Wolfram MathWorld. Accessed at http://mathworld.wolfram.com on 7 December 2009.

Williams, R. (1972). *Natural Structure*. Eudaemon Press.

Williams, R. (1995). *The PC is Not a Typewriter*. Peachpit Press, 1st edition.

Williams, R. (2003). *The Mac is Not a Typewriter*. Peachpit Press, 2nd edition.

Williams, R. (2008). *The Non-Designer s Design Book*. Peachpit Press, 3rd edition.

Woodbury, R., Datta, S., and Burrow, A. (2000). Erasure in design space exploration. In *Arti cial Intelligence in Design 2000*, pages 521–544, Worcester, Massachusetts. Key Centre for Design Computing, Kluwer Academic.

Woodbury, R., Kilian, A., and Aish, R. (2007). Some patterns for parametric modeling. In *Expanding Bodies: Art • Cities • Environment: Proceedings of the 27th Annual Conference of the Association for Computer Aided Design in Architecture*, pages 222–229, Halifax (Nova Scotia). Riverside Architectural Press and Tuns Press.

Woodbury, R. F. (1993). Grammatical hermeneutics. *Architectural Science Review*, 36:53–64.

Woodbury, R. F. and Burrow, A. L. (2006). Whither design space? *AIEDAM, Special Issue on Design Spaces: The Explicit Representation of Spaces of Alternatives*, 20:63–82.

Yorck (2002). The Yorck Project: 10.000 meisterwerke der malerei. DVD-ROM, Directmedia Publishing, GmbH. ISBN 3936122202.

Trademark notices

Adobe Creative Suite® is a registered trademark of Adobe Systems Incorporated.

ArchiCAD® is a registered trademark of GRAPHISOFT.

Autodesk®, AutoCAD®, Maya®, Revit® and Autodesk Showcase® are registered trademarks or trademarks of Autodesk, Inc., and/or its subsidiaries and/or affiliates in the USA and other countries.

Cinema4D® is a registered trademark of Maxon Computer.

form•Z® is a registered trademark of AutoDesSys Incorporated.

GenerativeComponents® is a registered trademark of Bentley Systems Incorporated.

Maple™ is a trademark of Waterloo Maple Incorporated.

Mathematica® is a registered trademark of Wolfram Research Incorporated.

Microsoft Excel® and Microsoft Word® are either registered trademarks or trademarks of Microsoft Corporation in the United States and/or other countries.

Rhinoceros® and Grasshopper™ are a registered trademarks or trademarks of Robert McNeel and Associates.

CATIA®, SolidWorks® and Virtools® are registered trademarks of Dassault Systèmes.

Index